DEFENDER OF THE UNION

Courtesy of the National Portrait Gallery, Smithsonian Institution, Washington, D.C.

DEFENDER OF THE UNION

The Oratory of Daniel Webster

Craig R. Smith

Foreword by Halford R. Ryan

Greenwood Press
New York • Westport, Connecticut • London

Library of Congress Cataloging-in-Publication Data

Smith, Craig R.
    Defender of the Union : the oratory of Daniel Webster / Craig
Smith.
        p.   cm. — (Great American orators, ISSN 0898-8277 ; no. 1)
    Bibliography: p.
    Includes index.
    ISBN 0-313-25860-0 (lib. bdg. : alk. paper)
    1. Webster, Daniel, 1782-1852—Oratory. 2. Political oratory—
United States—History—19th century. 3. United States—Politics
and government—1815-1861. I. Webster, Daniel, 1782-1852.
Speeches. Selections. 1988. II. Title. III. Series.
E300.W4S6   1989
973.5′092′4—dc19   88-21397

British Library Cataloguing in Publication Data is available.

Library of Congress Catalog Card Number: 88-21397
ISBN: 0-313-25860-0
ISSN: 0898-8277

First published in 1989

Greenwood Press, Inc.
88 Post Road West, Westport, Connecticut 06881

Printed in the United States of America

The paper used in this book complies with the
Permanent Paper Standard issued by the National
Information Standards Organization (Z39.48-1984).

10 9 8 7 6 5 4 3 2 1

To Senator Bob Packwood,
who teaches by example and
leads by achievement

Contents

Series Foreword

The idea for a series of books on great American orators grew out of the recognition that there is a paucity of book-length studies on individual speakers and their craft. Apart from a few notable exceptions, the study of American public address has been pursued in scores of articles published in professional journals. Yet, no matter how insightful their intellectual forebears, each generation of rhetorical critics must reexamine its universe of discourse, expand the compass of its researches, and redefine its purpose and methods. To avoid intellectual torpor, scholars and students cannot be content simply to see through the eyes of those who have gone before them. As helpful as article-length studies have been, none has or can provide a complete analysis of a speaker's rhetoric. Book-length studies, such as those in this series, will help fill the void that has existed in the study of American public address. In books, more than in articles, the critic can explicate a speaker's persuasive discourse that ranges over politics and history, theology and sociology, communication and law. The comprehensive research and sustained reflection that books require will undoubtedly yield telling examinations and enduring insights for the nation's most important voices.

This series chronicles the role of public discourse in the United States. American speakers shaped the destiny of the colonies, the young republic, and the mature nation. During each stage of the intellectual, political, and religious development of the United States, great orators, standing at the rostrum, on the stump, and in the pulpit, persuaded their audiences with word and gesture. Usually striving for the noble, sometimes achieving the base, they urged their fellow citizens toward a more perfect Union.

Each book is organized to meet the needs of scholars and students who would evaluate the effects of American public address. Previously, if one desired to assess the impact of a speaker or a speech upon history, the path was, at best, not well marked and, at worst, littered with obstacles. To be sure, one might turn to biographies to learn about an orator, but for the public address scholar these sources often prove unhelpful. Rhetorical topics, such as speech invention, disposition, style, delivery, and persuasive effect, are often treated in passing, if at all. Authoritative speech texts are often difficult to locate and the problem of textual accuracy is frequently encountered. This is especially true for early figures, or for those whose persuasive role, though significant, was secondary to other leading lights of the age.

Part I is a critical analysis of the orator and his or her speeches. Within the format of a case study, one may expect considerable latitude. For instance, in a given chapter an author might explicate a single speech or a group of related speeches, or examine orations that comprise a genre of rhetoric such as forensic speaking. But the critic's focus remains on the rhetorical considerations of speaker and speech, purpose and effect.

Part II contains the texts of the important addresses that are discussed in the critical analysis that precedes it. To the extent possible, each author has endeavored to collect definitive speech texts, which have often been found through original research in historical materials. In a few instances, because of the extreme length of a speech, texts have been edited, but the authors have carefully deleted material that is least important to the speech.

Each book contains a chronology of major speeches that serves several purposes. Pragmatically, it lists all of the orator's known addresses. Places and dates of the speeches are also given, although this information is sometimes difficult to determine precisely. But in a wider sense, the chronology attests to the scope of rhetoric in the United States. Certainly in quantity, if not always in quality, Americans are historically talkers and listeners.

Because of the disparate nature of the speakers examined in the series, there is some latitude in the nature of the bibliographic materials that have been included in each book. But in every instance, authors have carefully described historical collections, and have gathered primary and secondary sources that bear on the speaker and the oratory. By combining in each book critical chapters with bibliographic materials and speech texts, this series notes that textual and research sources are interwoven in the act of rhetorical criticism.

May the books in this series serve as a fitting memorial to the nation's greatest orators as students and scholars study anew the history and criticism of American public address.

Bernard K. Duffy
Halford R. Ryan

Foreword

It is altogether fitting and proper that the first book in the "Great American Orators" series should treat Daniel Webster's public persuasions. Without peer in the golden age of American oratory, Webster addressed the great issues of his era--the tariff question, secession, and slavery-- with language crafted to persuade his fellow legislators and countrymen to the keystone in his political philosophy: "Liberty and Union, now and forever, one and inseparable."

Craig R. Smith, president of the Freedom of Expression Foundation, explicates Daniel Webster's great speeches with the care and dedication to criticism that Webster devoted to creating and delivering his orations. As a former director of debate, Smith brings to Webster's legal oratory a keen analysis of his argumentation. At the bar, whether before the Supreme Court of the United States or in a rural courtroom, Webster crafted appealing arguments to justices on national issues confronting the young republic, or to bucolic jurymen on such a mundane matter as a murder. Smith demonstrates the incisiveness with which Webster could communicate his dissection of constitutional questions as well as the cleverness with which he could construct compelling narratives to convince a jury.

In academic courses, Smith has taught the issues that Webster addressed as a deliberative orator. But as a consultant and speech writer for contemporary persuaders in the United States Senate, presidency, and business, Smith conveys a reading of Webster's legislative speeches that a critic without Smith's experience might miss. One illustration may suffice. In the Compromise of 1850, Smith demonstrates the multiple national and congressional audiences Webster confronted. In order to gain a consensus on the compromise, the senator wove a rhetorical cloth that Unionist senators and citizens could wear comfortably; concomitantly, Webster did not court extremists on either side of the Mason-Dixon line who would find any compromise uncomfortably constricting. Nor does Smith overlook the important role that Webster's rhetoric played in the adoption of the omnibus bill when it was finally split into its constituent parts and passed as individual measures. Although not as famous as Webster's Seventh of March Address, these speeches, which were addressed to the senatorial mediating audience during the late summer and early fall of 1850, were more instrumental in securing

passage of the Compromise of 1850 than his more famous
oration in March.

Daniel Webster also excelled in epideictic address.
Other great American orators, such as the Reverend Henry
Ward Beecher who made his mark in the pulpit, or John C.
Calhoun who is remembered mainly for his deliberative
oratory, or Henry Clay who could address congressional or
stump audiences with equal ease, rarely distinguished
themselves in all three rhetorical genres. But Webster did,
and it is a mark of his oratory that he could move,
throughout his adult life, from setting to setting with such
facility and acclaim. (I let Smith state his ideas on
Webster and rhetorical genre; but in introducing the book, I
make a final commendation about his treatment of that
subject.)

Those who expect in these pages a slavish devotion to
Aristotle's tripartite division of oratory will be, it is
hoped, disappointed. It was Webster's genius that
synthesized form, purpose, and occasion to surpass genre.
It is Smith's perspicacity that explicates Webster's doing
so. For in truth the senator's persuasiveness, whether
before the bar or in Congress or on a platform, was
unparalleled in the first half of nineteenth-century U.S.
history.

Senator Robert Hayne of South Carolina, himself a
peripheral recipient of rhetorical fusillades from Webster
in 1830, is reported to have opined that an orator such as
Webster should never die. And on his deathbed, Webster is
reputed to have uttered his last words, "I still live."
Concerning the life of the spoken word, Abraham Lincoln, who
used in his First Inaugural Address constitutional arguments
that Webster made in his Reply to Hayne and Seventh of March
speeches, modestly noted at Gettysburg that "the world will
little note nor long remember what we say here." In fact,
the opposite occurred. Although Daniel Webster died
considerably more than four score and seven years ago, and
contrary to Lincoln's modesty about the effects of eloquent
language, in Smith's book Webster's rhetoric lives to speak.

Halford R. Ryan

Preface

Why write a book about Daniel Webster's oratorical career?
First, because it is a brilliant career from which we can
learn a great deal about effective and enduring speaking.
Second, because it reveals something about America's
heritage that is not available in most biographies about
Webster or in most histories of the time.

Like no other speaker in American history, Webster
dominated the courts, the legislature and the public
speaking circuit. He came to national prominence in 1812
and remained in the public consciousness until his death in
1852. His success is a given; by accounting for that
success, one can refine the theory by which we build
speeches today, particularly speeches in those arenas where
Webster did battle. It is not too much to say that
lawyers, legislators, and other public speakers who wish to
refine their rhetorical skills would be well served by a
close study of Webster's technique.

One can deduce a good deal about the American
consciousness in Webster's time by examining the evidence,
arguments, values, and style he used. Given that his
speeches were successful, one can assume that they were
highly adapted to his audiences. Thus, the values expressed
in the speeches were the same values held in the public
consciousness. By surveying his most effective addresses
and analyzing the audiences to which the speeches were
delivered, one can reconstruct the public consciousness of
the time. Such a reconstruction can only be achieved by the
careful examination of speeches because they are the only
artifact available which is so attuned to public attitudes.
Rhetorical analysis refines the understanding of the society
and thereby serves as an essential adjunct to any historical
study of the time. In the study that follows, several
standard historical positions are challenged because they do
not adequately account for the success of certain appeals in
the speeches of Webster.

Finally, Webster's story is fascinating because it is
about a man who is self-made and who understands how
important public speaking skill is to the self-creating
process. At almost every important juncture of his life,
Webster delivered a speech that enhanced his reputation,
saved the Republic, or changed the course of American
constitutional law. He was addicted to language because he

knew language shaped perception. It could bring reality into focus or it could convert division and disagreement into compromise. And what language could do for political issues, it could do for personal success. Webster was no romantic war hero; in fact, he believed they were of little use in the political realm. There, the need was for men who understood the power of language and could wield it on the legislative and forensic battlefield. Webster polished and refined his talent for words; then he sought to make his mark in a world where words were more important that swords and bullets. Luckily, he was raised in a country that believed in freedom of expression and had created a republican democracy in which deliberation and public speaking were highly valued. Webster's enormous success in that society should inspire those who today seek a country committed to reasoned decision making and who believe understanding of the state and nature of public issues is important to the proper functioning of the American system.

Craig R. Smith

I

CRITICAL ANALYSIS

Introduction

Daniel Webster was the most prolific of the great public orators of American history. His addresses of note are not limited to one genre but span the rhetorical spectrum. His forensic pleadings changed the course of constitutional law. His epideictic efforts reveal a mastery of style and form perhaps unsurpassed in American rhetorical literature. And his deliberative addresses are an integral part of the history of the nation.

Webster, like Henry Clay and John C. Calhoun, represents the second generation of American leaders. The first were the founders of the Republic; their rhetoric addressed the philosophy of governance and the justification for revolution. The second generation was faced with making the government work. Hence, they were more concerned than the founders with pragmatic questions. Like Clay and Calhoun, Webster addressed pragmatic questions but rarely lost sight of overriding values. He not only provided creative vehicles for his arguments, he lifted the standard of American public address to new heights. He succeeded in adapting the immediate consciousness of his audiences while also issuing transcendent appeals that excited the national spirit. He refined our civil religion by example and by adamantly proselytizing for a set of values unique to American culture.

TRAINING FOR GREATNESS

While Webster was born with a good deal of oratorical talent, he was also the product of extensive training and practice. Born on January 18, 1782, in Salisbury, New Hampshire, Daniel inherited the dark olive complexion and black hair of his father, who dubbed the boy "little black Dan." It was a visage that would fascinate the nation, and it was a nickname that would haunt him later in his life. Webster's father often declaimed the Bible to the boy and made sure his son understood its nuances. Young Dan memorized Watt's psalms and was soon taken with poetry. Before he was ten, Webster was reading the "good book" aloud to the citizens of the Merrimack Valley of New Hampshire. By age thirteen, he was an intern in the local law office of Thomas Thompson, where he memorized and used various legal

Latin phrases that would serve him throughout his
magnificent career. Thompson, a Harvard graduate, was the
first of a series of mentors that took Webster under their
wing. Older men of learning and skill were often so
impressed with Daniel Webster that they not only accpted him
as an apprentice, they guided him in his later adventures.
It was Thompson, for example, who encouraged young Daniel to
seek the best education available.
      Despite Thompson's help, Webster barely qualified for
entrance into Phillips Exeter Academy in 1796.[1] There, he
was very insecure about public speaking. In fact, in his
first year he was so distressed at being away from home that
he often found himself unable to stand before the class.
After these bouts of stage fright, he would return to his
room and weep over his plight. As an antedote to this
depression, he studied so hard that he won top honors among
his peers by the end of his first year. After a while
speaking began to come naturally to him. More important,
the next year he excelled in enough subjects that his father
agreed to send him to Dartmouth College if Daniel could
qualify.
      Webster threw himself into the effort. For example, he
refined his Latin with the help of Rev. Samuel Wood, a
tutor, in order to be sure he would meet the entrance
requirements. He studied Latin and Greek and is said to
have memorized Paradise Lost. His efforts were rewarded; at
age fifteen, Webster became a student at Dartmouth, only the
third person from Salisbury to go on to college.
      During his studies, he became familiar with "Cicero's
Select Orations" and his talent was further refined by
classes in oratorical composition and delivery and
membership in literary societies. For example, he became
United Fraternity's top debater. Classes under the
direction of Professor Charles Haddock were perhaps some of
the most rigorous in the new nation.[2] They included
instruction on all of the elements of rhetoric with special
emphasis on logic, the emotions, stylistic commonplaces, and
organization. Webster was required to take courses in
public address every year he attended Dartmouth,
culminating in legal and deliberative oratory in his senior
year. Almost in revolt, Webster wrote poetry, which was
well received by his classmates, if not his instructors.
Webster's popularity at the College led to gin, brandy,
port, and gambling. His eyes were opened to the vices as
well as the virtues of a college education. The habits
formed here, particularly the drinking and witty
conversation, stayed with Webster all his life.[3]
      Webster was chosen to be one of the commencement
speakers in 1801, but he turned down the opportunity because
he believed he was not placed prominently enough in the
program. Many agreed with the decision believing that
Webster was the best man in his class. So on graduation
day, Webster spoke before United Fraternity on the subject
of "Opinion." The speech revealed Webster's early talent
for ceremonial or epideictic oratory. It praised George
Washington and served as a precursor to later eulogies (see
chapter two) such as the "Centennial Anniversary of
Washington's Birthday" in 1832.[4]
      Webster began the study of law on his own at age
nineteen. But due to his father's financial difficulties,

young Webster was forced to teach school and delay his entry
to the bar. At Fryeburg, Webster taught so well that he
received a special bonus. The students were a wonderful
audience to whom Webster displayed his remarkable expository
talents. They allowed him to begin to hone his legal
talent. He studied Blackstone's <u>Commentaries</u> and often
raised issues of common law in the classroom. These same
teaching techniques would prove helpful when addressing a
jury. And Webster did not have to wait long for that
opportunity. Once he was financially able, he returned to
Salisbury and began an apprenticeship in the law under
Thomas Thompson. Webster stayed for two years.[5]
     On July 17, 1804, Webster moved to Boston to tutor his
brother Zeke in Greek and Latin and was luckily accepted as
an apprentice by the great Christopher Gore. Webster had
arrived unannounced at Gore's office on Tremont Street after
only a few days in town. Gore was a famed Federalist,
commissioner, and lawyer. His incredible library was soon
rifled by the young Webster, who worked diligently at
improving his use of the English language. He read Gibbon,
Boswell, Moore and many others. He translated Latin and
Norman common law commentaries into English and worked to
master case law. Gore taught Webster many useful things,
not the least among them was the ability to imitate the
sound practices of other lawyers and to mix with high
society in a civilized manner. The two were not
infrequently seen weaving down a cobblestone street together
after an evening on the town.[6]
     Webster was admitted to the bar in March of 1805 and
began practicing in Boscawen, New Hampshire, where he became
an instant success. Webster often argued before the
Superior Court that travelled to the various county seats of
New Hampshire. When Webster located his practice in
Portsmouth, New Hampshire, he found another mentor in
Jeremiah Mason, who often practiced before the same courts
with Webster.[7] Mason, a strong Federalist like Webster's
other mentors, believed him to be a fine orator and actor,
two essential talents for a great lawyer. Mason was superb
at common law and clear argumentation. Webster was not
above the sincerest form of flattery. Combining his talents
with those of Mason rounded Webster's forensic rhetorical
ability into a powerful and effective presence.
     At the same time, Webster became more active in the
Federalist cause, refining further his understanding of
Washington and Hamilton's principles. He delivered speeches
at Dartmouth on many a Fourth of July, and over an infinite
number of dinners where he expounded his Federalist
philosophy. He was soon known as the "Yankee Demosthenes."
     Although Webster never stopped learning, his entry into
the bar marked the end of his formal training and the
beginning of his illustrious career (see chapter one).
     That career was balanced by a rich personal life as
full of joy as tragedy. Webster was able to extract an
enormous amount of emotion from these experiences and to
relive them in other contexts before his audiences. In
1808, Webster married Grace Fletcher, and took up residence
in Portsmouth, New Hampshire. Portsmouth was the first
district that Webster would represent in the Congress; he
won election in 1812, the year in which the Federalists made

a comeback in the face of the unpopular war being conducted
by President Madison. As America went to war with England,
Webster, at age thirty-one, set off for the District of
Columbia, a city he found appallingly dirty and swamplike.
He lived in a Georgetown boarding house where his depression
at the sight of the city was relieved somewhat by the
friends he had there. Mason represented Massachusetts as a
senator and Gore lived at the same boarding house as
Webster. In May, 1813, he met Clay and Calhoun for the
first time. Little did he know how important they would be
to one another. Webster was reelected in 1814. But he did
not stand for election in 1816; the Federalists' popularity
declined with America's success in the war. Webster retired
from politics, moved to Boston, and returned to the practice
of law.[8]

Boston was a bustling city of 40,000 inhabitants at the
time. The Websters lived on Beacon Hill; his office was on
State Street, near the State House. By 1819, Webster was
earning over $20,000 a year, a sizeable sum for the time.
Yet it was not enough to support his extravagant life style.
Francis Lowell, the textile manufacturer who had befriended
Webster while the latter was in Congress, provided financial
support.[9]

Webster practiced law with a small but talented
fraternity. He found another Federalist teacher in the
eminent jurist, Joseph Story. Practicing before the highest
court in the land, Webster came into contact with the finest
minds in America. William Wirt's use of humor, historical
and poetic quotations impressed Webster. So did Wirt's
defense of Jeffersonian principles. Wirt, who was Attorney
General from 1817 to 1829, joined Webster as often as he
opposed him before the Supreme Court. David Ogden appeared
with or against Webster thirty-two times. And the eloquent
Rufus Choate, a few years behind Webster at Dartmouth,
joined him in Rhode Island v. Massachusetts.[10]

These men helped sharpen Webster's abilities and refine
his conceptualization of national conservatism, a platform
that would serve him well in the Congress. They forced
Webster to find the best ways to defend his fundamental
belief in due process, property rights, and federal
protection of contracts. The defense was almost always
rooted in constitutional issues because those issues were
the most current before the Supreme Court. Furthermore,
while a loose plan or an emotional argument might satisfy
some in the Congress, only a tightly reasoned argument
could pass muster before the Court. Any loose ends,
contradictions, or holes would be quickly taken advantage of
by adversaries and the sitting justices. Thus, Webster's
experience before the Court while he served in Congress
helped him to become the preeminent debater on the floor of
the Senate. He was often seen running from the Supreme
Court, which was then located on the ground floor of the
Capitol, up the steps to the Senate chamber. He would argue
a legal motion at one level and a legislative amendment at
the next.

Cast into such a world of luminaries, it was difficult
for Webster to avoid political discussions. Soon he became
active in the search for a new party structure to replace
the Federalists. The Union party would be national and
republican. It would stand for "measures, not men" unlike

the demogogic Democrats. National interests would be put before sectional interests. The great error of the Hartford Convention would be buried, or so Webster thought. On this platform, Webster was elected to the House in 1822. It is a measure of Webster's magnetism that he was able to move to a new state and come to represent it in Congress a short six years later.

Webster took his seat in December of 1823. The Monroe administration was in trouble. Webster, like Clay, sensed the opportunity to build a new national party. Webster contributed a framework of national conservatism, born of his Federalism and refined by his court presentations. Clay provided the American System, a pragmatic platform that united East and West. The former would gain the tariff; the latter would gain better transportation to markets and cheap land. Though some in the South would benefit from the new commercial possibilities of the System, the agrarian leaders opposed the program because of its dire economic impact. John C. Calhoun emerged as their leader.[11]

In the election of 1824, Clay and John Quincy Adams received enough electoral votes between them to block the election of Andrew Jackson and throw the election into the House. Clay then gave his support to Adams, who after his inauguration, named Clay Secretary of State. Webster had visited Jefferson just after the election and asked the aging founder whom to support in the House election. Jefferson must have thought Webster was being disingenuous since Webster would have been thrown out of Boston had he voted against Adams. Nonetheless, Jefferson recommended that Webster vote for Adams, warning that Jackson led a dangerous mob.

Webster became the administration's chief spokesman in the House. He proved effective, even though the administration was unpopular. In April of 1826, for example, Webster led the attack on Jacksonians who opposed the administration's initiative in Central America. He carried the day by a vote of 134 to 66.

In 1827, the Massachusetts legislature, loyal to Adams and solidly conservative, elevated Webster to the U.S. Senate. He had been instrumental in putting together the Union Ticket, which served as the foundation of the emerging Whig party. In the chapters that follow, relevant biographical details of Webster's life will be explored in more depth. Suffice it to say in this introduction that Webster's service in the Senate was immensely successful, particularly following his famous debate with Hayne in 1830. In 1841, he became Secretary of State to William Henry Harrison and contined after Harrison died, serving President Tyler until 1843. Having little use for the Polk Administration, he returned to the Senate in 1845. Upon the death of President Taylor in July of 1850, Webster was named Secretary of State by President Fillmore. Webster served with distinction until his death in October of 1852.

His first wife Grace had been reluctant to come to Washington, and had been very shy even at home in Portsmouth. In Boston, she became almost reclusive. Grace eventually bore Webster five children, who were a cause of great joy and sorrow for him. His daughter Grace died in 1817. Charles died at the age of four in the winter of

1825. His son Edward died in Mexico in February of 1848
just after the Mexican American War; and in April of the
same year, Webster's daughter Julia died of tuberculosis.
But most tragic of all was the death of his wife Grace in
January of 1828; Webster was at her side. He had barely
recovered from the tragedy when his brother Zeke died in
April of 1829. Webster loved Grace because she was a
delicate creature who needed to be taken care of. He loved
Zeke because as an older brother, Zeke had been a constant
source of moral support.

Webster mourned his wife's death for two years. Then
in his forty-seventh year, he married the lovely Caroline
LeRoy in New York City where her merchant father lived. He
had retained Webster on occasion and introduced the couple.
Caroline was sixteen years younger than her new husband, but
was, nonetheless, the perfect hostess. She was also more a
part of Webster's extravagant public life than Grace had
been. Caroline was able to control his depression and
diplomatically escort him from embarrassing situations. She
seemed to be the best of Grace and Zeke: she was beautiful,
strong, and supportive. Despite her best efforts, however,
Webster was plagued throughout his career by financial
difficulty and over-indulgence in alcohol. Political
cartoons of him with his hands in the pockets of wealthy
bankers were common. So were caricatures of Webster as a
mad scientist mixing as many liquors together as he could.
These unflattering portraits were printed until his death.
And even after his death, the Reverend Theodore Parker
condemned Webster's excesses in a mean-spirited eulogy.[12]

METHODOLOGY FOR AN ORATORICAL BIOGRAPHY

Before beginning the analysis of Webster's rhetoric, allow
me to define a few terms and outline the method of analysis
I employ. Rhetoric refers to the art of finding in any
given case the available means of persuasion. This
definition was first propounded by Aristotle and has served
speakers and critics well ever since. Aristotle's system
of analysis is audience based. For that reason, the
strategies Aristotle discusses are derived from the
particular audience for a speech. In order to know what
the available means of persuasion are for any particular
speech, the speaker or the critic of the speech must
endeavor to understand what potentialities lay in the
audience. What language did they speak? What were their
values? What excited them? What offended them? What were
they capable of comprehending? Because the answers to these
and other questions change with each audience, producing a
speech is difficult and analyzing it is even more difficult
without recreating the audience of the time.[13]

Aristotle also believed that rhetoric was an art, not a
science. That is to say, it is based on principles which
have exceptions but which nonetheless generate a useful
product. It is not based on rules that guarantee the same
result on every occasion. Persuasive speaking is creative
as opposed to derivative. It can be very ineffective if not
adjusted to audience, occasion, and message. These major
variables help us categorize the myriad of strategies that
go into the construction of a speech.

     A more refined way to examine those variables is to
organize them around the predominant form each speech
exhibits. Aristotle was the pupil of Plato. Plato believed
that perfect form, which existed in what he called the
numenal world, inspired artists. Aristotle brought Plato's
notion of form down to earth. He saw forms as useful
categories by which to talk about the actuality and
potentiality of all things, including speeches.[14] As with
any other artifact, a speech must have both matter and form.
The initial matter in the case of speeches is words and
thoughts; in the case of a statue, it is marble or bronze or
the like. This matter has the potential to become something
else, something beyond itself. Form determines the
particular realization of the potential entity. But once
the speech becomes a reality, that is, when it passes from
potential to actual form, it gains a second potentiality,
the potential to persuade an audience. Once this second
potential is fulfilled, the speech enters a third state of
actuality--it is instrumental, it affects. The critic
ultimately judges the effects of a speech to assess its
worth.[15]
     The matter with which we build a speech has the
potential of being used to enhance credibility, to activate
or allay the passions, and to arrange thought grammatically,
syntactically, and logically to captivate the understanding
of the listener. Form acts on this matter. Without form,
matter is shapeless and senseless. With form, it becomes
meaningful and persuasive. In Chapter Three of Book One of
the Rhetoric, Aristotle discusses the possible forms of
rhetorical discourse. These genre organize my analysis of
Webster's speeches. Aristotle tells us there are three
major forms for persuasive speeches: the forensic or legal
delivered to move judges; the epideictic or ceremonial
delivered to move spectators; and the deliberative or policy
delivered to move legislators. The first is concerned with
judging a past deed; the second with enhancing present
values; the third with deciding a future course of action.
These forms provide a way to segregate the matter of a
speech and assess how well it served the overriding aim of
the speech for a given audience.[16]
     But we should be careful not to fall into the trap some
so-called neo-Aristotelians have. They make the mistake of
assuming that Aristotle's categories are discrete, as they
are in science. But since rhetoric is an art, the forms can
overlap and even envelop one another. For example, a sermon
is a persuasive speech. But is it epideictic, forensic, or
deliberative? I would argue that it is all three. It is
epideictic because it seeks to reinforce present values
before a group generally viewed as spectators. Most sermons
address such values as humility, honesty, chastity, and
charity. A sermon is forensic because it seeks issue
judgments about past sins wherein the audience sits as
judges. And it is deliberative because it tries to move its
audience toward seeking salvation in the future, a
deliberative policy goal in a personal life. To assess the
merits of a sermon using only one form would be to neglect
its richness and persuasive power. Thus, while speeches in
this volume are divided by their major thrusts into
forensic, epideictic, or deliberative efforts, all three

forms are applied to each speech to see what other available means of persuasion were used by Webster on any given occasion.

The task before us is large and complex. Variables residing in the matter of the speaking situation, the audience, the occasion, the message, must be understood to determine how a speaker imposed a form by which he brought persuasive discourse out of chaos. This will require not only a careful examination of the texts of the speeches but also an understanding of the nature of issues in the society at the time and the audience present for the persuasion.

Once that is done, we can turn to an evaluation of the success of the speech. Here again we need to be very clear about the art form we are examining. Rhetoric is not literature. While literature discusses universal themes and appeals to universal audiences, rhetoric seeks to discuss specific messages for specific audiences. Rhetoric is successful if it changes the behavior of the listener in a way that was intended. Literature is successful if it transcends the mundane and pragmatic and takes us to higher realms of thought. Thus, while the Gettysburg Address is good literature because of its poetic quality, it was not successful rhetoric because it failed to move its specific audience concerning a specific message. And while Orwell's 1984 is not great literature, it is successful rhetoric because it makes us suspicious of paternalistic government. This is not to say that discourse cannot achieve both goals. Many wonderful novels have effective rhetorical passages and many effective speeches have transcendent passages. Again, we must be careful not to let the category blind us to the possibilities. And we shall see that Webster was the master of achieving rhetorical effect with literary flare.

Perhaps the best way to differentiate between long-term and short-term effectiveness of discourse is to assess it in terms of the audience's actual and potential consciousness. Actual consciousness refers to the attitudes and values of the moment. These can be discovered by examining what the audience watches, reads, enjoys, and espouses. Entertainment and advertising on television, perhaps more sensitive to audience ratings than anything in our society, gives one a picture of the actual consciousness of the American public. Determining the actual consciousness of Webster's audiences requires a reading of extant newspapers, popular entertainment, voting patterns and so forth. Adjusting to that consciousness in order to persuade the audience was Webster's chief goal.

Potential consciousness is deduced from the highest aspirations of an ideal audience. This is the level to which great literature aspires. Potential consciousness is represented in the highest art a culture produces. It can be summoned by a speaker seeking to move his audience beyond the present goal or seeking to leave a legacy by which his tenure might be judged. When summarizing a case before a jury, or praising a past patriot on a national holiday, or making the case for new legislation in a crisis, a persuader often finds it necessary to appeal to what Lincoln called the "better angels of our nature." Webster was able to do all of these things and do them better than any American speaker before or after him.

ORGANIZATION

     I began this study by examining the education of
Webster to see what kind of rhetorical training he received.
Now we can move to his forensic speaking before the Supreme
Court and in one famous criminal trial. The second chapter
analyzes Webster's ceremonial speeches. Chapters three and
four center on his deliberative speeches with a special
emphasis on audience analysis, the Webster-Hayne Debate, and
the Compromise of 1850.
     Webster presents us with the opportunity to examine not
only the actual consciousness of the first half of the
nineteenth century, but the potential consciousness as well.
An examination of his rhetoric should enlighten our
understanding of America's past as well as enrich our
understanding of the roots of our current civil religion.
During his lifetime, Webster saw the nation double in size,
open the frontier, strengthen as an international power, and
consolidate into a more perfect Union. He debated with the
great men of his era in the courts and in the Congress. He
had a formidable impact on the domestic development of the
country; twice as Secretary of State, he guided foreign
policy at crucial periods in our history. Perhaps this is
why he is more remembered than most presidents and revered
as one of our most important senators.
     Many of our leaders have proven that America is the
land of opportunity by rising from poverty and obscurity to
power and fame. Webster is such a leader. But it was not
economic freedom that provided Webster with his opportunity
to rise; it was the free and open marketplace of ideas. Few
of our leaders have understood that marketplace so well or
have made a larger contribution to it.

1

Forensic Speaking

From his first case, Webster caused a stir. He displayed
his forensic achievements in the county courts of New
Hampshire, then in the First Federal Circuit in Boston, and
then before the Supreme Judicial Court of Massachusetts.
His prodigious training in the law served him well at the
bar.

It was no different before the Supreme Court.
Starting in 1814, the persuasive force of Webster's briefs
was very helpful to Chief Justice John Marshall's efforts to
build a consensus on constitutional questions. Marshall was
delighted to use Webster's unionist arguments to inculcate
the Constitution with Federalist dogma. In his opinions,
he went so far as to compliment and plagiarize Webster's
arguments.[1]

Webster's early cases before the Supreme Court
centered on admiralty law. His knowledge of maritime
jurisprudence would later give his deliberative speeches on
trade, tariffs, and foreign policy added credibility. It
may also explain his penchant for using nautical metaphors
to open his speeches on the floor of the Senate. This
expertise was certainly useful to him when he served as
Secretary of State under President Tyler and negotiated the
Maine boundary dispute with England.[2]

While admiralty law was greatly diminished as a part of
his case load after 1820, he occasionally took one on when
he thought it might set an important precedent. The
Lexington case (1848) and Luther v. Borden (1849) served to
strengthen admiralty law thanks to Webster's forensic
ability.[3]

Of the 168 cases Webster argued before the Supreme
Court, only 24 involved major constitutional questions. Of
these, Webster won 13, most of them while Marshall was
sitting as Chief Justice. Webster success in the courts led
to his Chairmanship of the House Judiciary Committee when he
returned to the Congress during John Quincy Adams'
presidency in 1825.

CONSTITUTIONAL CASES

Perhaps the three most important Supreme Court cases
Webster argued were Dartmouth College v. Woodward, decided

in 1819, <u>McCulloch v. Maryland,</u> also in 1819, and <u>Gibbons v. Ogden</u> in 1824.   Each of these cases set precedents that affect the American jurisprudential system to this day. Each also served to reinforce and refine Webster's vision of national conservatism.

In <u>McCulloch</u> and <u>Dartmouth</u>, Webster faced the same panel of justices sitting on the Court.   By the time of <u>Gibbons</u> in 1824, only one change had occurred and that justice was absent for the decision.   Thus, it is not difficult to describe the audience that Webster faced in these important forensic situations.   This Supreme Court was dominated by Marshall, who had been appointed to the Court in the closing days of John Adam's administration.   Though a cousin to Jefferson, Marshall, who had served in the Revolutionary War, was a Federalist through and through.   He argued only one case before the Supreme Court, <u>Ware v. Hyton</u> in 1796, which may be why he declined a seat on the Court in 1798 to become a member of the House of Representatives from Virginia, and then Secretary of State in 1800.[4]

Marshall was known to be the master of syllogism and believed in the power of demonstrative argumentation.   His colleagues refer to his "web of argumentation" as gentle, delicate but ensnaring.   He used argumentation to construct justifications for his position as well as to refute the arguments of others.   In closed chambers, Marshall gently riddled positions of opposing justices and prodded them into consensus.   Perhaps that is why he wrote 519 of the 1,215 opinions issued during his tenure as Chief Justice and was in the minority on only one involving an important constitutional question.[5]

In 1801, Marshall instituted the practice of having the majority speak for "the Court" through the Chief Justice or his designee.   In 1803, he authored the landmark <u>Marbury v. Madison</u> decision which established the Court's judicial review authority.   After 1809, Marshall's decisions came under attack more and more often by Democratic-Republicans who believed he was undercutting state authority.   Every Congress from 1821 on tried to weaken Marshall and expand the Court.   President Jackson once said of Marshall, "He has made his decision, now let him enforce it."

Marshall was surrounded by an able group of associate justices.   Though they were appointed by different presidents, they had much in common.   Most were related to the Founding Fathers; most fought in the Revolutionary War; and most had served in their state legislature or the Congress.   Marshall's strongest ally was Bushrod Washington, appointed to the Court by John Adams in 1798.   Washington had served under his uncle George during the revolution and had inherited Mount Vernon when his aunt Martha died.   He had been a strong supporter of ratification of the Constitution during the Virginia debates on the matter in 1788.[6]

H. Brockholst Livingston was appointed to the Court by Jefferson in 1806.   He had been a classmate of Madison's at Princeton where he became a state's rights Republican. Prior to his appointment, he served on the Supreme Court of New York, where he was known for his Jeffersonian views.   He was an active anti-Federalist and particularly distrusted Hamilton.   Perhaps no justice was more hostile to Webster's positions during the period from 1819 to 1824.[7]

Thomas Todd was appointed by Jefferson in 1807; he had been Chief Justice of the Kentucky court system. He allied himself with western landed interests and specialized in real estate law. He followed Marshall's lead on Constitutional questions.[8]

William Johnson was the brother of a South Carolina bank president. In 1804, Jefferson moved him up from the South Carolina court of common pleas to which Johnson had been elected in 1798. Though he often disagreed with Jefferson's presidential policies, he remained close to Jefferson and wrote a flattering eulogy upon the Founder's death in 1826.[9]

Joseph Story, appointed by Madison in 1811, believed the Constitution should protect propertied interests. They were, in his mind, the bulwark of representative democracy. Story had socialized with many of the Justices prior to his appointment. His addition to the Court strengthened its sense of comaraderie. At thirty-two, Story was the youngest person appointed to the Court to that time. He had served in the Congress for one year during the 1808-09 session and then returned to the Massachusetts Assembly. He had strong ties to the banking community which threw him together with Webster often. He respected Webster's mind and ability to argue, but dismissed Webster's style and sentimentality. Webster was partially responsible for Story's strong commitment to the sanctity of contracts. Even though they were from different parties, Story wrote the Crimes Act of 1825, which Webster succeeded in getting passed into law. It was the first reform of the Criminal Code since 1790.[10]

Like Story, Gabriel Duvall was appointed to the Court in 1811. After these two, no new appointments were made until 1823. Thus by 1819, the seven members of the Court knew one another well and had established a set way of working with one another. Duvall was from Maryland and had served with its militia in the battles of Brandywine and Morristown. He was elected to Congress in 1794 from the Maryland House of Delegates. He served two terms and then became Chief Justice of the Maryland General Court and was Jefferson's Comptroller of the Treasury.[11]

In 1823, Smith Thompson replaced Livingston. That was the only difference between the Court Webster faced in 1824 and the one he argued before in 1819. Thompson had been Secretary of the Navy for Monroe and was politically ambitious. While sitting on the Court, for example, he ran against Martin Van Buren for Governor of New York in 1828. This was viewed by many as unseemly and Thompson lost what little credibility he had with his colleagues.[12]

Though the Court consisted of appointees of different presidents from different parties, they were nonetheless a group that held key values in common. They respected the Constitution; they believed in natural rights; and they espoused certain liberties obtained througn the revolutionary war. They were close friends and had many friends in common. Webster was a part of their social world, and they were a part of his. This intimate audience of seven provided most lawyers with a difficult persuasive challenge. But with Marshall as Chief Justice, Webster's burden was greatly reduced.

Dartmouth College v. Woodward

As a graduate of Dartmouth College, Webster had a particular interest in seeing that the institution carried the day.[13] The state of New Hampshire, newly controlled by the Democratic- Republicans in 1816, had ousted Dartmouth's president and placed the College under the jurisdiction of its new board of trustees. However, Dartmouth held a royal charter that predated New Hampshire's becoming a state, and since Dartmouth was a private eleemosynary institution, the original board of trustees argued that the state could not regulate it.

The case was first argued in the Superior Court at Exeter in 1817 by Jeremiah Mason and Jeremiah Smith. They did the fine legal work that laid the basis for Webster's later victory. He was first brought in to summarize the case in Exeter. Though he reduced the spectators to tears, the politicized jury voted against Webster. His peroration in the case became the basis for his concluding argument when the case reached the Supreme Court in March of 1818. There Webster argued that contractual obligations were based on natural law and were therefore immune to man-made law. A right, such as the charter of Dartmouth, once invested, became a natural right and could not be divested through legislation. The New Hampshire legislators argued that Dartmouth became a public corporation because it served the people of the state. Webster said the argument was radical and ludicrous: by such reasoning, almost any private entity could be converted to public property.

Webster relied on the briefs of Mason and Smith from the earlier presentations of the case. But he added eloquence and emotion that had been lacking during the early rounds. He also drew heavily on English common law. On March 10, 1818, with the gallery and the justices intently listening, Webster said in his peroration:

> This, sir, is my case. It is the case, not merely of that humble institution, it is the case of every college in our land. It is more. It is the case of every eleemosynary institution throughout our country--of all those great charities founded by the piety of our ancestors, to alleviate human misery, and scatter blessings along the pathway of life. It is more! It is, in some sense, the case of every man among us who has property of which he may be stripped, for the question is simply this: Shall our State Legislatures be allowed to take that which is not their own, to turn it from its original use, and apply it to such ends or purposes as they in their discretion shall see fit? Sir, you may destroy this institution; it is weak; it is in your hands! I know it is one of the lesser lights in the literary horizon of our country. You may put it out. But if you do so, you must carry through your work! You must extinguish, one after another, all those great lights of science which, foᵢ more than a century, have thrown their radiance over our land! It is, sir, as I have said, a small college. And yet there are those who love it. . . . Sir, I know not how others may feel, but, for myself, when I see my Alma Mater surrounded, like Caesar in the Senate house, by those who are reiterating stab upon stab, I would

not, for this right hand, have her turn to me, and say,
Et tu quoque, mi fili! And thou too, my son!
Webster made Dartmouth represent larger and larger
categories of private privilege. It stood for all colleges,
then all charities, and then all private property. All the
while, he portrayed Dartmouth as a small, simple school that
could be snuffed out by the powerful court. Also woven
through this argument is the "light" metaphor, a standard
symbol of learning. It served to unify the logic of his
position into a stylistic whole.[14]

The case gave Marshall an opportunity to strengthen the
federal government at the expense of the states. Webster
was unusually successful, especially when he appeared before
the Supreme Court presided over by fellow Federalist
Marshall.   In fact, it is said that Marshall often had his
decisions ready before Webster presented his oral arguments
to the Court because Marshall was so impressed with the
briefs Webster filed. Despite William Wirt's fine defense
of the earlier opinion, Marshall knew that this decision
would reinforce the Federalist commitment to protect private
and natural rights from encroachment by the states. Given
that the Republicans had controlled the White House since
1801, and Congress for most of that period, Marshall was the
last Federalist in a position to convert ideology into
public policy. But the Court deferred its decision to the
next session in order to give Marshall a chance to build a
consensus among the justices. He eventually persuaded the
hostile Livingston to go along.[15] But he failed to carry
Duvall, Johnson and the absent Todd.

Webster promptly had his speech printed and
distributed, a practice he would follow on the legislative
front and in the epideictic forum. He believed in the power
of opinion leaders to influence political and judicial
opinions. Webster and Timothy Farrar soon published the
Report of the Case of the Trustees of Dartmouth College
against William H. Woodward. This persuasive tract rallied
support behind the victorious College. Curiously, the
pamphlet did not include Webster's emotional peroration.
Thanks to Professor Chauncey Goodrich of Yale who
transcribed it, the peroration over-shadowed the Report.
More important to this study, it initiated a technique
Webster used again and again. After delivery, he polished
texts of his speeches and then published them for general
consumption in order to gain adherents to his cause. This
tactic was used after the Webster-Hayne debate and after the
March Seventh Address of 1850 (see chapter four). The most
lasting tribute to Webster's effort in this case can be
found on a bronze plaque at Webster Hall on the Dartmouth
campus that reads, "Founded by Eleazer Wheelock, Refounded
by Daniel Webster."[16]

On February 2, 1819, the Supreme Court agreed with
Webster that the original charter had been violated. All
but one of the justices agreed that the contract clause of
the Constitution prohibited the states from enacting laws
that impaired "the Obligation of Contracts." The Court
applied this clause to the New Hampshire legislature at
Webster's urging. Chief Justice Marshall, writing for the
majority, held that the charter was a contract, and
therefore, the covenants in the charter were inviolable even
though the holders of the charter, the board of trustees,

had no beneficial interest in the instrument.

To be fair, Webster used arguments developed earlier in the case by associates.   But his brilliant stylization of these arguments and his appeal to the sentiment of his listeners was credited with making the landmark decision possible.   It also made Webster's reputation as a constitutional lawyer.

McCulloch v. Maryland

McCulloch v. Maryland was very different from the Dartmouth case, though it was also decided in 1819.   Just three weeks after the Dartmouth victory, Webster defended the constitutionality of the Bank of the United States, for which he received a fee of $2,000.[17]   A second bank had been chartered by President James Madison to deal with the economic woes caused by the unfortunate War of 1812.   Many states were opposed to the national bank because it preempted their ability to operate banks and tax revenues. Maryland was one of those states.   It had enacted a tax on bank notes from banks not chartered by that state.   When the national bank refused to apply for a charter or to pay the tax Maryland imposed, Maryland brought an action against the cashier of the national bank.

Webster represented the national bank before the Supreme Court.   It is important to note that in April of 1816, Webster had voted against the bank bill, fearing it gave too much power to the president.   The Bank was established anyway and Webster eventually became one of its most avid defenders.   The Bank came under renewed attack during 1819 when its anti-inflationary policies were blamed for the panic of that year.

Webster's argument before the Court is short, to the point, and not nearly as stylized as some of his other rhetorical efforts.[18]   Nonetheless, his statement reveals the arsenal of argumentative tools Webster kept at his disposal when before the Court.   He knew how to enhance the credibility of his position, increase the gravity of the situation, insert an important argumentative summary, use precedent, create winning definitions, argue from analogy to specific cases, extend arguments established earlier, and to build a case from Aristotle's topic of "more or less."   All of these strategies are evident in the McCulloch summary.

At the beginning, Webster made sure the Court understood the gravity of the questions involved.   He told the Court that it faced not only the question of state versus federal power,
but the question of who controlled "private property."   To settle these questions, Webster was forced to go back to the "first Congress," where he claimed this issue was decided.

At this juncture, Webster further enhanced the credibility of his position by arguing that until this case, the issue had been decided in favor of the federal government in everyone's mind.   Using negative evidence, he argued that neither the House nor the Senate had ever challenged federal preemption on the question of a national bank to collect revenue.   Quoting Hamilton from 1791, Webster defended the proposition that Congress had the power to create a national bank, that the first Congress did just

that, the courts had sustained it, and that even those who
opposed this position had later agreed with it. These
opening passages revealed Webster at his very best. He
built the credibility of his case, reinforced it with
precedent, and then argued that even those opposed to his
position had been won over. His internal summary was
powerful and clear: "When all branches of the government
have thus been acting on the existence of this power nearly
thirty years, it would seem almost too late to call it in
question, unless its repugnancy with the constitution stare
decisis were plain and manifest." Even in this summary,
Webster could not resist adding yet another element to the
debate: the doctrine of stare decisis. The government's
method of operating had gone on so long, that to change it
would be disruptive and fly in the face of precedent.
     As was his wont, Webster then turned back and
reinforced his position that the Congress did in fact have
the power to create a bank. This argument was multifaceted
in order to capture every possible justice's opinion. It is
based on an "even if" strategy. The Congress is sovereign
"within the scope of these powers." But even if a justice
did not accept that, then the "general clause" gave the
Congress the power to create a bank. And even if one did
not accept that, then the power to declare war gave Congress
the power to collect money for the war and that meant it
could create a bank to do the job. Overlaying this basic
structure was the argument that Congress could use "all
usual and suitable means for the execution of the powers
granted." Finally, Webster extended the argument to the
question of orginial intent in order to pre-empt an attack
by the other side. He claimed that the Founders did not lay
out every means the government could use to carry out its
commission because they were not clairvoyant and could not
determine every eventuality. Instead they established a
framework adaptable to new situations and new inventions.
This framework allowed Congress to use any means "not being
specifically prohibited."
     With that line, Webster touched on one of the most
important constitutional issues in American history: Is
Congress limited to specifically delineated powers? Or is
it limited only when specifically precluded from taking
action by language in the Constitution? The issue is
important because it decides which side must carry the
larger burden of proof in the debate over implied powers.
Webster shifted the burden to the states, Maryland in this
case, which was a common strategy of the Federalists. This
position flowed directly from Webster's "framework" analogy.
If the Constitution is meant to be a flexible frame built to
last through the ages, then Congress must have the widest
latitude in adapting to new eventualities. Should it be
limited by the narrower interpretation, the government would
fail in a very short time. This argumentative synthesis set
the tone for the rest of Webster's argument.
     Webster next moved to the specific case at hand to see
if it fit his definition. First, he tried to show that a
bank is "a proper and suitable instrument" for the
government to use. He supported this contention in several
ways. He showed that it is the Congress' right to determine
the nature of the bank, not the Court's. All the Court
could do was settle whether creating a bank was

constitutional. Next, he answered an opposition point and
advanced his argument by showing that creating a corporation
was a normal way of doing governmental business.   All
governments have used corporations to conduct business, they
are merely a means to an end.   Furthermore, state
governments have the right to use corporations, so the
federal government should have even more of a right to
create and use them.   One would not deny a method of
operation to the federal government that one would grant to
the states.   At this point, Webster again felt the need for
a summary to reinforce his position.

He then moved to the second major question: Does
Maryland have the right to tax the federal bank?   Webster
argued that the "people" divided sovereignty between the
states and the federal government.   Since the bank was
carrying out the will of the people, the states have no
right to interfere with the bank.   The federal government is
supreme in this case because it is charged with carrying out
its obligations under the Constitution that is the "supreme
law of the land." On this question, the Supreme Court could
and must rule or else the system would fall into chaos.

The Court should rule for the national bank because if
it did not the states would have the power to destroy it.
Here Webster reduced the opposition position to absurdity by
arguing that if the Court allowed some taxation, it must
allow any taxation.   And if it allowed any taxation, then
the states could tax the national bank out of existence,
which would be the aim of at least a few of them.   Webster
believed that Maryland's tax eroded the congressional
authority, which, according to Article VI of the
Constitution, was the supreme law of the land: "An
unlimited power to tax involves, necessarily, a power to
destroy; because there is a limit beyond which no
institution and no property can bear taxation." He repeated
this argument, applying it to other government properties
that the states could attack, including bonds, lands,
"permits, clearances, registers, and all other documents
connected with imposts." At this juncture, Webster was not
far from the position he would take years later in his
reply to Hayne: state power is dangerous, it will destroy
the federal government if left unchecked.   The case here was
state taxation of federal property, the case in 1830 would
be nullification of federal laws.

Webster forced the Court to choose between the collapse
of the federal system at the hands of the voracious states,
or the strengthening of the young government by allowing it
to create and use a national bank to carry out its
functions.   He quickly retreated to a very reasonable
position that enhanced his credibility and gave the Court a
way out of the dilemma:

> A bank may not be, and is not, absolutely essential to
> the existence and preservation of the government.   But
> it is essential to the existence and preservation of
> the government that Congress should be able to exercise
> its constitutional powers at its own discretion,
> without being subject to the control of state
> legislation. . . . To hold otherwise, would be to
> declare that Congress can only exercise its
> constitutional powers subject to the controlling
> discretion, and under the sufferance of the state

governments.
The bank, then, was just an example of a larger problem that
the Court must address to save the nation. Thus did Webster
conclude as he began by bringing as much gravity to the case
as the situation would allow.
    William Pinkney's conclusion of the Bank's case was
highly stylized; it upstaged Webster with the gallery and
with some justices.[19]   Nonetheless, it was Webster who
influenced the thinking of Marshall. Marshall wanted to
widen the scope of the government's powers, much in the way
Alexander Hamilton had first envisioned them. Hamilton,
like Madison, was one of the Founders who recognized the
inadequacy of the Articles of Confederation.
    Webster argued that the "necessary and proper" clause
of the Constitution established the legitimate role of the
federal government in dealing with national problems.
Marshall accepted Webster's argument and held the Maryland
tax to be unconstitutional. He noted three distinct areas
of federal power: the federal government draws its
authority from the people, not the states; the "necessary
and proper clause" gives Congress broad powers to implement
the enumerated powers of the federal government; and any
state legislation that interferes with the existence of
legitimate federal powers is invalid. Marshall shamelessly
borrowed Webster's allusion to Hamilton and the argument
that "the power to tax involves the power to destroy."
Webster was delighted to have won the case and took great
pride in pointing out Marshall's plagiarism to friends.
    There were several other cases involving the bank in
which Webster participated. Webster, who often defended the
bank on the floor of the Senate (see chapter three), took
these cases upon receiving a hefty retainer from Nicholas
Biddle, the president of the Bank. Between 1819 and 1839,
Webster defended the bank ten times and opposed it twice.
In Osborn v. Bank of the U.S., for example, he was joined by
Clay. They defeated the state of Ohio's attempt to tax the
bank.[20]   The bank cases vastly expanded the rights of
corporations to operate across state borders and to seek
federal protection from state taxation.[21]

Gibbons v. Ogden

    As in the previous cases, Webster's arguments in
Gibbons v. Ogden stretched the powers of the federal
government by extracting implicit meaning from explicit
language.[22]   In this case, the commerce clause was at issue.
Webster believed the Constitution granted the Congress
exclusive power to regulate interstate commerce. The
founding fathers had taken this position because the state
legislatures had so badly managed commercial affairs,
particularly those between states. In fact, it was the
dispute between Virginia and Maryland over fishing rights in
the Potomac River that had led to the Annapolis Convention,
which in turn recommended a Constitutional Convention to
amend the Articles of Confederation. The inability of the
Articles to solve interstate problems served to reinforce
the need for a new national constitution. The commerce
clause, according to Webster, was perhaps the most strongly
mandated, given the way the Constitution evolved.

     The facts behind the case involved other historic
figures.   Robert Livingston and Robert Fulton had been
granted exclusive rights to operate a steamboat line on New
York waters.   In the absence of a federal law to the
contrary, no action was taken to restrict that license.
Livingston and Fulton sold their rights to Aaron Ogden.
Thomas Gibbons, however, operated a steamboat between New
York and New Jersey, and refused to stop when Ogden claimed
Gibbons was stealing his business.   Gibbons argued that his
license under the Federal Coasting Act justified his action
and negated the monopoly granted to Fulton by New York.
Ogden sued Gibbons for encroachment.
     With the talented Wirt at his side, Webster argued
Gibbons' case for five hours before the Court in February of
1824.   He said that congressional regulatory power in
commerce was complete and exclusive, the Coasting Act was
commercial regulation, and that the state of New York was in
conflict with this power.   Again Webster relied on
quotations from Hamilton to support a Federalist
interpretation of the Constitution.[23]   These passages no
doubt pleased Justices Marshall and Washington.   Webster
recited the reasons for the failure of the Articles of
Confederation and argued that they motivated the founders to
insert the commerce clause into the Constitution:
"Henceforth, the commerce of the States was to be a unit."
He went on to argue that interference with this form of
transportation would occur unless the Court remedied the
situation.
     Again Marshall sided with Webster, as did the majority
on the Court.   Justice Thompson was absent due to the death
of his daughter.   Congress had the power to regulate "that
commerce which concerns more states than one."   Therefore,
New York could not limit the scope of the federal powers by
creating a state monopoly over an interstate waterway since
that would effectively render the federally conferred
license useless.   But the Court did not go as far as Webster
desired.   It did not decide the issue of exclusivity;
instead, it found the state of New York in conflict with the
Federal Coasting Act of 1793.   Nonetheless, the case was a
historic victory of enduring impact because of its
affirmation of congressional power over interstate commerce.
Eventually this ruling was used to justify legislation
proposed during the New Deal.
     Webster argued over twenty cases before the Supreme
Court from 1819 to 1824.   The important ones strengthened
the hand of the federal government and further confined the
power of the states to regulate their own internal affairs.
Thus, Webster's forensic position complemented the political
position he would espouse as a senator.   Both in the courts
and the Congress, Webster stood for the Union.
     In the years that followed these cases, he argued many
others before the Court that had important impact, including
Ogden v. Saunders (1827).[24]   George Ogden refused to pay
bills and claimed he was protected by a New York insolvency
act dating from 1801.   A team of seven lawyers including
David Ogden, William Wirt, and Henry Clay, defended George
Ogden.   Henry Wheaton and Webster were on the other side.
The main question in the case was: Could a state enact
bankruptcy laws that affected future, private contracts?
Again the question of national jurisdiction came to the

fore.

The contract clause is the Tenth Section of Article I of the Constitution. Webster argued that the clause implied that bankruptcy laws were the exclusive right of the federal government. Moreover, no regulation, state or federal, claimed Webster, could be triggered until a contract was broken. Thus, the New York law was invalid because of its prospective nature.[25] In making the best case he could, Webster drew an overbroad interpretation of the contract clause, much the same way he had done with the commerce clause in Gibbons v. Ogden.

In this case, Marshall, supported by Story and Duvall, agreed with Webster but found himself on the dissenting side for the first and only time as Chief Justice. The decision caused many states to institute new and differing bankruptcy laws. The confusion that resulted was one of the causes of the Panic of 1837. After that depression, Webster again called for a national bankruptcy law to bring order out of the chaos. Like many conservatives, Webster was justified in taking up the cry of "I told you so." It was one of the many instances where his legal experience influenced his legislative agenda.

Also in 1837, Webster had a chance to deal with the contract clause again, in Charles River Bridge v. Warren Bridge. Webster defended the Charles River Bridge's exclusive right to the traffic crossing the river between Boston and Charlestown. He opposed the state's claim of eminent domain, again trying to protect private corporate rights.

With Taney sitting as Chief Justice, Webster lost the case. However, Story and two others filed a strong dissent supporting Webster's position, which was eventually incorporated in majority decisions. This was another in a string of cases that prepared him for the legislative battles with Calhoun, Clay, Benton, Seward, and others. Webster's forensic presentation of national conservatism surrounded the states' rights position on two sides. On the one side, Webster knew that a strong federal government was essential for national defense, internal improvements, and healthy commerce. He would keep the states from usurping or infringing upon federal powers that were clearly granted in the Constitution and that protected an orderly free enterprise system. On the other side, Webster defended the natural rights of citizens and corporations against their states. Not since Hamilton had anyone so adamantly argued for court decisions and legislation that would contract the power of the states.

By 1850, as we shall see in chapter four, Webster had become so used to defending the Union that he placed it above the other values that had once justified creation of the Union in the first place. Union served as a means to an end for Webster from 1819 to about 1838, but at that point, Union became the end in itself. No doubt the Webster-Hayne debate of 1830 was a major turning point in Webster's thinking on this matter. The overwhelmingly favorable response to Webster's performance undoubtedly reinforced Webster's commitment to the Union. It is surely the point where Webster shifted from pre-eminent Supreme Court lawyer to pre-eminent legislative debater.

This emphasis on the legislative arena was further

encouraged by Taney's arrival on the Court in 1835. With
Marshall as Chief Justice, Webster usually won his cases.
But when Marshall died in 1835 and was replaced by Democrat
Roger Taney, Webster's winning percentage began a decline
that would eventually put his lifetime average before the
Supreme Court at 48 percent. Webster said, "Taney is smooth
and plausible but cunning and Jesuitical and as thorough
going a party judge as ever got on to a bench of justice."[26]
Taney first came to prominence by leading a dissenting group
of Federalists who favored the war of 1812.   Ironically,
though he would pen the Dred Scott decision, Taney actively
defended the rights of blacks, including slaves.   He
believed the commerce clause should be interpreted narrowly.
Unlike Webster, Taney often favored state regulations over
federal regulations.[27] It is important to note that Webster
had acted to keep Attorney General Taney from becoming
Secretary of the Treasury in 1833 and off the Court when he
was first nominated in March of 1835 as an associate
justice. When Marshall died, President Jackson nominated
Taney for Chief Justice and the nomination was approved by
the Senate over the objections of Clay, Calhoun, and
Webster. Thus, it is no surprise that Taney was less than
enthusiastic about Webster's appearances before the Court.
From that point on, Webster would score his points for Union
and national conservatism as a senator and as a Secretary of
State.

CRIMINAL CASES

      Webster mastered argumentation before the Supreme
Court, but he was also persuasive in criminal and civil
cases. He demonstrated his versatility in many courtrooms.
He was able to produce enormously persuasive narratives in
criminal cases before a jury, a tactic not likely to impress
a Supreme Court justice.
      The most famous criminal case argued by Webster was the
Knapp-White case of August, 1830. Captain Joseph White, a
well-to-do entrepreneur, was found murdered in his bed on
April 7, 1830, in Salem, Massachusetts, and panic swept the
town.   Eventually the police apprehended three men: Richard
Crownshield, Joseph Knapp, and Frank Knapp.   Under
questioning, Joseph Knapp, who was married to White's niece,
admitted to hiring Crownshield to commit the murder in order
to gain White's inheritance.   Crownshield then committed
suicide in prison, and Knapp quickly retracted his
confession.[28]
      Because of the fervor in the community, the prosecution
invited Webster to represent their interests in the three
trials that followed. Several trials were necessary because
of the complexity of the indictments and an early mistrial.
Frank Knapp was tried first; the result was a hung jury.
Tension increased substantially in Salem and spread to
nearby communities.   Knapp was convicted at his second
trial. Webster's five-hour summation in this trial won him
acclaim.   To a packed courtroom, Webster performed well.
The Knapp brothers were publicly executed while a mob of
10,000 looked on. Webster's legend grew.[29]
      Webster's success in this forensic effort was marked by
his ability to recreate scenes before the jury. He played
on their powers of imagination by building a coherent

scenario of the crime. This strategem was essential because
one of the problems in the case was proving that both
brothers were involved in "a cool, calculating, money-making
murder." By recreating scenes in the mind's eye of jurors,
Webster was able to sustain the claim that the brothers were
in league with the murderer. Furthermore, enacting the
scene helped incite the jury against the conspirators since
the victim was eighty-two years old and helpless. The
following passage reveals Webster's strength at narrative:

> The deed was executed with a degree of self-possession
> and steadiness equal to the wickedness with which it
> was planned. The circumstances now clearly in evidence
> spread out the whole scene before us. Deep sleep had
> fallen on the destined victim and on all beneath his
> roof. A healthful old man to whom sleep was sweet, the
> first sound slumbers of the night held him in their
> soft but strong embrace. The assassin enters through
> the window already prepared, into an unoccupied
> apartment. With noiseless foot he paces the lonely
> hall, half lighted by the moon; he winds up the ascent
> of the stairs, and reaches the door of the chamber. Of
> this he moves the lock by soft and continued pressure,
> till it turns on its hinges without a noise; and he
> enters and beholds his victim before him.

Webster knew that the case would be made or broken on the
question of motive. So he worked throughout the speech to
establish the motive of the crime. Webster brought to bear
on the question of motive not only scenic recreation but
psychological analysis and the force of repetition. At one
point he said:

> Whoever shall hereafter draw the portrait of a murder .
> . . let him not give it the grim visage of Moloch, the
> brow knitted by revenge, the face black with settled
> hate, and the bloodshot eye emitting livid fires of
> malice.   Let him draw, rather, a decorous,
> smooth-faced, bloodless demon.

Webster's object was to engrave the attitude of a
conspirator on the minds of the jury. The passage is not
untypical of Webster; the repetitious, periodic phrasing
gave a driving force to the vivid picture. The conspiracy
theme was picked up, repreated, and extended, much like a
theme in fugue. Webster used this strategy to reinforce
the evidence, all circumstantial, that this "extraordinary"
case involved a cold-hearted deal for money.

The strategy emerged again and again as Webster moved
through the speech. For example, to sum up the facts
supporting a meeting of the conspirators, he said:

> It was their place of <u>centrality</u>. The club was found
> near the spot, in a place provided for it, in a place
> that had been previously hunted out, in a concerted
> place of concealment. <u>Here was their point of</u>
> <u>rendezvous</u>; here might the lights be seen; here might
> an aid be secreted; here he was within call; here might
> he be aroused by the sound of the whistle.   [his
> emphasis]

The thesis, that this was the location, is reinforced by the
repetition of the word "here."   The opportunity for the
crime is reinforced by the repitition of the word "might."
Again, the drum beat of Webster's phrasing, when combined
with his sonorous delivery and dark eyes, must have been

impossible for any member of the jury to resist. And it was critical that they accept Webster's version of the facts that placed the conspirators in the same street near the house of Captain White. The jury accepted Webster's scenario.

CONCLUSION

   In January, 1830, Webster had gained national attention with his "Reply to Hayne." With the Knapp-White case in August, his reputation as a criminal lawyer swept Massachusetts. Webster was the consummate lawyer. He had proven himself in the highest court in the land and in a simple courtroom in Salem, on constitutional issues, and on criminal matters. In each instance, he had demonstrated an ability to link the specific issues of the case at hand with transcendent Constitutional and/or moral issues. Webster persuaded justices of the Supreme Court and jurors of Salem that his vision of those issues was the correct one.
   His forensic powers not only served him well, they helped strengthen the young Union and set a model for criminal prosecution. Late in his life, Webster confessed, "You will find, in my speeches to juries, no hard words, no Latin phrases, no _fieri facas_; and that is the secret of my style if I have any."[30] But Webster was also the consummate speaker. His success at forensic oratory was matched by his talent to produce moving ceremonial speeches and unparalleled deliberative addresses. To these masterpieces we now turn.

2

Ceremonial Speaking

Many of Webster's addresses have been examined by
rhetorical critics; but most ignore questions of genre.[1]
Those who do attempt some judgment of form analyze only a
single genre.[2]   Thus, when critics discuss Webster's
forensic speaking, they ignore epideictic and deliberative
elements in forensic speeches.   And yet Webster's arguments
before the Supreme Court are known to have influenced
Justice Marshall's decisions on deliberative matters, and
reflected Webster's own political positions.[3]   Similarly,
although many have studied Webster's deliberative speaking,
no attention has been paid to forensic and epideictic
elements in these addresses.   For example, in the replies to
Hayne, Webster praised noninterference and Union, while
making a forensic case for disposition of public lands.   In
the first reply, Webster's discourse was epideictic: he
"deprecated and deplored" the tone of Hayne's rhetoric.
During the debate over the Missouri Compromise, he spent a
good deal of time explaining the "injustices" done to the
New England states.   During the 1850 Compromise debates,
Webster had praise for some senators and states, and blame
for others.   In fact, one would be hard pressed to find a
deliberative effort that did not contain forensic and
epideictic aspects.   Throughout Webster's ostensibly
deliberative speeches, the reader finds references to
precedent, certain "injustices," and the Constitution--all
forensic subjects.   One also finds references to freedom,
liberty, progress, hard work, and conciliation--usually
epideictic subjects.
     Much less research has been dedicated to uncovering the
strategies that Webster used in ceremonial addresses.   An
examination of them makes clear that Webster used epideictic
form to house elements of the other genres in order to
accomplish his rhetorical end.   Webster's ceremonial
speaking demonstrates that effective discourse has elements
of all three forms of address and that interaction among
forms within an address may explain its effectiveness or
lack thereof.   For instance, on August 5, 1812, he delivered
the Rockingham Memorial.   It was based on his July 4 address
before a group of leading Federalists.   In this polished
version, which was set for printing and distribution,

Webster attacked in a deliberative sense the administration's prosecution of the war and defended the Constitution: "Resistance and insurrection form no parts of our creed. The disciples of Washington are neither tyrants in power, nor rebels out of it." The address was quickly printed and widely distributed. Within the month, it was revised into a "memorial" or letter of resolution to President Madison by Webster in his role as delegate to the Federalist county convention. The memorial included words which would embarrass Webster in his legislative debate with Hayne and on several other occasions: "If a separation of the states shall ever take place, it will be, on some occasion, when one portion of the country undertakes to control, to regulate, and to sacrifice the interest of another." New England's support for a tariff, argued Hayne in 1830, was just such an occasion. An analysis of Webster's major ceremonial addresses demonstrates the effective fusion of deliberative and forensic elements in an epideictic form.

THE PLYMOUTH ADDRESS

On December 22, 1820, Webster gave the "Plymouth Address" (also known as "The First Settlement of New England") to celebrate the bicentennial of the landing of the Pilgrims. People came from almost every part of the country for the event. Webster delivered the oration in First Parish Church, which was too small for the attending crowd. Twelve hundred people were jammed inside; the rest craned to see Webster through the windows and cupped their ears to hears his words. This speech, like many other of his ceremonial addresses, revealed Webster's ecumenical Protestantism. His belief in God, the Ten Commandments, and the righteousness of revenge was softened by his faith in New Testament redemption. But these values, while undoubtedly deeply held by Webster, usually played a secondary role to his political philosophy. Webster's political values were refined before the Supreme Court and tested in the caldron of legislative debate, and some ideas, like his notion of "national conservatism," were original. They were also enriched by Webster's reading material, including the best of Bacon, Macaulay, Dryden, and Moore.

Webster spoke for two hours, enthralling the audience and reinforcing his already growing reputation for great speaking. Many in the audience said that Webster burned with an inner fire as he spoke as if inspired by the spirits of the Pilgrims. Earlier in the day, most of the members of the audience had visited Plymouth Rock and what was left of the Pilgrim's village. Webster's emotional style and vivid imagery brought back to the audience not only the place they had visited, but the reality of the Pilgrims' suffering and sacrifice:

> We cast our eyes abroad on the ocean, and we see where the little bark . . . made its slow progress to the shore. We look around us, and behold the hills and promontories, where the anxious eyes of our fathers first saw the places of habitation and of rest. We feel the cold which benumbed, and listen to the winds which pierced them.

Perhaps no orator has ever been better at bringing a picture
alive before an audience, nor better at adapting to a
particular location or occasion.

The speech is full of historical allusions and
analogies. For example, Webster compared the Pilgrims'
journey to earlier efforts at colonization by the Greeks and
Romans. But most true to the epideictic form was Webster's
praise for certain values:

> [T]here is also a moral and philosophical respect for
> our ancestors, which elevates the character and
> improves the heart. Next to the sense of religious
> duty and moral feeling, I hardly know what should bear
> with stronger obligation on a liberal and enlightened
> mind than a consciousness of alliance with excellence
> which is departed; and a consciousness, too, that in
> its acts and conduct, and even in its sentiments and
> thoughts, it may be actively operating on the happiness
> of those who come after it.

This respect for past generations and traditions is
traceable directly to Edmund Burke, whom Webster greatly
admired. It comprises one of the most persistently
mentioned tenets of Webster's philosophy. It is without
doubt his firm belief that history, tradition, and
generational loyalty are the mystical cords that bind a
people into a nation:

> Standing in this relation to our ancestors and our
> posterity, we are assembled on this memorable plot, to
> perform the duties which that relation and the present
> occasion impose upon us. We have come to this Rock, to
> record here our homage for our Pilgrim Fathers; our
> sympathy in their sufferings; our gratitude for their
> labors; our admiration of their virtues; our veneration
> for their piety; and our attachment to those principles
> of civil and religious liberty with which they
> encountered the dangers of the ocean, the storms of
> heaven, the violence of savages, disease, exile, and
> famine, to enjoy and establish.

In form, this passage reveals the periodic cadence that
typified Webster's style. In substance, this perspective on
what citizens owe their ancestors framed the obligation that
Webster's audience owed to future generations. "Advance,
then, ye future generations," said Webster.

Having reinforced transcendent values and a sense of
linkage with the past, Webster moved to the course he
believed the nation should take. Here he most clearly fused
deliberative argument with epideictic form. He endorsed
protection of property as the foundation of constitutional
law. Like Aristotle, Webster claimed that property provided
the stake in the nation that guaranteed the loyalty and
productivity of the electorate. But not to be
misunderstood, he added:

> If there be, within the extent of our knowledge or
> influence, any participation in this [slave] traffic,
> let us pledge ourselves here, upon the Rock of
> Plymouth, to extirpate and destroy it. It is not fit
> that the land of the Pilgrims should bear the shame
> longer. I hear the sound of the hammer, I see the
> smoke of the furnace, where the manacles and fetters

are still forged for human limbs. I see the visages of
those, who by stealth, and at midnight, labor in this
work of hell, foul and dark, as may become the
artificers of such instruments of misery and torture.
Let that spot be purified, or let it cease to be of New
England.

Not only was praise involved, as one might expect, but
Webster recommended a course of action for the country and
at the same time condemned slavery.[4] He thereby concealed a
deliberative and a forensic argument in the epideictic form
by reinforcing the seminal value of New England's Puritan
founders, who would cleanse impurities in the body politic.

Like most of Webster's ceremonial speeches, this was
rewritten, polished, and then published. The speech brought
Webster national attention, adulation in the North and West,
but hostility in the South. John Adams was effusive in his
praise of the address in calling Webster "the most
consummate orator of modern times." Adams said the speech
would live for "five hundred years hence." This event did
nothing to diminish Webster's credibility as he returned to
the Massachusetts Constitutional Convention to debate its
provisions. The Plymouth Address and his actions at the
Convention mandated a political career. Two years later he
was returned to the House to represent Boston; five years
after that, he would enter the U.S. Senate from
Massachusetts.

THE BUNKER HILL ADDRESSES

On June 17, 1825, in his "First Bunker Hill Address,"
also known as "Laying the Cornerstone of the Bunker Hill
Monument" (see text in Part II) Webster argued for Greek
independence and speculated on South American revolutions.[5]
But first Webster set the scene, celebrated the occasion,
and excited the enormous crowd of at least twenty thousand
that had gathered for the event in Charlestown, across the
river from Boston. Said Webster:

If, indeed, there be anything in local association fit
to affect the mind of man, we need not strive to
repress the emotions which agitate us here. We are
among the sepulchres of our fathers. We are on ground
distinguished by their valor, their constancy, and the
shedding of their blood.

Webster played to New England pride in this address even
more than in his tribute to Adams and Jefferson, which
followed a little more than a year later.

Fifty years earlier, the first major battle of the
Revolutionary War had been fought on nearby Breed's Hill.
Webster's father had been close to the battle, in charge of
a company of volunteers. He was later with Washington at
White Plains. Webster's adoration for his father often
colored his narration of the Revolutionary War. On this
day, Webster commemorated the laying of the cornerstone of
the monument to be erected to celebrate the battle. The
Marquis de Lafayette, the most noted foreign ally of the
war, and two hundred veterans of the battle sat on the stage
near Webster. This situation allowed Webster to place the
moment into the context of the American heritage and then

use it to reinforce the most important values in civil life.
"We consecrate our work to the spirit of national
independence, and we wish that the light of peace may rest
upon it forever."

At the same time, Webster praised America's fifty years
of growth and new found strength.

We have a commerce that leaves no sea unexplored;
navies which take no law from superior force; revenues
adequate to all the exigencies of government, almost
without taxation; and peace with all nations founded on
equal rights and mutual respect.

One of the reasons Webster was so convincing in this passage
was that he reinforced the message with a periodic and
parallel construction that progressed to a natural
conclusion. (If one delivers the words out loud, one will
sense that the style and thought flow together so well that
the message is almost irresistible.) Certainly, on this
occasion, with Webster facing thousands of sympathetic
listeners seated on the hill below him, it was transcendent.

In the next section of the speech, Webster contrasted
American values and successes with European ones. He
claimed that the Revolution was only the beginning of a
great victory that the New World would achieve over the Old
World not only in terms of military might but in terms of
legislation, commerce, arts, letters, "and above all, in
liberal ideas."

Then returning again to the event itself, a step
Aristotle said was essential for effective epideictic
oratory, Webster emotionally called out the names of the
leaders at the battle and remembered the other crucial
battles of the War. He recounted the circumstances that led
to the battle of Bunker Hill and once more brought the
speech back to the local audience and Boston:

You see the lines of the little redoubt thrown up by
the incredible diligence of Prescott; defended to the
last extremity, by his lion-hearted valor . . . . You
see where Warren fell, and where Parker, Gardner,
McCleary, Moore, and other early patriots fell with
him. Those who survived that day, and whose lives have
been prolonged to the present hour, are now around you
. . . . Behold! they now stretch forth their feeble
arms to embrace you. Behold! they raise their
trembling voices to invoke the blessing of God on you
and yours forever.

This metaphysical appeal worked because of Webster's
sincerity, because the crowd was with him, and because
sitting on the stage with him were the withered survivors of
the battle whose feeble arms and trembling voices gave
substance to Webster's rhetorical ghosts. The scene was
recreated in the minds of his listeners and they gladly
received the benediction of the dead patriots. (In the
eulogy to Adams and Jefferson, soon to be discussed, Webster
became Adams and uttered what has been called the greatest
"ghost speech" in American public address. Perhaps
Webster's success at Bunker Hill gave him the courage to be
even more daring with invented dialogue at Faneuil Hall a
year later.)

Once Webster had fixed the moment at Bunker Hill, once

the values he preferred were endorsed, he moved on to
espouse the spread of democratic revolution and the manifest
destiny of civilized men.   Throughout his defense of
revolution, Webster contrasted American democratic values
with the autocratic tendencies of the Old World.   While
Europe fought wars to maintain alliances and power, America
fought for freedom.   Webster then praised the Greek
Revolution and the revolutions underway in Latin America as
part of a new wave of freedom sweeping from the cradle of
liberty to the New World.
     In the end, Webster reinforced the ideals he believed
would deliver America to her destiny.   These included
liberty, progress, duty, defense, peace, and union.
Throughout the two-hour address, he rarely glanced at the
few scribbled lines he kept on a small podium beside him.
Like most of Webster's ceremonial speeches, this one was
polished, then published and widely distributed.   Proceeds
were donated to the Monument Association.   Most important,
the speech helped to establish the genre of ceremonial
speaking in America.   The Cyclopedia of American Biography
states, "Achieving another great oratorical triumph at the
laying of the cornerstone of the Bunker Hill monument on
June 17, 1825, he made popular the occasional oratory that
was to thrive for decades."[6]
     A generation later, on June 17, 1843, Webster returned
to the same spot to deliver the "Completion of the Bunker
Hill Monument Address."   He reiterated his favorite themes
and proclaimed that the newly completed "column stands for
the Union."   Given just before the hostilities that led to
the Mexican-American war, Webster used the opportunity to
rationalize Manifest Destiny, though he would oppose the war
with Mexico.   Webster's ambivalence over this issue stemmed
from his sense of loyalty to the president he had served and
his own fears that acquisition of territory from Mexico
would jeopardize the North-South balance.   This speech was
also hampered by the appearance of President Tyler at this
event.   Webster had resigned a month earlier as Tyler's
Secretary of State and a year earlier, he had attacked the
Whig leaders for criticizing Tyler.   Most Whigs believed
Webster had stuck with Tyler too long.   They also despised
Tyler for abandoning Whig principles.   John Quincy Adams was
so appalled at the spectacle of Tyler appearing at the
ceremony that he refused to attend.   Webster was upset, too.
He drank a tumbler of brandy before the speech and another
just after it, although neither seemed to have an effect.
His delivery was brilliant and the audience was moved.
However, the speech was not known as one of his most
memorable.[7]

THE CHARACTER OF WASHINGTON

     In 1832, in his "Character of Washington Address,"
Webster used an ostensibly epideictic occasion to attack
John C. Calhoun's doctrine of nullification.   Again, Webster
used an epideictic occasion to make a deliberative point.
The speech was delivered two years after the famous
Webster-Hayne debate (see chapter three) in which Webster
soundly thrashed the doctrine of nullification.   But

nullification would not die as long as Calhoun was around to
flog it, and he proved more able to the task than the
hapless Hayne. Webster's replies to Hayne in 1830 were full
of praise for Washington because Webster had enormous
admiration for the General. The nation's first president
also provided ample support for Webster's call for Union.
Thus, it was expected that Webster would rise on February
22, 1832, to praise the occasion of the "Centennial
Anniversary of Washington's Birthday." As usual, Webster
tied the event to the immediate audience:

> We perform this grateful duty, gentlemen, at the
> expiration of a hundred years from his birth, near the
> place, so cherished and beloved by him, where his dust
> now reposes, and in the capital which bears his own
> immortal name.

As in previous speeches, Webster talked about the progress
of the New World and its unique values. In contrast, the
Old World seemed to stagnate. Many of the values mentioned
in the speech were supported in the biographical section of
the speech. Washington's life was used to demonstrate the
character of those values and how they manifest themselves
in national leadership. The strategy culminated with the
following sentence: "We cannot wish better for our country,
nor for the world, than that the same spirit which
influenced Washington may influence all who succeed him."
The line served as a turning point in the speech and
foreshadowed Webster's underlying message: to honor
Washington properly, we must live by his principles, and
those principles inevitably lead to Union. Webster built to
this message subtly and carefully.

He began by associating Washington with simple values
no one could reject. "[H]e told the country . . . that
honesty is the best policy. . . . He had no favorites; he
rejected all partisanship; and, acting honestly for the
universal good, he deserved, what he has so richly enjoyed,
the universal love of his countrymen." Then Webster moved
to Washington's principles of foreign policy with which few
could quarrel.

Once he had established admiration for and
identification with Washington, his "great character," and
his foreign policy, Webster could reinforce his own agenda:

> The domestic policy of Washington found its pole-star
> in the avowed objects of the Constitution itself. He
> sought so to administer that Constitution, as to form a
> more perfect Union. . . . [T]here was in the breath
> of Washington one sentiment so deeply felt, so
> constantly uppermost, that no proper occasion escaped
> without its utterance. For the letter which he signed
> in behalf of the Convention when the Constitution was
> sent out to the people, to the moment when he put his
> hand to that last paper in which he addressed his
> countrymen, the Union—the Union was the great object
> of his thoughts.

The remainder of this speech supported Union, further
identified it with Washington, and stressed the values
important to maintaining it. As in the Webster-Hayne debate
and the first speech on the Compromise of 1850, Webster
argued that all good things flow from the Union. Ending the

Union would end its benefits as well.
     In an emotional conclusion he refered to the opening of
the address and prayed that in another hundred years, the
nation would still be moving toward its glorious destiny.

ADDITION TO THE CAPITOL

     Even Webster's last critically acclaimed speech,
"Addition to the Capitol," is full of legislative
recommendations and forensic attacks on slavery. This
speech was delivered at the laying of the cornerstone of the
addition to the Capitol building on July 4, 1851. Nearly a
year had passed since the passage of the Compromise of 1850
(see chapter four) and Webster's selection for a second time
to be Secretary of State. Webster had a little more than a
year to live. President Fillmore, a Webster prote'ge',
preceded Webster to the rostrum in an acknowledgment of who
was the most important speaker of the day. But while he
enjoyed fame in Washington, Webster was snubbed by Whigs in
Boston. His ostracism from the Boston Whigs would be
complete by the time of his death in October of 1852. Thus,
when he rose to speak, those assembled realized that the
Secretary of State was in the twilight of a great career,
which Webster believed might yet earn him a presidential
nomination. He acknowledged his warm reception in his
opening remarks, "I see before and around me a mass of faces
glowing with cheerfulness and patriotic pride. I see
thousands of eyes, all sparkling with gratification and
delight." As always, Webster adapted his rhetoric to the
occasion, the audience, and location. In this case, he used
a narrowing perspective that came to focus on the assemblage
before him: "This is the New World! This America! This is
Washington! and this is the Capitol of the United States!"
     The body of the address, like that of the First Bunker
Hill Address, stressed the story of the Revolution and its
attendant values to reinforce Webster's transcendent vision
of a democratic Union leading the rest of the world to peace
and freedom. "Fellow citizens, this inheritance which we
enjoy today is not only an inheritance of liberty, but of
our own peculiar American liberty." Webster then
differentiated American experiences from that of other great
nations and concluded with the ancient Greeks. That example
allowed him once again to make his case for Union, "And let
it ever be remembered, especially let the truth sink deep
into all American minds, that it was the want of Union among
her several States which finally gave the mastery of all of
Greece to Philip of Macedon." This lesson gave Webster the
opportunity to review again what he believed "American
political principles in substance to be." The list included
representative government, equality, and maintaining the
will of the majority in harmony with the rule of law. Then
echoing Washington and previewing Theodore Roosevelt,
Webster added, "Individual virtue is a part of public
virtue."
     At this juncture, Webster turned to his official duty,
the commemoration of the laying of the cornerstone. George
Washington, Webster's great hero, had laid the first
cornerstone fifty-eight years earlier, and Webster used that

fact to bring his speech back to the moment at hand by
comparing the state of the Union in 1793 to its state in
1851.   Again, Webster claimed that Union made all of the
expansion and prosperity possible.   He called on the South
in general, and Virginia, just across the Potomac, in
specific to support a working federal system.   Webster
concluded his speech by quoting Cicero in Latin and then
saying,

> And now, fellow citizens, with hearts void of hatred,
> envy and malice toward our own countrymen . . . or
> toward the subjects or citizens of other governments,
> or toward any member of the great family of man; but
> exalting, nevertheless, in our own peace, security, and
> happiness . . . let us return to our homes, and with
> all humility and devotion offer our thanks to the
> Father of all our mercies, political, social, and
> religious.

The closing plea was remarkable because it reversed the
opening focus.   Instead of closing to the immediate
audience, it began with "countrymen" and opened to "the
great family of man."   The progressive strategy tied the
speech together and gave it an elegant unity rarely attained
in American public address.

CEREMONIAL SPEECHES ON THE CAMPAIGN TRAIL

Webster's epideictic speeches were often part of grand
tours arranged out of the many invitations he received.
1837 was a banner year for him in this regard.   In New York
City he was given the equivalent of a ticker-tape parade
along Broadway and then spoke on the future of the Whig
party, which had lost yet another presidential election.
The speech was delivered to 3,500 people in a huge and
popular saloon.   In the speech, Webster opposed annexation
of Texas, attacked Jackson and the new president, Martin Van
Buren, and predicted a recession.   When the economic panic
did come later that year, the Democrats claimed that
Webster's speech had encouraged New York banks to
precipitate a panic.   Webster said he was merely farsighted
and that the Democrats were to blame for the economic
collapse.
        Caleb Cushing financed Webster's western tour that
began in Pittsburgh in May.   It included St. Louis, Chicago,
Detroit and many stops in between, including a visit to
Lexington, Kentucky to see Henry Clay, who had headed the
unsuccessful Whig ticket.[8]
        In his "Reception at Madison Address," in Indiana,
Webster argued for Western expansion, the American System,
and nationalism.   The hour-long speech was delivered from an
elaborately decorated platform on June 1.   Above the
platform was a large banner that read, "Liberty and Union,
now and forever, one and inseparable" in tribute to the
stirring finish of the Webster-Hayne debate.
        This invitation to speak in the West afforded Webster
the opportunity to promote nationalism, the constitution,
and his own presidential aspirations.[9]   But the text reveals
that it was easier for Webster to praise General Washington

or a historic battle than to advance his own name. His attempts at adapting to his immediate audience seem somewhat awkward and contrived. For example, he said he had "lived on terms of great intimacy and friendship with several western gentlemen, members of congress, among whom is your estimable townsman near me [Governor Hendricks]. I have never before had an opportunity of seeing and forming an acquaintance for myself with fellow-citizens of this section of the Union." Beside the fact that the lines contradict one another, the wording is unusually wooden for Webster.

Webster was known by 1837 as a spokesman for the propertied, rich, industrial and banking interests of prosperous Boston, yet his audience was composed basically of small landholders and farmers. Throughout the speech, his attempts to identify with these simple folk missed the mark. "[Y]ou far surpass in fertility of soil and in the widespread and highly-cultivated fields, the smiling villages and busy towns. . . . [Y]ou will reap a rich reward for your investment and industry. . . . [Americans] plough the land and plough the sea." Webster devoted the first part of the speech to praising Indiana's accomplishments and making sure his audience understood that he had supported the American system of internal improvements that facilitated settlement in Indiana and transportation of its crops to market. As in other speeches, Webster made clear that the American system was made possible by a national Constitution.

A second problem Webster faced in this situation was the fact that William Henry Harrison, the hero of the battle of Tippecanoe and potential presidential nominee, was from Indiana. Webster avoided antagonizing Harrison's supporters by concentrating his fire on the legacy of the Jackson and Van Buren administrations. The second part of his speech discussed national economic problems and how leadership was needed in the White House to overcome the financial depression. His answer was to facilitate commerce wherever possible and to continue to build roads, bridges, and canals all across the country. These improvements would not only spur the economy, they would also serve to unite the country, which meant a stronger Union. Here again, Webster used a ceremonial occasion to advance deliberative themes.

The grand tour of 1837 was a great success in terms of publicity and in promoting Webster for the party's nomination of 1840. But since the nomination was three years off, Clay took offense at Webster's show of ambition. So did Southern Whigs who disagreed with Webster on Texas, the tariff, and slavery.[10]

The point of this review is to show that categorizing a speech into one and only one of the forms recommended by Aristotle limits the criticism of that discourse. In Webster's case, this limitation is particularly damaging to understanding his oratory since he was a master of encasing elements of one form in another. Aristotle described the strategy when he wrote:

> To praise a man is in one respect akin to urging a
> course of action. The suggestions which would be made
> in the latter case become encomiums when differently
> expressed. . . . Consequently whenever you want to
> praise anyone, think what you would urge people to do;

and when you want to urge the doing of anything, think
what you would praise a man for having done. Since
suggestion may or may not forbid any action, the praise
into which we convert it must have one or other of two
opposite forms of expression accordingly.[11]
Recognizing that the interplay of the various forms produces
a unique speech for a rhetorical situation, the critic is
more likely to make useful and complete judgments.
Webster's eulogy to Adams and Jefferson demonstrates this
thesis and gives one a chance to examine his epideictic
oratory in more detail. Unlike the previous speeches, the
eulogy lacks prominent forensic or deliberative elements;
therefore, it should lend itself more readily than the
others to Aristotle's formulation. This apparent
faithfulness to one form may be explained by noting the time
of the speech. It came before Webster was solidly committed
to national conservatism and six years after the Missouri
Compromise. The slavery issue had ebbed. The address came
midway between presidential election years, thus somewhat
removing the occasion from national politics. Finally, the
event was so mystical and so concerned with national heroes
that it easily lent itself to the epideictic form. It is
not difficult to understand why the speech is Webster's most
purely epideictic; he had less need for forensic or
deliberative strategies on this occasion than on the others
reviewed above.

EULOGY OF ADAMS AND JEFFERSON

On July 4, 1826, exactly fifty years after the
Declaration of Independence, Thomas Jefferson and John Adams
died. On August 2, 1826, Daniel Webster chose to speak of
this event and about the lives it concerned. Edward
Everett, who was gaining a reputation for oratorical skill
himself, had planned to speak about this event in New
Hampshire a few weeks earlier, but Webster talked him out of
it, not so subtly implying that speaking before Webster
would be politically unwise. Four thousand people tried to
crowd into Faneuil Hall in Boston's financial district near
the harbor. The balconies were draped in black. Near
Webster on the stage sat John Quincy Adams, the former
president who retained membership in the House of
Representatives. It was his father who would receive most
of Webster's attention.[12]
The event not only captured the national imagination
but seemed marked by providence. It would become part of
American civil religion, and any speaker addressing the
moment needed to tread carefully.
The task was doubly difficult because Jefferson and
Adams represented very different personalities and political
philosophies. The eulogy was Webster's most successful
ceremonial address because it artfully welded occasion and
subjects into one piece of discourse.[13] This union was
enhanced by employing the epideictic form with only a few
traces of forensic and deliberative elements in the speech.
Aristotle's advice on epideictic form was given
throughout the Rhetoric. He specifically recommended

appeals to honor and dishonor for the epideictic address,[14] and his discussion of the other virtues indicates that they were to support the strategies surrounding honor or dishonor. Furthermore, the Rhetoric includes advice on how to make all of these claims believable.[15]

Aristotle's recommendations for arrangement in epideictic speaking began with a call for a preview of ideas. The Rhetoric recommends that themes be integrated into the text to insure continuity. Consistent with this advice is the recommendation that the narration be intermittent throughout the speech, and that eulogy and argument be interwoven.[16] In these passages, one sees the emergence of flexible form over mere prescription; that is to say, Aristotle seemed concerned not only with an organizational structure appropriate to the occasion, but a structure that demonstrated some sense of proportion.

The Rhetoric also recommends that the speaker bring his audience into the occasion. One suspects that Aristotle realized how easy it would be for a speaker to exclude his audience while eulogizing the dead, a past event, or while vilifying an opponent, a nasty deed, or a place. Of the three forms, Aristotle claimed that the epideictic "is the most literary, since it is meant to be read."[17] We find support for Aristotle's claim among modern critics and in Webster's practice of not publishing his speeches until he had revised them.[18] Thus, of the three forms, the epideictic is likely to be the most lasting and thereby the most controlled.

Webster's eulogy is evidence of this thesis. Not only does it meet all of the overt criteria of the form by dealing with a present occasion and praising its subjects, but in subtle ways it meets the standards of structure crucial to Aristotle's notion of epideictic form. The proportioning of the speech is almost poetic. If the letter A represents discourse devoted to Adams, the letter J discourse devoted to Jefferson, and AJ the discussion of the two together, the following general pattern emerges:

Introduction: AJ.
Body: A then J, then AJ, then A, then J, then AJ, and AJ again.
Conclusion: AJ, digression, AJ, peroration.

The introduction is concerned with describing the extraordinary coincidence that has brought the audience together. Then the parallel lives of the two patriots, who died on the same day on the fiftieth anniversary of the Declaration of Independence, were generally explored as a kind of preview of what will come. Already in the introduction, Webster had created a pattern that would guide him through the speech. The audience would be involved in the speech by references to the occasion. The occasion would be explored by references to the parallel lives of the two patriots. Also foreshadowed in the introduction was a wonderful metaphor that surfaced several more times in the speech and culminated at the end. Webster refered to the stars in the sky, and then a little later to orbits and planets. This universe allowed the patriots to shine like stars.

The first section after the introduction was devoted to John Adam's life to the year 1776. The following section

explored Jefferson's life to the same year. Webster knew
Adams better than Jefferson and certainly preferred the
politics of the former to the politics of the latter. But
during his Christmas vacation in 1824, Webster visited
Jefferson, ostensibly to seek his advice on the presidential
selection process that had been thrown into the House.
During their meeting at Monticello, Webster was delighted to
learn that Jefferson believed Andrew Jackson to be a
dangerous demagogue. Webster had been predisposed to
support John Quincy Adams for president, and now could do so
enjoying the blessings of one of the nation's founders.

The praise of both men centered on their particular
accomplishments as evidence of honor. Jefferson's role as
leader-statesman, philosopher and founding father was
compared to Adams' political commitments and service on the
Massachusetts Supreme Court. Other accomplishments were
used to demonstrate virtues attendant upon honor. For
example, Jefferson was said to have received the highest
honors at William and Mary College, an obvious attempt on
Webster's part to demonstrate the intelligence of his
subject. Adams was said to have argued before his state's
Supreme Court at the early age of twenty-four. Jefferson
was pictured as just in representing his constituents. With
Adams, Webster was more direct, "Mr. Adams himself seems
never to have lost the feeling it [justice] produced, and to
have entertained constantly the fullest conviction of its
important effect." Courage and sacrifice were also imputed
to the two patriots in the early sections of the speech and
then re-established as Webster moved toward the conclusion.
Praise was contained within the AJ proportion and reasserted
to maintain continuity and consistency.

Webster also showed great skill in making the virtues
he attributed to his subjects believable. The central AJ
section is composed of Webster's nearly forty-five-minute
review of the writing and approval of the Declaration of
Independence. His recollection of Jefferson's involvement
was easily researched; historians knew that Jefferson was
the major drafter of the document. It was not difficult for
Webster to render Jefferson's contribution believable. But
with Adams he faced a larger challenge. Though no record of
the debates was extant, Webster contended that Adam's
debating skill was crucial to the passage of the
Declaration. Webster solved the problem by recreating the
debates and inventing a speech for Adams. Webster claimed
to have written the "ghost speech" over breakfast and that
his stationery was wet with tears when he finished.

The impersonation of Adams worked for a number of
reasons. First, Webster's ethopoiia (impersonation of
another giving a speech) was dynamic and well fashioned: it
is perhaps the best example in all of American public
address.19 Second, the exposition of Jefferson's
involvement is historical and dry in contrast to the
explosive and dramatic "ghost speech." Third, the use of
the ethopoiia reinforced the AJ structure, keeping the lines
of organization clear while filling the units with exciting
discourse.

Webster maintained continuity by referring to certain
virtues throughout the speech. He also maintained

continuity with two striking metaphors. The first appears
in other Webster speeches. It involves the turbulent ocean
and role of the mariner in bringing his ship safely home.
The metaphor had great appeal to Americans at the time
because the great bulk of the population lived in such ports
as Boston, New York, Philadelphia, and Charleston.

The second metaphor concerned the growth cycle and
helped unify various elements in the speech. In its
simplest form, the metaphor is a reference to the past, the
present, and the future. In this speech, it concerned the
seed, the sapling, and the tree. The seed is the
accomplishments of the two patriots; the sapling is the
present and the audience's understanding of virtue; and the
tree, which reaches to heaven, is the future guiding the
living and providing a lasting tribute to the dead patriots.
This is the stream of time that leads to greatness. It
allowed Webster to say that while Jefferson and Adams "are
no more," "they live" nonetheless. The oxymoron is
transcended by the metaphor of time.

The same strategy is evident with the themes he
manipulated. Webster's use of "liberty" was typical. The
concept, which was introduced in paragraph one, reappeared
in paragraphs nine and fifteen in the beginning, and was
still evident in paragraphs sixty-nine, seventy-one, and
seventy-two at the end.

Webster's approach to narrative material was equally
adept. Adjusting to his Massachusetts audience, he
consistently spent more time per unit on Adams than he did
on Jefferson. But in each case, the story was interrupted
in order to hold attention or to involve the audience once
again in the occasion. His ability to weave eulogy and
argument followed the same pattern. Paragraph thirty-nine,
for example, not only praised the patriots for their
eloquence, but argued that "True eloquence, indeed, does not
consist in speech. It cannot be brought from far. Words
and phrases may be marshalled in every way, but they cannot
compass it."

Thus, within the epideictic form, Webster was able to
satisfy the needs of this particular rhetorical situation
with proportion and grace. The subjects were treated
separately, and then united: "Both had been presidents,
both had lived to great age, both were early patriots, and
both were distinguished and ever honored." Paragraph
twenty-eight rendered an example of the same strategy but
with the use of historic events instead of thematic
material: "Mr. Jefferson . . . had received the highest and
Mr. Adams the next highest number of votes. The difference
is said to have been but a single vote." Near the end of
the address, Webster succeeded in expanding the strategy to
include the occasion when he spoke of the common death day.
Thus, in substance and in form, the A, J, AJ structure is
evident.

Perhaps because he was so effective, writers have
ignored the possibility that deliberative and forensic
elements might also surface in this epideictic address.
Possibly the concealment was so subtle as to mask the
elements. After all, Webster was steeped in the classical
tradition. Not only had he read Cicero and Quintillian on

rhetoric, he was fond of Bishop Richard Whately's <u>Elements of Rhetoric</u>. [20]

Webster learned well Aristotle's lesson concerning praising a man for a course of action the orator would have others follow. He used this device to organize the deliberative themes around praise of Adams and Jefferson. Thus, while he was being deliberative, he contained the deliberative advice inside the AJ structure. Examine the following passage:

> They live in their example; and they live, emphatically, and will live, in the influence which their lives and efforts, their principles and opinions, now exercise, and will continue to exercise, on the affairs of men not only in their country, but throughout the civilized world.

This passage appears early in the speech (paragraph six) and previews Webster's use of "principles and opinions" for deliberative ends. Subsequent paragraphs reinforced this preview, which seems both to justify and to mask Webster's deliberative remarks. When Webster finally translated the patriots' "principles" into a course of action, the deliberative advice seemed natural to the discourse: "Be it remembered . . . that liberty must, at all hazards, be supported." As the speech continued, the deliberative advice became more intense.

The climax of deliberative messages came in the "ghost speech" where Webster put his thoughts into Adams's mouth:

> Sink or swim, live or die, survive or perish, I give my hand and my heart to this vote. . . . Why put off longer the Declaration of Independence? That measure will strengthen us. It will give us character abroad. . . . But while I do live, let me have a country, or at least the hope of a country, and that a free country. . . . Independence <u>now</u>, and <u>Independence for Ever</u>! [his emphasis]

One can hardly read the passage without recalling "Liberty and Union . . . now and forever," which was Webster's conclusion to the "Reply to Hayne," a deliberative speech of 1830.

This and other themes were reiterated and further developed with less passion in the beginning of the conclusion and in the peroration that followed a digression. The epideictic mask was thin in the next-to-the-last paragraph of the eulogy when Webster said:

> And now, fellow citizens, let us not retire from this occasion without a deep and solemn conviction of the duties which have devolved upon us. This lovely land, this glorious liberty, these benign institutions, the dear purchase of our fathers, are ours; ours to enjoy, ours to preserve, ours to transmit.

In the last paragraph, Webster admitted that he might have spent too much time on these themes, but continued to discuss them anyway. He argued that America was a model for the world, that it embodied a new approach to government, that its citizens must preserve its institutions, and that all must be guided by God. Only Webster's references to the occasion and the forefathers maintained an epideictic veneer over a deliberative message concerned with the ways to

achieve and preserve happiness, with the good in society,
with forms of government, and with duties of citizens. Each
of these themes was treated by Aristotle under the
deliberative heading in Book One, Chapters Five through
Eight of the <u>Rhetoric</u>. Thus, Webster demonstrated that he
was a master of concealment and thereby accomplished
deliberative persuasion in the epideictic form.

Less crucial to the speech were the forensic elements.
While accusation and defense were rare, they were employed
to set the scene for the all-important "ghost speech." And
throughout the speech the defense of the forefathers was
employed as reinforcement of praise and a backdrop for the
deliberative themes.

Any praise or blame of person is closely akin to
forensic pleading. This passage near the end of the speech
reveals the ambiguity:

No men, fellow citizens, ever served their country with
more entire exemption from every imputation of selfish
and mercenary motives, than those to whose memory we
are paying these proofs of respect. A suspicion of any
disposition to enrich themselves, or to protect by
their public employment, never rested on either.

The setting and the audience as part of the controlling
form make this passage epideictic; however, were the same
passage uttered before a jury, it would be forensic. Here
is a case where the form transforms the matter to create a
reality appropriate to the particular rhetorical situation.
The issue of England's treatment of the colonies is more
clearly forensic. Paragraphs twenty-nine through thirty-two
condemn the unjust action of Parliament and the King and
vindicate the just actions of the patriots. The section is
used to establish Webster's crediblity regarding the debate
over the Declaration, its intent, and composition. Thus,
the masking of forensic elements works to make the
epideictic persuasion more effective.

The speech was an enormous success. One result was
that henceforth Webster was often referred to as the
"Godlike Daniel." Webster had moved beyond being a great
lawyer; he became a man of letters, a force in American
literary circles. Few political leaders have equalled that
achievement. The most noted, Abraham Lincoln, never
produced the variety or volume of work that Webster did,
although he was able to match the quality of Webster's best
poetic lines.

CONCLUSION

This analysis reveals several important strategies that
Webster used in ceremonial addresses. First, the overlap
between genres occurs in two theoretically distinct ways:
(1) a masking process where purposes proper to one genre are
developed in a speech ostensibly belonging to another genre,
and (2) a borrowing process in which the purposes of one
genre are served by using the devices from another. The
latter case is exemplified in the above analysis where
Webster in the body of the address uses deliberative and
forensic elements to reinforce the epideictic <u>telos</u> or end.

Second, there is always a controlling or <u>dominant</u> form.

Generally, audiences that gather to hear a speech are often called upon to serve in a loose sense as jurors, observers, or deliberators, but they may also serve a secondary function at the same time with or without the encouragement of the speaker. For example, those gathered as observers of Webster's "Eulogy" could think as jurors or policy makers at various points in the address. Thus, audience role stands out as one of the major constituents by which we can identify the controlling form. Setting is also useful; that a speech is given in court, or in Congress, or in celebration of a holiday helps the critic determine the dominant form shaping the discourse. But again we should note that while one setting may dominate, another may be called to mind. Webster's conversion of Faneuil Hall into the Congress for the "ghost speech" is a case in point.

Aristotle also used time as a determinant of controlling form. If one intended to issue a judgment about the past, the forensic form was useful. Speaking to the future necessitated deliberative utterance, and endorsing values for the present was epideictic. Yet again while one time period may be emphasized, and thereby help us identify the controlling form, secondary time periods often appear. Webster's vindication of Jefferson's past was part of an overall strategy to reinforce present values so that future policies would be improved.

The notion of form examined here is useful in explaining why Webster was so successful. He adapted epideictic rhetoric to fit the audience, subject, time, and setting. He understood that Aristotle's three genre cast three different lights on the persuasive situation. Each light revealed different strategies that Webster employed. Since he incorporated Aristotle's view into his arsenal of strategies, his public address was complex, effective, and enduring.

Webster's first major public speech was epideictic, as was his last. In the first, he struggled to contain his enthusiasm for the grand style and poetic language. Like a young Marc Antony, he demonstrated his cleverness at figures and wore his patriotic fervor on his sleeve. The mature Webster was a man of letters, able to craft a ceremonial address that was pleasing to hear and memorable to read. Whether celebrating a national holiday, laying the cornerstone of a new monument, or praising the virtues of the Founders, Webster advanced themes that shaped the national consciousness.

Through Webster, the Federalist virtues of Union, opportunity, and propertied rights have not only survived but flourished in the birth of the new Whig party. Webster played a key role in the evolution of America's representative federal system. His ceremonial speeches brought this message to the public where he reinforced values that devolved from the Revolution and the ratification of the Constitution. These same values would serve later presidents well, particularly Lincoln as he preserved and protected the Union a decade after Webster's death.

3

Deliberative Speaking to 1845

To analyze Webster's deliberative oratory, the next two chapters will concentrate on two of his most successful persuasive campaigns in the United States Senate: the debate with Senator Robert Y. Hayne in 1830 and the debate over the Compromise of 1850.

Webster's conservative nationalism was inherited from his father, reinforced by Christopher Gore, and refined in practice before the Supreme Court. His first defense of the Federalist agenda came in a pamphlet published in February of 1805. In 1809 Webster campaigned for Federalist Jeremiah Smith, who won the governorship of New Hampshire. And in March of 1812, Webster became the first Federalist elected town moderator of Portsmouth in thirteen years; he won by twelve votes. He believed that representative republican government could best serve the needs of a rapidly growing country. He was dedicated to seeing that the expansion continue and that commercial prosperity be assured. His patriotism extended to an impulsive defense of nationalism and territorial acquisition.[1]

But Webster opposed the War of 1812 because it jeopardized New England and was begun by the Democratic-Republicans. In 1813 Webster went to Congress. In his early speeches, Webster made clear his belief that the American Revolution was a conservative one that preserved rights gained over a period of years.[2] Even members of the opposing party were impressed with Webster's skill at argument. When he succeeded in getting resolutions passed condemning President Madison's conduct of the war, he was praised by the New York Herald as "second to none" in the House. William Plumer, a Republican Representative from New Hampshire, said:

> His manner is forcible and authoritative. Nothing is left at loose ends in his statements of fact or in his reasonings; and the hearer passes from one position to another with the fullest conviction that the result must be correct, where the steps leading to it are so clear and obvious.[3]

He believed, and quoted Aristotle to the effect, that agriculture was the foundation of all successful democracies. He was easily re-elected on the "American Peace ticket" in 1814. New England was preoccupied with the Hartford Convention. It called for interposition as a

state's right.   Though Webster did not attend the
Convention--he was in Washington surveying the damage the
British had inflicted on the Capitol--he had encouraged the
Federalist stance as the only hope of regaining power
against the Jeffersonian Democrats.[4]

Webster's New Hampshire roots sent shoots into Boston's
business community.   Francis Lowell, who invented the power
loom and created the Boston Manufacturing Company, induced
Webster to redirect his attention from agriculture, per se,
to national development.   All through 1816, when tariff
proposals were being hotly debated in the Congress, Lowell
suggested new positions for Webster and helped him
rationalize support for selective tariffs.   Lowell was also
instrumental in Webster's moving to Boston and developing a
new party.[5]

Webster also took up New England's position on the
question of expanding slavery into the territories.   In 1819
Webster said at a public meeting in Boston that the Missouri
question presented the opportunity to put "a barrier to the
further progress of slavery."   In 1820 he supported Clay's
compromise.

In the same year, the United States was recovering from
a financial panic.   The Federalist party was dead; Monroe
was unopposed for re-election.   During the campaign,
however, many expressed the belief that regulation of the
economy was in order.   Webster was not one of them.   In
three major speeches, Webster set out his laissez-faire
position on trade.   He delivered the first speech at Faneuil
Hall to the Boston financial community on October 2, 1820.
He claimed that the tariff led to an unhealthy "reliance on
government," and it divided the country, rural against
industrial.   Furthermore, a tariff "tended to make the poor
both more numerous and more poor, and the rich less in
number, but perhaps more rich."[6]   These words would later be
used against Webster in his debate with Hayne.

Webster became a delegate to the Massachusetts
Constitutional Convention, which met in the winter of
1820-21.   His speeches there introduced him to the
influential leaders of Massachusetts and paved his way for
re-entry into Congress.   Sitting at the convention were such
Federalist luminaries as former President John Adams, Josiah
Quincy, and Justice Story.[7]

Webster's first battle with Clay occurred in 1824 a
year after his return to the House.   Because the wool mills
of Massachusetts were very efficient, they did not need
protection.   So Webster opposed a general tariff that was
crucial to fund Clay's American System of internal
improvements. In the same year, Webster spoke out for Greek
independence, relying heavily in his speeches on his
education in the classics.   He portrayed the Turks as
barbarians and supported a resolution favoring Greek
liberty.   The administration killed it.

In 1825 Congressman Webster opposed a tariff on raw
goods because it would have raised the price of wool for the
mills of New England.   At that time, Webster attacked the
alliance between the West, led by Senator Thomas Hart Benton
of Missouri, and the South, led by John C. Calhoun of South
Carolina.   In 1827 Webster was made a Senator and in the
same year the English began dumping wool at low prices into

the American market. Webster fully supported a new tariff. It passed the House but lost in the Senate when Vice President Calhoun broke a tie and voted against it. Nonetheless, Webster was a hero in Boston.[8]

THE WEBSTER-HAYNE DEBATE

The tariff proposal of 1827 was followed by an even higher, and therefore, more intolerable one to the South in 1828. It affected the importation of flax, hemp, iron, lead, molasses, and raw wool. Webster duly represented Boston shipping and wool manufacturers in Senate negotiations. He knew that incentives in the tariff bill would provide enough votes for passage. It was tied to Clay's American System of internal improvements, another set of incentives for many to support the tariff. Webster would ensure that money was appropriated for dredging and maintaining harbors important to Boston shippers.
Once New Englanders saw the advantages of the internal improvements supported by revenues from the tariff, they encouraged Webster to continue cooperating in the design of the legislation. The American System, which would speed the opening of the West and help farmers move their produce to Eastern markets, became a firm plank in the Whig platform and gave Webster a way to pierce the alliance between the South and West.[9]

Senator Robert Y. Hayne of South Carolina perceived this intent as did Vice President Calhoun. Calhoun responded with the South Carolina Exposition of 1828. It claimed to advance Jefferson's and Madison's famous Resolves of 1798 by protecting a minority represented in a state government and by giving that state the power to nullify heinous federal acts. In late 1829 and 1830, Hayne tried to maintain the West-South axis and attack the North as a conspirator against the South. But because he had supported internal improvements, Webster could argue that he was a friend of the West and give the lie to Hayne's charges. Furthermore, the call for Union above separatism, reinforced by the American System and the tariff, was irresistible to the patriotic frontiersmen and farmers of the West, while slavery was considered a necessary evil at best.[10]

What began in December of 1829 as a debate over the disposition of public lands in the West spilled over into the question of the tariff, states' rights, and slavery in January of 1830. Senator Foot of Connecticut proposed legislation to halt surveys and sales of western lands. Senator Benton took this move as an assault on the growth of the West. He referred to Foot and his compatriots as "yankees" trying to maintain their control of the Congress. Senator Hayne on the advice of Calhoun, used this moment to attempt to cement the West-South alliance. As Hayne reached the middle of his speech on January 14, 1830, Webster arrived on the floor of the Senate from the Supreme Court downstairs. Taking his lead from Benton and his thoughts from Calhoun, Hayne alleged that there was a conspiracy afoot among manufacturing states to retain poor laborers in the North and consolidate their power at the same time.[11]

Webster was appalled and asked to reply formally the next day. He woke up early the next morning, as was his custom, and jotted three pages of notes. In this short reply to Hayne on January 15, Webster carefully avoided antagonizing the West while drawing Hayne out on the issue of states' rights. Webster also alluded to Calhoun's role as Hayne's mentor. Calhoun glowered from the presiding officer's chair throughout Webster's first reply to Hayne.

After his introductory remarks, Webster supported his claim that New England had always supported Western development. He pointed out that Nathan Dane of Massachusetts had composed the Ordinance of 1787, which not only allowed development of the west, but precluded slavery in the new territory. He demonstrated the unity between North and West with a discussion of the tariff of 1816. He then justified his support of the tariff of 1828 by arguing that tariffs had become established national policy thanks to the support of them by the South in general and Calhoun in particular. The question was not whether or not there would be a tariff, but rather on what goods and at what level. Furthermore, the tariff provided funds for internal improvements, which were important to the nation as a whole but particularly to development of the West, and enhanced manufacturing capacity, which while important to the North benefitted the national treasury and American commerce in general.[12]

Webster then proceeded to attack disunionists in South Carolina. Hayne's talk of a conspiracy justified this sudden shift in tone. Webster was hoping to lure Hayne into debating the issues that would alienate the West. New England had historically favored Western growth, and the West had been free of slaves. Webster claimed that Hayne's so-called conspiracy was nothing more than a national and natural tendency toward consolidation. Since George Washington, America had consistently moved toward "true, constitutional consolidation," by which he meant "whatever tends to strengthen the bond that unites us and encourages the hope that our Union may be perpetual." Slavery and nullification did not support America's dream of unity and nationhood, a dream Webster traced back to the Founders.

In replying to Webster, Hayne made the mistake of flying full force at the issue of slavery and hooking himself on Webster's line. While his speech brought nods of approval from Calhoun, it helped Webster frame the debate around issues splitting the West from the South, mainly states' rights, nullification, and slavery.

Hayne's second speech took parts of two days. This small man became shrill on occasion and at one point grabbed his heart and said that Webster's speech "rankled" in his bosom. In his calmer moments he defended Calhoun's "Carolina doctrine." Webster sat at his desk throughout taking copious notes, looking much like a collegiate debater. Hayne's reply to Webster was ironic, biting, often ornate and proud.

While Hayne spoke, Calhoun was not above passing notes to help his student defend slavery. And when Hayne spread his accusations of conspiracy to all those who opposed slavery, Webster knew he could force the West to choose between embracing a slave-holding ally or one who supported

Union and the American System.   After Hayne finished,
Webster told associates that he would "grind" Hayne into a
"pinch of snuff."[13]
     The Second Reply to Hayne was the most memorable speech
ever delivered on the floor of the Senate.   It took two
afternoons for Webster to complete.   Anybody who was
somebody in Washington attended the speech.   Webster dressed
immaculately in a dark blue coat with shiny brass buttons, a
cream-colored vest, and a white cravat.   In full regalia,
Webster played to the galleries.   His highly stylized lines
pleased the bonneted ladies in the gallery.   His lines of
argument were pressed home to his colleagues on the floor.
And not infrequently, Webster would shake a finger at
Calhoun.[14]
     One of the most remarkable features of Webster's Second
Reply to Hayne is its refutative structure.   Webster, like
most good parliamentary debaters, knew that it is more
effective to argue on your own ground rather than on your
opponent's.   There are, in fact, several allusions to this
strategy in the speeches of Hayne and Webster.   So why is it
that Webster relies so heavily on Hayne's organization of
the arguments in this second reply?
     First, Hayne's second speech was a response to
Webster's first and as such refuted Webster's issues.   Thus,
Hayne was already on Webster's ground.   Moreover in the
second reply, Webster pretended he was using Hayne's
structure, as any diligent and fair debater would, when in
fact the arguments were the very ones he wanted to raise.
Second, there is an aspect of bravado here that increases
Webster's credibility with his audience.   He as much said,
"I will not only win this debate, but I will win on my
opponent's terms."   And third, and most obvious, Hayne's
structure was clearly on the minds of those present.
Webster might risk confusing them if he reorganized the
whole sum and substance of the arguments before them.
     Webster accepted the organization of Hayne, refuted him
point by point, but all the time scored points in terms of
credibility by advancing lines of argument useful to his
persuasive strategy.   This structure forced Webster to use
fugal form of argumentation.   When Webster introduced an
argument, he did not develop it fully; later when he
reintroduced the argument, he extended it a little further;
later still, he introduced it again and extended it further.
This method gave the speech a feeling of progress, persuaded
by repetition, and built the best arguments to a crescendo
at the conclusion.   The strategy is not unlike the one he
used in his eulogy to Adams and Jefferson (see chapter two).
     Using one of his favorite metaphors, Webster began by
comparing the legislative debacle to a storm-tossed sea.   He
sought to bring calm to the situation.   But no sooner had he
gained attention than he began to ridicule Hayne, a tactic
that is evident through two-thirds of the speech.   Webster's
first complaint is rather ironic.   He said that Hayne had
talked about "everything but public lands," the ostensible
topic of the debate.   Of course, to achieve his persuasive
purpose, Webster had to wrench the debate from the issue of
public lands to the questions of slavery and states' rights.
Although this attack was disingenuous, it reinforced

Webster's stature.

Webster stated that Hayne claimed he "had a shot" to discharge, but Webster was still standing. Hayne interrupted to clarify the remark, but Webster waved him off arguing that it is not what he said but what he intended that was important:

> I will not accuse the honorable member of violating the rules of civilized war--I will not say that he poisoned his arrows. But whether his shafts were, or were not, dipped in that which would have caused rankling, if they had reached, there was not, as it happened, quite strength enough in the bow to bring them to their mark. If he wishes now to gather up those shafts, he must look for them elsewhere; they will not be found fixed and quivering in the object at which they were aimed.

This passage set the tone for the running personal attack on Hayne. Webster opened with an <u>apophasis</u>, that is, a denial of what he was actually doing; then he developed an extended metaphor, dripping with sarcasm, that painted a picture of a weakly armed opponent using unethical methods. From this moment on it is clear that the speech will contain a vast array of stylistic devices and persuasive strategies. Those seeking entertainment would not be disappointed.

Webster was intent on refuting every point made by Hayne. He even disputed Hayne's charge that Webster needed "to sleep" on Hayne's speech before replying. Webster claims he was ready to reply but Benton adjourned the Senate before a response could be made. Webster then answered Hayne's "taunt" about seeking to debate Hayne instead of Benton. "Sir, the gentleman seems to forget where and what we are. This is a Senate; a Senate of equals."

With Hayne's credibility and sense of decorum in tatters, Webster turned to Hayne's more serious charge that there is a conspiracy afoot. He ridiculed the charge by pointing out that Hayne's use of Banquo's ghost is misinformed: "It was not, I think, the friends, but the enemies of the murdered Banquo, at whose bidding his spirit would not down." Webster carried on for several paragraphs using Hayne's erroneous reading of <u>Macbeth</u> to reduce his opponent's credibility to pulp. The argument about a conspiracy would be introduced again and extended, but at this juncture, it is clear that the purpose of Webster's opening remarks was to damage Hayne's credibility as much as possible. By the end of this onslaught, the audience was left with the impression that Hayne is ill-mannered, poorly educated, and unable to keep his mind on the legislation before the Senate.

Having demolished Hayne, Webster began to examine more substantive matters although he still retained the refutative organizational pattern for his remarks. He mentioned the Northwest Ordinance by pointing out that it favored the development of the West and was drafted by Mr. Dane of Massachusetts. Hayne had belittled Dane after Webster cited the New Englander in his First Reply. Webster seized the opportunity to reinforce the ties between the West and New England while further ridiculing Hayne:

> [Dane] is of Massachusetts, and too near the north star to be reached by the honorable gentleman's telescope. If his sphere had happened to range south of Mason and

Dixon's line, [Dane] might . . . have come within the
scope of [Hayne's] vision!

After citing the provisions of the Northwest Ordinance,
Webster claimed he had not said "a single word which any
ingenuity could torture into an attack on the slavery of the
South." Webster clearly stated that while the federal
government could not interfere with slavery in the South, he
regarded it "as one of the greatest evils." Webster then
turned Hayne's attack on the American System back on him and
used it to stress New England's support for the West:

> "What interests," asks he, "has South Carolina in a
> canal in Ohio?" . . . On his system, it is true, she
> has no interest. On that system, Ohio and Carolina are
> different governments and different countries. . . . On
> that system, Carolina has no more interest in a canal
> in Ohio than in Mexico.

Webster then defended New England's national approach, and
added enormous credibility to his cause because a few days
earlier Webster had supported federal underwriting of the
stock of the South Carolina Canal and Railroad Company.

Webster next explained the alleged inconsistency in his
record on the tariff. Once the tariff became national
policy, he worked to support his constituents' interests,
but never, even when opposed to the tariff, did he threaten
nullification. Hayne, claimed Webster, used "metaphysical
scissors" to patch together a misleading version of his
position. This argument will be extended into an elevated
theme that pervades the speech. By the conclusion, New
England's willingness to play by the rules will be
contrasted with South Carolina's unsportsman-like conduct.

Then Webster undercut Hayne by quoting Calhoun's
nationalistic sentiments of 1816 and later. This part of
Webster's speech was undoubtedly his weakest. Everyone knew
that Senators change their mind and the argument over past
positions of Webster and Calhoun was old territory. This
was simply an obligatory passage that needed to be dispensed
with quickly.

Webster never lost sight of his goal to tie New England
and the West to the cause of Union, and to tie Hayne to
Calhoun, South Carolina, and the cause of disunion. An
internal summary at this juncture brought everything back
into focus: "The real question between me and him is: Has
the doctrine been advanced at the South or the East, that
the population of the West should be retarded. . . . Is this
doctrine, as has been alleged, of Eastern origin?" Webster
then explained the basic Whig position on Western lands.
Lands should not just be given away but should help finance
and/or promote internal improvements and education in all of
the states. He contended that historically lands have
always been distributed to serve the common good.

This question aside, Webster demonstrated that New
England "has supported measures favorable to the West." In
1820, for example, New England favored reduction in the cost
of public lands by a vote of 33 to 1 among its House
delegation. He also pointed out that South Carolina
supported internal improvements as early as 1816 and had
supported a tariff at that time.

Calhoun, who was sitting as the President of the

Senate, interrupted to ask: "Does the chair understand the gentleman from Massachusetts to say that the person now occupying the chair of the Senate has changed his opinions on the subject of internal improvements?" Webster responded that Calhoun had not changed but that either South Carolina has, or Hayne "has misled" me. In fact, claimed Webster, Hayne had misled people about Webster's position on the national debt and his reference to national consolidation. Webster explained that he meant consolidation of the Union, not the North, as Hayne had alleged. A close reading of Webster's First Reply bears out his version.

Webster next returned to the issue of the tariff and states' rights. If Webster could make the issue one of patriotic loyalty to the Republic, he was sure he could carry the votes of western Senators. They were highly dependent on a national system of roads, canals, harbors, and other internal improvements. They were frontiersmen and farmers who hailed mainly from the North; they knew that the federal government had protected and promoted their interests, and that the individual states had not.

Webster again defended New England against Hayne's conspiracy charges by extending the argument a little more. In this case, the extension was the result of an attack on Hayne's evidence. Hayne had quoted from selected pamphlets, sermons, and speeches which he said proved that the North was out to diminish the influence of the South. Webster was disgusted with Hayne's use of selected evidence. He said he would not answer point by point nor would he stoop to using such evidence from the South, of which he asserted there was an abundance: "I employ no scavengers; no one is in attendance on me, tendering such means of retaliation; and, if there were, with an ass's load of them with a bulk as huge as that which the gentleman himself has produced, I would not touch one of them."

Thus, Webster avoided Hayne's trap. It would not be consistent with the tone of Webster's speech to insult the South and annoy the North by reading from inflammatory Southern tracts. Instead he defended New England's loyalty to General Washington, to the Constitution, and to the Union thereby foreshadowing his stirring peroration. Webster then praised South Carolina for her past patriotism, thus introducing a strategy he will visit again before the end of the speech. He would seek unity with those Southerners and Westerners who support Union and all the benefits it can bring. He will not be lured into partisan or sectional strife.

This was the perfect moment to "state and to defend what I conceive to be the true principles of the Constitution." The question to be resolved was when and under what circumstances can a state legislature interfere with the authority of the federal government. Webster answered that it can only do so when "this government transcends its constitutional limits."

Does Hayne's case fit the criteria? To answer this question, Webster restated Hayne's position in four paragraphs, and he began each with the phrase, "I understand him to . ." Hayne interrupted, pointing out that he had used the Virginia Resolution of 1798 written by Madison as his authority.

    Webster responded that he knew the Resolution written
by James Madison. Webster explained that there was a
crucial difference between the problem the Virginia
Resolution was trying to solve, the Alien and Sedition Acts,
and the current problem, a tariff. In the former case, the
government had become too oppressive and the public had a
right to revolt. But the latter case is part of established
government policy. Hayne interrupted again to say that the
"right of constitutional resistance" was more important than
the "mere right of revolution. . . . Plain, palpable
violation of the Constitution by the general government"
justified interposition. Hayne attempted to place the
rights of the states to interpose above the rights of its
citizens to revolt. Webster, whose whole argument was the
fact that the Constitution is for the people not the states,
would not allow Hayne to succeed with this ploy. He stated:
    I say the right of a state to annul a law of Congress
    cannot be maintained but on the ground of the
    inalienable right of man to resist oppression. . . .
    But I do not admit that under the Constitution . . .
    there is any mode in which a State government, as a
    member of the Union, can interfere and stop the
    progress of the general government, by force of her own
    laws, under any circumstances whatever.
In other words, states do not have the same rights as common
citizens. Webster ridiculed Hayne's system in which there
would be "four and twenty masters, of different wills and
different purposes." The decision as to the supremacy of
states or the federal courts had been decided when the
Constitution was ratified as "the supreme law of the land."
Furthermore, the federal government had been given judicial
power over "all cases arising under the Constitution."
Webster in case after case before the Supreme Court had
helped to solidify this power, at the expense of the states.
This power was the "keystone of the arch" for Webster. In a
slashing attack on states' rights, he hit on the nub of the
issue when he said: "It is, Sir, the people's Constitution,
the people's government, made for the people, made by the
people, and answerable to the people." This line influenced
Lincoln's Gettysburg Address. Webster's speech was
circulated widely, especially among Whigs, of which the
young Lincoln was one of the most ambitious.
    Hayne's plan for the Union was portrayed as unworkable
because the Constitution confined certain activities such as
making war, coining money, and agreeing to treaties, to the
federal government exclusively. Webster scoffed at Hayne's
notion of nullification as selective. South Carolina would
nullify the tariff of 1828, because it did not like it, but
not the tariff of 1816 because it protected South Carolina
cotton from imports from Calcutta. With a flurry of
rhetorical questions, Webster reduced Hayne's doctrine to
anarchy.
    Webster then compared the "New England school" of
protest to the South Carolina school. Massachusetts
responded to the Virginia Resolution of 1798 by defending
the Union and has not wavered from that course.
"Misgoverned, wronged, oppressed as she felt herself to be,
she still held fast her integrity to the Union."

Massachusetts protested vehemently, then submitted to the
will of Congress. That is the way it should be. Such
reasoned submission makes the Union work. Webster concluded
this argument by pointing out that Madison did not believe
the tariff to be an excessive exercise of federal power.
Once again Webster turned Hayne's own authority against him.
After the debate, Webster and Hayne submitted their speeches
to Madison. The former President sent a four thousand word
rebuttal to Hayne. He sent Webster a cautious letter that
discussed the need for checks and balances. While he
opposed secession, Madison thought Webster assumed too much
power for the federal government.[15]

As Webster moved toward his conclusion, he marshalled
his various arguments into a major summary and extended each
important one. If the South Carolina doctrine had been
exercised in the past, "The government would very likely
have gone to pieces, and crumbled into dust." The
Constitution formalized the Union, and the Union had its
roots in the revolution. The states ceded their sovereignty
to the Union and to its people when they ratified the
Constitution. Says Webster: "For myself, sir, I do not
admit the jurisdiction of South Carolina, or any other
state, to prescribe my constitutional duty; or to settle,
between me and the people, the validity of laws of Congress
for which I have voted. I decline her umpirage." Webster
admitted that the federal government is limited, but it is
supreme when operating within those limits imposed by the
Constitution, and establishing a tariff is clearly within
those limits. At this point, Webster again visited the
question of workability and reduced Hayne's position to
absurdity by asking what the customs collector is to do when
torn between federal and state authority. He compared
nullification of Congressional law to Fries' rebellion and
implied it is nothing short of treason. "If John Fries had
produced an act of Pennsylvania annulling the law of
Congress, would it have helped his case!" Realizing he had
scored a point, Webster extended it with gallows humor. He
speculated on what might happen if the Senate refused to go
along with Hayne: "[S]hall we swing for it? We are ready
to die for our country, but it is rather an awkward
business, this dying without touching the ground! After
all, that is a sort of hemp tax worse than any part of the
tariff." The remedy to any serious problem, said Webster,
is not nullification, but rather amending the Constitution.

As a transition to his peroration, Webster sought unity
by reminding the states that they had fought together in the
Revolution and if they had not, surely the enterprise would
have been lost. Had not South Carolina and Massachusetts
together defeated the tyrant George III? Webster
dramatically underscored this historic loyalty to Union in
his memorable peroration:

> Would to God that harmony might return! Shoulder to
> shoulder they went through the Revolution, hand in hand
> they stood round the administration of Washington, and
> felt his own great arm lean on them for support. . . .
> When my eyes shall be turned to behold for the last
> time the sun in heaven, may I not see him shining on
> the broken and dishonored fragments of a once glorious
> Union; on States dissevered, discordant, belligerent;

on a land rent with civil feuds, or drenched . . . in
fraternal blood!   Let their last feeble and lingering
glance rather behold the gorgeous ensign of the
republic, now known and honored throughout the earth,
still full high advanced, its arms and trophies
streaming in their original lustre, not a strip erased
or polluted, not a single star obscured, bearing for
its motto, no such miserable interrogatory as "What is
all this worth?" nor those words of delusion and folly,
"Liberty first and Union afterwards"; but everywhere,
spread all over in characters of living light, blazing
on all its ample folds, as they float over the sea and
over the land, and in every wind under the whole
heavens, the other sentiment, dear to every American
heart--Liberty <u>and</u> Union, now and forever, one and
inseparable!

When he concluded, all present knew that Webster had
elevated a legislative quarrel from the slag heap of
regional concern to the transcendent question of national
spirit.   He had done it in the past and he would do it
again, particularly in 1850, but never as forcefully or as
effectively as he did on that winter afternoon in January of
1830.

Webster spoke extemporaneously from twelve pages of
notes that were the culmination of his thought and argument
on the subject of Union.[16]   Those thoughts and arguments had
been rehearsed in ceremonial speeches and in many cases
before the Supreme Court where John Marshall incorporated
them into his decisions.   But in 1830, they came together in
one triumphant rhetorical moment.   They thrilled those in
the audience who longed for a defense of the Union.   They
established Webster as the chief advocate of Union.   And he
clearly defeated the forces of states' rights by frustrating
their attempt to link arms with the representatives of the
West.   The South was isolated.   Calhoun would soon resign
the Vice Presidency to return to the Senate as the chief
defender of nullification.   He would battle for it and
against Webster until his death in March of 1850.

Webster polished the speech before having it published
in three parts in the National Intelligencer in late
February.   Luckily for Webster, Joseph Gales, sometime
editor and part owner of the Intelligencer, recorded the
speech and had his wife transcribe it.[17]   Edward Everett
then reviewed the text before it was published.   The demand
for the document was overwhelming; 60,000 copies were
distributed by the spring.   Unauthorized versions reached
well beyond 100,000.   It was undoubtedly the most widely
distributed speech to that time.   Webster was flooded with
honors, with requests to speak, and with praise from
established patriots.   James Madison said this "very
powerful" speech crushed secessionist sentiment.   Even
Hayne, in later years, said Webster had proven himself the
greatest orator of all time with that one set of speeches.

Most important in any assessment of the effectiveness
of this speech is that Webster helped to lead the American
public toward its potential consciousness of freedom and
Union.   He helped to reify its respect for Constitutional
order.   He elevated the people above the states in phrases

that Abraham Lincoln would echo at Gettysburg. This speech achieved the highest goal of rhetorical literature: it touched the actual consciousness of the immediate audience on a specific topic, and it moved the potential consciousness of the audience toward lasting, transcendent values.

WEBSTER'S DELIBERATIVE EFFORTS AFTER 1831

New England continued to support a tariff that would protect its mills, pay for the dredging of harbors and the building of canals and roads. The West benefitted from the internal improvements program but suffered from the inflated cost of American goods, as did the South. In 1832 South Carolina held a convention and vowed not to collect tariff duties. President Jackson became so incensed by this action that he threatened to hang Calhoun. Instead he introduced the infamous "force bill." Clay tried to work out a compromise; Webster supported the President before a cheering crowd at Faneuil Hall. William Lloyd Garrison began publication of the Liberator in 1831 and quickly organized a corps of radical abolitionists in Boston. Webster's support of Jackson on the tariff identified him with a president who had violated the First Amendment by refusing to allow abolitionist tracts to be sent into the South. This was the beginning of Webster's split with the radicals.[18]

The crisis intensified in February of 1833 when Calhoun returned to the Senate representing South Carolina. (Hayne was "promoted" to Governor.) On February 16, Calhoun, in his first speech on the Senate floor in sixteen years, advocated a "constitutional compact" to resolve the crisis. Webster replied immediately with a pragmatic speech that avoided Calhoun's logical snares. Webster's lucid explanation of the Preamble of the Constitution undercut the compact theory:

> They executed that agreement: they adopted the Constitution, and henceforth it must stand as a Constitution until it shall be altogether destroyed. . . . The truth is, Mr. President, and no ingenuity of argument, no subtlety of distinction, can evade it, that, as to certain purposes, the people of the United States are one people. They are one in making war, and one in making peace; they are one in regulating commerce, and one in laying duties and imposts.

Webster defended majoritarian democracy and mocked Calhoun's proposal as "wholly unknown to our Constitution." Later in this two-and-a-half hour speech, Webster pounded home his contention that the government was adopted by the people. It was not a confederation of states. He reviewed the evolved relationship between the people and the government, and claimed that no state had the authority to sunder those ties and responsibilities. "What is a constitution? Certainly not a league, compact or confederacy, but a fundamental law."

Calhoun was ready to avenge Hayne's loss of three years earlier. He listened to Webster's reply and took notes the whole time. He studied them and wrote a response over the

next ten days. In the meantime, the Force Bill had passed
and South Carolina was supremely isolated. Calhoun's
subsequent speech was syllogistic and highly effective.
Webster made the mistake of trying to respond at once;
Calhoun's logic was too hard to crack. Many considered
Webster the loser in the exchange. Furthermore, when the
Force Bill failed in the House, it had to be brought back to
the Senate for softening. Clay worked out a compromise
which led to a heated exchange with Webster. The new bill
passed both houses but not before Webster became tainted
with the brush of extreme protectionism. Furthermore, few
believed the compromise between Unionists and nullifiers
would last for long.[19]

The National Bank of the United States became another
bone of contention between the President and the Congress.
Nicholas Biddle, the Bank's president, wanted to renew the
charter of the Bank early to force President Jackson's hand
while Biddle had enough votes in the Congress on his side.
Jackson vetoed the renewal in 1832 claiming the Bank was the
embodiment of all that was evil in the American System of
the Whigs. Biddle turned to Webster for help. It was a
natural friendship since Webster had defended the
Constitutionality of the establishment of the Bank before
the Supreme Court.[20] Webster condemned Jackson's veto
message for inciting the poor against the rich. "It
wantonly attacks whole classes of people, for the purpose of
turning against them the prejudices and the resentments of
other classes." Webster was attacked for taking money from
Biddle to deliver the speech. Furthermore, Webster accepted
Biddle's offer to publish the speech. In the Presidential
campaign of 1832, Clay led the Whigs (National Republican
Party), including the young Lincoln, down the road to defeat
defending the Bank along the way.[21]

In 1833 Jackson instructed his Secretary of the
Treasury, Roger B. Taney, to remove U.S. deposits from the
Bank. Biddle responded by retaining Webster, the Chairman
of the Senate Finance Committee, and then by tightening
credit. This caused a panic in 1833 and 1834 that the Whigs
then blamed on Jackson. Vice President Martin Van Buren
responded by accusing Webster of instigating the entire
crisis. Webster was accused of the same tactics in 1837
(see chapter two). Webster referred to his attackers as
Catalines "greedy of other men's property." Biddle finally
loosened credit and the Senate passed a resolution censoring
Jackson for removing the deposits from the Bank.[22] The
whole controversy was put before the voters in the election
of 1836 when Van Buren, with 170 electoral votes, defeated a
host of opponents including Webster, who received only 14.

Much of the business of the Senate, the forming of
opinions and consensus, was achieved at dinner parties and
private meetings. Webster was as impressive in these small
gatherings as he was on the floor of the Senate. He was
warm and witty at dinner parties, content to drown his
ambition and clear vision in the deep red port of
hospitality. His forceful mind was barely able to tolerate
the mediocrity that often surrounded it. A little dulling
of the senses with alcohol was a constant necessity which at
times proved an embarrassment. Webster's elitism, as much

as his geographic commitment and his taunting of the South, prevented him from gaining the Whig nomination for President. He was qualified and no doubt could have generated a national following, but he was neither a frontier hero like Jackson, nor a middle-state compromiser like Clay. And so his party's nomination was denied to him again and again.

The 1837 session of the Congress was dominated by the slave issue and unresolved questions about the Bank. Van Buren strongly opposed the Bank and slavery, dividing himself from Whigs and Southern Democrats. The fracturing of the Democratic party was matched by smaller cracks in the Whig party over the question of slavery. For example, Webster would protect the institution "where it existed" but would not allow it to spread. Clay would allow slavery and the slave trade to continue in the District of Columbia. All of these issues would come to a head in 1850.

Another panic swept across the nation in 1837 further weakening the Van Buren administration. Webster lost money on land speculation, an experience that changed his opinion about government regulation and opened him to the influence of special interests. He now saw that the federal government had a role to play in economic development. He expanded his defense of a carefully crafted tariff, a national bank, and the use of revenues for internal improvements. He believed the Bank was critical to a stable currency that was essential for economic expansion. The Bank could assure steady loan rates that would allow farmers and merchants to plan and prosper. It is not unfair to say that the panic of 1837 helped Webster bring elements of his "National Conservatism" together into a grand vision with weight and consistency far beyond the parochial needs of New England.[23]

In 1839, Webster sought to settle the score with Calhoun. The topic again was the tariff, the Bank, and nullification. Webster did not take his opponent lightly, nor did he try to match his logic. Instead, he resorted to wit and ridicule:

Where am I? In the Senate of the United States? Am I Daniel Webster? Is that John C. Calhoun of South Carolina, the same gentleman that figured so largely in the House of Representatives in 1816, at the time the Bill creating the National Bank passed that body. What have I heard today? The Senator attempting to maintain his consistency?

He then called Calhoun the "engine car" on the nullification train.

The speech was hailed as Webster's best by the National Intelligencer and Clay concurred. Calhoun's response failed because he left his fortress of logic and tried to match Webster on the fields of style and credibility. The personal attacks of the humorless Calhoun took on a mean and artless quality that ruined his rebuttal.

In 1840 many believed that the Whigs' time had come. Webster, having lost all hope for the nomination by 1838, stepped aside and threw his support behind William Henry Harrison, the hero of the battle of Tippecanoe. It was time the Whigs became less elitist and supported a popular candidate. Just after Clay was beaten for the nomination,

Webster began a vigorous campaign for Harrison with a speech
in Saratoga, New York, on August 19, 1840. The platform
collapsed under the weight of the dignitaries and pitched
the assembled Whigs to the ground eight feet below. Webster
leapt up and declared the Whig platform was much more solid
than the one that had just collapsed. He climbed into a
wagon and carried on for two and a half more hours
enthralling the crowd.[24] Some passages brought tears to his
eyes as well as the audience's:

> Gentlemen, it did not happen to me to be born in a log
> cabin; but my elder brothers and sister were born in a
> log cabin, raised amid the snowdrifts of New Hampshire,
> at a period so early that, when the smoke first rose
> from its rude chimney, and curled over the frozen
> hills, there was no similar evidence of a white man's
> habitation between it and the settlements on the rivers
> of Canada. Its remains still exist. I make to it an
> annual visit. I carry my children to it, to teach them
> the hardships endured by the generations which have
> gone before them. I love to dwell on the tender
> recollections, the kindred trees, the early affections,
> and the touching narratives and incidents, which mingle
> with all I know of this primitive family abode. I
> weep.

The picture drawn is exquisite and it is reinforced by the
internal rhymes (recollections and affections) and emotional
delivery.

During the campaign, Webster made over twenty-five
speeches for the Whig ticket. He spoke to fifty thousand
people at Bunker Hill, a mob on Wall Street, and over ten
thousand in Richmond, his first major address in the South.
There Webster pressed home the Whig case in periodic prose:

> Tell it to all your friends that standing here, in the
> capitol of Virginia beneath an October sun, in the
> midst of this assemblage, before the entire country,
> and upon all the responsibility which belongs to me, I
> say there is no power, direct or indirect, in Congress
> or the general government, to interfere in the
> slightest degree with institution of the South.

This sentiment expressed again and again in the campaign
further infuriated abolitionists against Webster. But this
campaign speech, like the others, strongly endorsed the
economic principles of the Whig platform. This integrated
"American System" required a National Bank, Western
development, and a sensible tariff. These speeches, as
reported in the New York Herald indicated that Webster had
learned to leave the language of the U.S. Senate and the
Supreme Court behind. Instead he took up the rhetoric of
simplicity and sentiment when speaking to the common man.
This concern for the most appropriate style permeated his
being. In at least one speech, he said, "I come to make no
flourishes or figures, but to make a plain speech to the
intelligence of the country." Almost seventy thousand
copies of this speech alone were distributed in pamphlet
form.[25]

Thanks to campaigners like Webster and the national
mood, William Henry Harrison was elected President and
inaugurated on March 4, 1841. A second party had emerged at

last and Webster could take great credit for it. He was
rewarded by being named Secretary of State, head of the
cabinet. But all soon turned to gloom. Harrison's ride
down Pennsylvania Avenue through the freezing rain after his
inauguration led to his death a month later. Except for
Webster, who had been named Secretary of State, the entire
cabinet resigned. The new President, John Tyler of
Virginia, relied on Webster to build a new administration.
Webster dominated not only the cabinet but the controversial
President for the next three years.
      This situation put him at odds with Clay who remained
in the Senate and sought to isolate the unpopular Tyler.
Webster hoped to use his post to advance his presidential
candidacy. Clay used his position in the Senate for the
same purpose.
      Webster got off to a slow start when he supported the
president's plan for establishing a national bank that
required permission of the states to open branches in them.
This position contradicted the Whig platform and Webster's
past arguments before the Supreme Court. The Whig press
accused Webster of betraying constitutional principles.
Clay stepped in and offered a compromise, which was promptly
vetoed by Tyler. The outcry of Whigs against Tyler and his
administration was overwhelming. Webster cut his losses by
helping to pass a national bankruptcy law, long a favorite
project of the Whigs. But when Tyler vetoed a second bank
bill, four members of the cabinet resigned, Whig caucuses
were called to condemn the president, and Webster's stock
plummeted. He travelled to Faneuil Hall to defend his
reputation; the hall was filled to capacity. Webster
enhanced his credibility by talking about foreign policy;
then he launched into a bitter tirade against the Whig party
leaders. It was his least popular speech to date, thought
by many to be petty and arrogant. The speech was the
culmination of Webster's difficulty in trying to defend the
administration and yet remain loyal to the Whig party.
      He was more successful in foreign policy. In 1842 he
negotiated a treaty with Great Britain that resolved the
Maine boundary question. It passed the Senate by a vote of
39 to 9 and was a great success. Nonetheless, the New York
Courier and Enquirer, a paper run by pro-Clay Whigs, and the
Washington Globe, a voice for Western Democrats, criticized
Webster's diplomacy. The Eastern Argus and the National
Intelligencer supported him.[26]
      In 1843 the question of how to deal with the crisis in
Texas divided the Whigs. Webster tried to divert attention
to the question of what to do with the California and Oregon
territory. But this strategy failed, and Webster, who
disagreed with Tyler on these issues, resigned on May 1,
1843. He was sixty-one and had no where to go but
Marshfield. His career was revived only slightly at this
juncture when on June 17, 1843, he delivered a speech to
dedicate the Bunker Hill Monument (see chapter three). The
appearance of President Tyler at the event ruined it for
Whigs. Tyler realigned himself with the Democrats a few
months later.
      Webster was cheered for a speech he gave in Rochester,
New York in September of 1843 wherein he attempted to build
a base for his presidential bid. But it was too late. By

1844, Webster realized he had little stature in his own party. Webster wisely sought rapprochement with Clay.

The Whigs nominated Clay for President in 1844.   Polk defeated Calhoun and Tyler for the Democratic nomination. He went on to win the general election despite Webster's gracious effort in support of Clay.   Throughout the campaign, Webster warned that annexation of Texas would divide the country.   But America continued to favor expansionism, and common sense was not going to stand in the way of patriotic fervor.

In January of 1845 Webster persuaded the Massachusetts legislature to returned him to the Senate.   Business interests were particularly influential in this effort. Upon election, Webster was funded by so many special interests that he could resume living well in Washington.   By 1846 forty businessmen had subscribed to Webster's $37,000 fund.[27]   For this and the use of the Secret Service Fund when he was Secretary of State, Webster often had to endure attacks.   Said Alabama Senator William Yancey, "Mr. Webster has two characters, which Proteus-like he can assume as his interests and necessities demand--the 'God-like' and the 'Hell-like'--the 'God-like Daniel' and 'Black Dan'!"[28]   The label stuck because of Webster's dark eyes, dark hair, and dour demeanor.

In December of 1845 Texas was admitted to the Union despite Webster's objections.   The Senate was divided between thirty Northern and thirty Southern Senators. "Manifest Destiny" became the slogan of the Democratic party, and war with Mexico was not far off.   The territory obtained in the settlement of that war would help to produce one of the greatest crises in American history. It would also provide Webster with a stage for his last persuasive campaign in the Senate.

4

The Compromise of 1850

The United States Senate has faced many crises, but few were as difficult or as protracted as the debate over slavery in 1850. Riots broke out in major cities. Southern states threatened to secede. And the president of the United States threatened to force his views upon the nation regardless of the consequences.

Webster's two major speeches on the floor of the Senate in 1850 were part of a larger campaign of persuasion.[1] While the Seventh of March Address helped create an atmosphere of compromise in influential segments of the population, it was not nearly so effective in Congress.[2] The July Address was delivered to move Congress toward compromise, thereby accomplishing what Webster had failed to do on March seventh. The first played mainly to the public and to preservation of the Union; the second mainly to legislative action in the Senate and to the pragmatic survival of the Union. Obviously, in introductions and perorations, both addresses raised themes common in Webster's career. A close reading, however, shows the thrust of each speech to be different. Furthermore, when the latter address is examined along with the former, it becomes clear that in achieving consensus, Webster expanded the use of public deliberation to produce compromise, and the use of freedom of expression to bring about conciliation in the nation and compromise in the Senate.[3]

To understand the significance of Webster's achievement, we need to understand the men who worked with him and against him, and the events that provided opportunities and obstacles through the course of the crisis.[4]

The politicians elected to the House of Representatives in 1848 consisted of a large group of freshmen who were divided almost evenly between Whigs and Democrats with enough Free Soilers present to make consensus practically impossible. Because of this partisan division, the House was unable to select a speaker through sixty-three ballots when it tried to organize itself in early 1849. The fractured Senate had organized more quickly, but the tension was no less severe. As the 1850 session got under way in January, 55 percent of the Senate was Democrat, 42 percent

Whig, and 3 percent Free Soil. Of the Democrat total, 54 percent were from slave states; of the Whig total, 48 percent were from slave states. Further complicating the situation was the fact that several of the Southern senators were from border states such as Missouri and Maryland. Constituents of border states' senators were divided between strong Union and strong slavery sympathies, and therefore, these senators, fearing a split within the borders of their states, were more open to compromise than their Deep South colleagues.[5] This set of · coalitions was further destabilized by the fact that a change of leadership was taking place. The 1850 Compromise debate would prove the last hurrah for Henry Clay, John C. Calhoun, and Daniel Webster. Each had been elected to the House of Representatives prior to 1815; each had served as Secretary of State; each had sought but never attained the presidency; and each would die within two years of the others: Calhoun in 1850, Clay in 1851, and Webster in 1852. The Compromise debate would serve to initiate such future leaders as William Seward, Stephen A. Douglas, and Jefferson Davis. Such colorful debaters as Henry Foote of Mississippi, Thomas Hart Benton of Missouri, Salmon P. Chase of Ohio, and John Hale of New Hampshire would also be on hand.

Another meaningful way to represent the fracturing is to break down the Senate according to which groups preferred what solutions to the slavery question. The Southern Democrats, headed by John C. Calhoun and Jefferson Davis, wanted to extend slavery into the territories. They believed that the South had been treated unfairly, was inadequately represented in the House, and needed the extension of slavery into new states to survive. About one quarter of the Senate belonged to the group that wanted to extend slavery. The United States were, to use the idiom of these Southerners, divided equally between fifteen "free" states and fifteen "slaveholding" states. To admit a single new state would upset the balance and put one section of the country or the other at a disadvantage.

A second group, led by Lewis Cass and Stephen A. Douglas, favored "popular sovereignty." That is, each territory should vote on its own to decide whether slaveholding would be allowed within its borders. In the presidential campaign of 1848, Cass had called for "squatter sovereignty" to determine whether the new territory acquired from Mexico should be organized as free or slaveholding. (Douglas euphemized the term to "popular sovereignty" and would use it with great success until the presidential campaign of 1860.) This group generally worked behind the scenes and tried to shift the slavery question from the federal government to the citizens of the states-to-be. This faction comprised another quarter of the Senate, and they were predominantly Democrats from the North.

Northern hardliners were another faction. They supported President Zachary Taylor in his effort to exclude slavery from the territories and newly admitted states. (Taylor, the hero of the Battle of Buena Vista, had, as the Whig nominee, beaten Cass in the 1848 election.) Led by William Seward of New York, this group tended to be radical in their views. They were among the delegates to the Whig Convention who had nominated Taylor over Webster. Webster had opposed Taylor's nomination and would now oppose his obstinate stand.[6]

The remainder of the Senate was divided between those who sought equitable compromise through omnibus legislation, like Webster and Clay, and those who were simply undecided. These "undecideds" were mainly from the South and were crucial to hopes for a compromise.

But if the Senate was a tangle of political prejudices, the issues were no less complex. They can be traced back to the war with Mexico (1846-48) wherein the United States defended its annexation of Texas and expanded the size of the country by approximately 25 percent. Under the leadership of Sam Houston, Texas had won its independence from Mexico in 1836. Texas had immediately petitioned for annexation by the United States, but President Andrew Jackson feared that admitting Texas would have an adverse effect on the presidential election of that year. Jackson's Vice President and successor, Martin Van Buren, was from New York and opposed slavery in the territories. He knew the admission of Texas would strengthen the South and the cause of slavery. Once again annexation was shelved. So Texas turned its attention to Europe in order to obtain necessary capital for development of its vast territory. England and France were eager to recognize the Republic of Texas. The three nations established strong ties that would last through the Civil War. By 1844, President John Tyler and his new Secretary of State, John C. Calhoun, who replaced Webster, believed annexation of Texas was possible. But Calhoun's florid and pro-slavery message to the Senate led to the defeat of the treaty.[7]

Finally, by a joint resolution of both houses of Congress, Texas was admitted to the Union in February and became a state in December, 1845. However, the resolution of admission contained three provisions that would become nettlesome in the 1850 debate: 1) Texas could be sub-divided into as many as four states; 2) Texas had to pay debts it incurred prior to joining the Union; and 3) Texas had to turn its boundary disputes over to the U.S. Government. The joint resolution passed the House by a vote of 120 to 98, and squeaked through the Senate on a 27 to 25 vote.

The foundation had been laid for a war with Mexico. When Mexico turned down offers of money for California and the New Mexico Territory in 1846, President James Polk ordered General Zachary Taylor's army to cross the Nueces River on January 13, 1846, and proceed to the Rio Grande. Diplomatic relations reached a crisis stage. Mexico abruptly broke off relations with the United States when news of the annexation was received in its capital. As Polk was drafting a war message to send to Congress, he received word that Taylor's troops had been attacked. Congress declared war on May 13, 1846, and soon after, American forces crossed the Rio Grande. The war with Mexico became a training ground for the future military leaders on both sides of the Civil War.

Like Congressman Abraham Lincoln, Senator Daniel Webster not only opposed the war with Mexico, but as early as 1837 publicly said that slavery should be excluded from the acquired territory.   This position was made into a congressional bill by David Wilmot during the war with Mexico.   Although it passed the House, it was blocked in the Senate.

On February 2, 1848, the treaty of Guadalupe Hidalgo was signed, whereby Mexico ceded the New Mexico Territory and California to the United States.   Ironically, in January, gold had been discovered in the Sacramento Valley and eighty thousand new settlers began their emigration to California.   These events spurred California politicians to clamor for statehood.   But admitting California would have thrown the evenly divided Senate out of balance.[8]

A period of rapid expansion led to the crisis of 1850. Besides Texas in 1845, Iowa (1846) and Wisconsin (1848) had been admitted as states.   Title to Oregon had been affirmed in 1846, preserving the Oregon Trail.   And in August, 1848, after heated debate that rehearsed the arguments of 1850, Congress passed and Polk signed the Oregon Bill.   It asserted Northern power by refusing to extend the Missouri Compromise line into the West.   The gold rush to California helped to bring new traffic to the Santa Fe Trail, which had seen commercial use as early as 1821.   It was Congress's responsibility to organize all of these new territories.

In early 1849, a group of Northern senators initiated stringent legislation outlawing slavery.   Senator Joseph Root of Ohio requested that the Committee on Territories effect legislation that would establish territorial governments in New Mexico and California that would prohibit slavery.   In direct messages to the territories, President Taylor supported this initiative.   But in so doing, Taylor usurped congressional authority.[9]

Californians were delighted and acted precipitously. By October of 1849, only seven months after Taylor's inauguration, and without waiting for the required congressional approval, California had passed an anti-slavery constitution, elected a state government, and sent members to Congress! The other territories in the west followed California's lead and began to set up provisional governments.

When criticized in the Senate and the press for the secrecy surrounding his messages, Taylor became defensive. On January 23, 1850, he notified the Senate of his action: "I did not hesitate to express to the people of those Territories my desire that each Territory should . . . form a plan of a State constitution and submit the same to Congress with a prayer for admission . . . but I did not anticipate, suggest, or authorize the establishment of any such government without the assent of Congress."[10]   The ensuing controversy centered on the organization of New Mexico and Deseret (today Utah, Nevada and parts of Idaho and Wyoming) and the admission of California as a state.

By the end of January, these and other issues enmeshed the Senate in a legislative gridlock.   The Congress was ready to stand up to the new president, believing he had usurped their powers.   They faced tough questions: should the slave trade continue in the District of Columbia? should fugitive slaves be returned to their owners?   should California be split in two?   should Texas, as was allowed under the annexation treaty, be split into four slave

states?   should the federal government assume the Texas
debt?   This last issue would prove particularly useful to
Webster because northern Whigs held the bonds on this
debt.[11]   Should a compromise pass, they would collect at
inflated rates.   Should it fail, they stood to lose a good
deal of money.   Since the bondholders were influential
businessmen, they could exert pressure by lobbying for the
Compromise.   Webster not only took money from them, he also
suggested ways by which they could succeed in changing
votes.   Furthermore, over port and in letters, Webster
warned business leaders that no tariff legislation was
possible until a compromise was passed.

Southern interests opposed any compromise short of
splitting Texas into more states and extending slavery into
the territories.   They used every argument to defend the
last vestiges of their power.   For example, on the question
of abolishing the slave trade in the District of Columbia,
they claimed that such a move would require the permission
of the state of Maryland since Maryland had donated the land
for the District's formation in the first place.

The national audience was as divided as the Congress.
Cotton Whigs and Democrats were balanced against Conscience
Whigs and Democrats.   Free Soilers and Abolitionists were
even more strident than Southern secessionists and
slaveholders.   Northern Free Soil and Abolitionist sentiment
favored legislation directly opposed to Southern cotton and
slave interests.   Southern hardliners supported legislation
inflammatory to the Northern moralists.   Each tried to put
the other on the defensive.   The depth of the division over
slavery was evident early and surfaced in the most sacred
beliefs of Americans.   By the 1840s, for example, the
Baptist and Methodist churches had split into separate
Northern and Southern organizations over the slavery
question.   In 1843, Henry H. Garnet called for slaves to
resist their owners.   In 1849, John Brown printed Garnet's
address and distributed it in the South.   Here are some
excerpts: "Slavery! How much misery is comprehended in that
single word. . . .   Unless the image of God be obliterated
from the soul, all men cherish the love of liberty. . . .
Brethern, the time has come when you must act for
yourselves. . . .   You had far better all die--die
immediately, than live [as] slaves.   Let your motto be
resistance!   Resistance!   Resistance!"   This inflammatory
document enraged Southerners.   One Southern clergyman, in
response to a speech by Henry Clay, defended slavery in the
summer of 1849 this way: "The degraded state and squalid
condition of poor negroes in the so called free States, show
them to be greatly injured, civilly and morally. . . . Hence
the wisdom and prudence of the free negro . . . as desiring
to sell himself into slavery, valuing his freedom at the
moderate price of $150."[12]

Passions ran high for many reasons, not the least of
which was that 1.7 million of the 6 million people who lived
in the South were members of slaveholding families.   This
count does not include the more than 3 million slaves who
were counted at a rate of three-fifths each for purposes of
apportioning seats in the U.S. House of Representatives.
Slaves were essential to profitably raise cotton because

cotton was much more labor intensive than other crops. It
not only required picking and baling, but carding,
separating, and spinning. In 1850, the South also supplied
half of the nation's corn, 87 percent of its hemp, 80
percent of its beans and peas, but these were not the money
crops. Those were tobacco, rice, sugar, and "King Cotton."
(By 1860, for example, Southern cotton brought $190,000,000
on European markets alone, while rice brought only
$2,000,000.) The entire social and economic structure of
the South was imperiled by emancipation of the slaves.[13]

With the president threatening to veto anything but
unconditional statehood, and claiming he would hang all
"traitors," the situation became hopelessly deadlocked.
Throughout this period, tempers grew short in the Congress
and often exploded into physical confrontations. Senators
Foote and Benton became so heated in one exchange that Foote
drew a pistol when Benton charged toward him. Both men had
to be physically restrained by their colleagues. Anxiety
intensified in the money markets of the nation and among
concerned citizens. The newspapers fed daily on the
deepening crisis. Thus, those seeking a compromise faced an
uphill battle. The House, the Senate, and the nation were
seriously divided by party, by region, and by policies.

Perhaps earlier than any of the other members of the
United States Senate, Henry Clay saw the impending danger of
the 1850 legislative session. In fact, he had come out of
retirement for the 1850 session, and had returned to his
familiar desk in the Senate chamber. On a cold, wet night
in January of that year, the elderly Clay toddled out of his
home to be helped into his carriage and driven to the home
of Daniel Webster. Over port, they discussed the crisis.

Clay was anxious to gain Webster as an ally. The two
men had known one another for more than forty years. They
had battled three times for the nomination of the Whig Party
with disastrous consequences. In 1848, Clay tried again
with the political omens pointing to a Whig victory this
time. The Whigs met in Philadelphia confident they would be
victorious in the general election. The nomination fight
soon became a battle between the old guard, represented by
Clay and Webster, and the new guard, represented by two
heroes of the Mexican-American War, Generals Winfield Scott
and Zachary Taylor. Webster was eliminated before the
convention; he was heartbroken at the lack of support he had
generated. In the end, he supported Clay. The delegates,
however, remembered Clay's previous loss and the fact that
they had won by running a war hero in 1840. So in 1848 they
did it again by nominating Taylor on the fourth ballot. The
conservative forces were allowed to balance the ticket with
Webster's friend from New York, Millard Fillmore.

Thus, on the very cold night of January 21, 1850, Clay
and Webster had a good deal about which to reminisce. They
had both lost sons in Mexico, Clay's being bayonnetted to
death by Mexican regulars. They had both been excluded from
the president's inner circle; and they had both sought to be
the nominee instead of the president. As Clay warmed
himself beside Webster's fire, he warned his old colleague
that this crisis was worse than the others. The South had
helped win the war with Mexico and it wanted its share of
the spoils. But President Taylor, a slave owner himself,

had surprised Southerners by making it clear that he would
refuse to extend slavery into the newly formed territories.
At the end of their meeting, Webster agreed to support
Clay's compromise.

When President Taylor learned that Clay had returned to
the Senate after an absence, he was suspicious of the old
politician's motives. Taylor was a blunt man, short of
stature and temper. He had been a hero in the War of 1812,
in the Indian Wars that followed, and in the war with Mexico
where he had captured Monterrey, Buena Vista, Palo Alto, and
Resaca de la Palma. Having dispatched the Mexican army, he
had little patience for the U.S. Senate. When he learned of
Clay's compromise plan on January 29, he was outraged. He
met with Senator William Seward of New York and encouraged
the young firebrand to block Clay's proposal. In a
reference to Taylor's interference, Clay said, "At a moment
when the White House itself is in danger of conflagration,
instead of all hands uniting to extinguish the flames, we
are contending about who shall be its next occupant." Clay
was implying that his colleagues should help him control
Taylor rather than jockeying among themselves for the 1852
presidential nomination.

Clay, looking thin and pale, began his lengthy oration
in support of a compromise on February 5, 1850, and
finished the next day. Below, Webster was arguing a case
before the Supreme Court. Calhoun was in his sick-bed. To
a crowded gallery and nearly full Senate chamber, Clay
outlined the causes of the crisis and offered his solutions:

First, admit California with no predisposition as to
slavery. If slavery worked in California, so be it.
If it was not economically viable, then the citizens of
that state would not introduce it there. (This was
disingenuous of Clay since the California organizers
had already declared themselves opposed to slavery.)

Second, reject the Wilmot Proviso, which called for
prohibiting slavery in the territories.

Third, settle the New Mexico boundary with Texas,
granting to New Mexico her claim east of the Rio
Grande.

Fourth, the United States should assume the Texas debt
incurred during the war with Mexico.

Fifth, the Congress should prohibit the slave <u>trade</u> in
the District of Columbia, but allow <u>slavery</u> in the
District.

Sixth, fugitive slaves should be returned to their
rightful owners.

Clay concluded thusly: "[That] if the direful event of the
dissolution of this Union is to happen, I shall not survive
to behold the sad and heart-rending spectacle."

Clay's prophesy would come true. And as early as
mid-February, 1850, he knew that his speech had failed;
abolitionists condemned the speech, Southern extremists
attacked the California plan, Northern Whigs supported
President Taylor. Even Southern Whigs, who were Clay's
natural allies, began to pick the omnibus package to pieces.

Then on February 23, 1850, President Taylor sealed the
fate of Clay's plan. In a meeting with Congressmen Stephens
and Toombs from Georgia, Taylor promised to hang all

"traitors," and made clear he meant those who talked of secession. Toombs and Stephens told their colleagues that Taylor was referring to the Southern extremists. The rumor, which Webster found to be true, disrupted all attempts at conciliation between the emerging factions.

The press had speculated that Senator John Caldwell Calhoun of South Carolina was too weak to participate in the 1850 session. So when he came to the Senate chamber on March 4, 1850, to oppose Clay's omnibus proposal, the gallery was packed and the chamber was electric with excitement. Calhoun's leonine mane of white hair contrasted sharply with his formal black coat. Those assembled watched as the once-noble War Hawk of the House of Representatives was helped to his seat by a colleague.

The gaunt Calhoun rose, thanked his colleagues, and asked Senator Mason of Virginia to read the address to the Senate on his behalf. The speech was one of Calhoun's most impressive. It rationalized Southern obstinacy on the slavery issue, stiffened resistance to compromise, and incited radicals from the North (like Seward) to oppose compromise from their side. Most important, in an interesting use of metaphor and metaphysics, Calhoun seized the high ground in the debate over compromise. He decided that he would not go on the defensive, but instead, he would aggressively argue that the South's position was morally right and was derived from the intent of the founding fathers of the nation.

Calhoun then denounced the Clay proposals as well as the plan of President Taylor as hopeless. He spent little time on Clay's omnibus bill, claiming other senators had dealt with it adequately. But he went on at some length with a detailed attack on the president's plan.

Finally, Calhoun concluded by offering his solution, noting to the dismay of Webster and Clay that the South had "no compromise to offer, but the Constitution; and no concession or surrender to make. She has already surrendered so much that she has little left to surrender." He called on the North to concede to the South "an equal right in the acquired territory . . . to do her duty" by returning fugitive slaves, ending Abolitionist agitation, and "to provide for the insertion of a provision in the Constitution, by an amendment, which will restore to the South, in substance" equal power with the North. Thus Calhoun shifted the burden of the debate back to the North. His demands were so extreme, his challenge so strong, that compromise seemed an impossibility should southern senators embrace his position.

But what concerned Webster and others seeking a compromise were Calhoun's ominous last words: "Having faithfully done my duty to the best of my ability, both to the Union and my section, throughout this agitation, I shall have the consolation, let what will come, that I am free of all responsibility." Webster knew at that moment that Calhoun had washed his hands of the idea of compromise. "[Let] what will come" was a clear reference to war. If the rest of the South followed Calhoun's lead, the battle was surely lost, just as Clay had feared earlier.

To the cheers of Southerners in the gallery and on the floor, Calhoun rose and, leaning on the arm of a friend,

left the Senate. At his boarding house, he could not sleep
that night, so he wrote to a friend about his "speech . . .
among my most successful." He was never to return to the
Senate alive. Twenty-seven days later, as he lay dying, he
uttered his last words, "The South, the poor South." On
April 1, his body lay in state in the Senate chamber while
mourners, including Daniel Webster, paid their last
respects. The head of the pride had departed from the field
of battle, and now the hunt was left to the young lions.[14]

THE SEVENTH OF MARCH ADDRESS

     As early as 1847, Webster had warned that the
acquisition of territory from Mexico would lead to strife.
He had lost his son Edward in Mexico and was in fact
notified of the horrible news on February 23, 1848, the very
day the Senate voted on ratification of the treaty with
Mexico. (On the day Edward's coffin arrived from Mexico,
Webster's daughter Julie was buried, having died of
consumption.) Webster opposed the treaty, saying it brought
alien and barren territory into America's domain. In 1847
and 1848, in quest of the Whig nomination, Webster travelled
the country from South Carolina to New Hampshire. Wherever
he spoke, he had stressed compromise and national unity to
preserve local ways of life.
     Thus it is not surprising that before entering the
controversy of 1850, Webster enjoyed a favorable press and a
large following. "Webster's name became symbolically
attached to the concepts of Constitution, Union, and the
wisdom and virtue of the age of Washington," according to
Bartlett.[15] Webster's identification with American civil
religion helped him elevate his arguments to a transcendent
level, while providing him with unprecedented credibility.
     The night before the speech, Webster worked on the
draft with his son Fletcher and two close friends, Ned
Curtis, and Peter Harvey. He began the three and a
half-hour speech plainly: "I speak today for the
preservation of the Union. 'Hear me for my cause.' I speak
today for the restoration to the country of that quiet and
that harmony which make the blessings of this Union so rich
and so dear to us all." Webster was not asking the North to
preserve some abstract form of liberty but rather that
system of government which had ensured prosperity in the
past. Near the end of the speech he pointed out that the
alternative to Union would be a war that threatened every
man, North and South.[16]
     Throughout the speech, Webster discussed the causes of
the crisis and how to avoid the specter of secession while
restoring harmony and peace. Concerning the limitation of
slavery by law, he said: "There is not at this moment . . .
a single foot of land, the character of which, in regard to
its being free soil territory or slave territory, is not
fixed by some law, and some irrepealable law, beyond the
power of action of this government." He clarified what he
meant by "irrepealable law" in his discussion of slavery in
the California and New Mexico territories: "I hold slavery
to be excluded from those territories by a law superior to

that which admits and sanctions it in Texas. I mean the law
of nature, of physical geography. . . .   That law settles
forever . . . that slavery cannot exist in California or New
Mexico." Like Clay, Webster was certain that these arid
territories could not support the crops that required slave
labor and thus would not prove profitable for slave holders.

Webster took delight in scolding "Northern Democracy"
for having supported the admission of Texas in 1845 in their
greed for land. He observed that according to the
agreements made, the state of Texas could be divided into
four slave states. Webster hinted that it was up to
Congress to decide when those states could be formed.

Webster set the stage for his version of popular
sovereignty when he reviewed the history of slavery. In his
biography of Webster, Henry Cabot Lodge wrote that he
believed Webster wasted time reviewing such a familiar
subject.[17] Yet Webster not only de-escalated the moral
implications of slavery but, more important to Free Soilers
and Cass supporters, he tied the expansion of slavery to the
expansion of cotton. He argued that social and economic
conditions in the North led to the moral judgment against
slavery, and that the South only defended slavery after it
was justified economically: "It was the cotton interest
that gave a new desire to promote slavery, to spread it, and
to use its labor." The strategy may have defused the fear
of "Slave Power" while deflating the righteous indignation
of the Abolitionists. Hence, Webster not only diminished
the moral issue, but sought identification with his audience
through the pragmatic economic issue. Webster concluded
this argument by stating: "Sir, wherever there is a
particular good to be done, wherever there is a foot of land
to be stayed back from becoming slave territory, I am ready
to assert the principle of the exclusion of slavery. I am
pledged to it from the year 1837; but I will not do a thing
unnecessary, that wounds the feelings of others."
Obviously, Webster hoped the North would understand that
adopting the Compromise would not expand slavery but would
preserve the Union.

Webster tried to identify with his audience by
appealing to latent attitudes in his review of grievances
produced by the North and the South which had "alienated the
minds of one portion of the country from the other."[18]   No
legislative action could be taken to correct most of the
offenses, according to Webster. But there was one Southern
complaint that Congress could correct: the North's
unwillingness to   return fugitive slaves. Webster
suggested that when each Northerner stopped to investigate,
he would understand that he had a constitutional obligation
to return fugitive   slaves. Although Lodge believed
Webster's argument was "merely legalistic," it probably
appealed to most Northerners. People who were interested in
preserving the Union and the prosperity that went with it
would have been interested in preserving the constitutional
principles that held the Union together. Webster's argument
in this context hardly seems "legalistic."

Webster knew that the Southern moderates would be
placated further if Abolitionists were criticized. So he
characterized Abolitionists as men who "think what is right
may be distinguished from what is wrong with the precision

of an algebraic equation." If they detected a spot on the
sun, Webster surmised, they would strike it down from
heaven. Although he conceded that there were thousands of
"perfectly well-meaning men" in the societies, they had, by
their vicious attacks, helped strengthen Southern support
for slavery instead of weaken it.[19] Webster's strategy was
to separate the moralistic Abolitionists from the rest of
the North in order to minimize their influence. This tactic
particularly annoyed the Abolitionists and motivated their
intense hostility toward the speech.

Webster's arguments were consistent with most Northern
attitudes. Like most reformers, he thought that elimination
of slavery was impossible. Many Northerners saw "Negro
colonization" (an enforced emigration to Africa or to
Central America) as the only real answer to the slave
problem. Many of the clergy believed that although "slavery
was a moral problem, abolition was not the moral way to
solve it."[20] The Abolitionist societies had strengthened
slavery sentiment in the South and rejected the advice of
pragmatists.

Even though Congress could not resolve Northern
grievances, Webster discussed them in an effort to identify
with the North. He charged the South with extending and
extolling the blessings of the institution of slavery. He
objected to several Southern claims, especially those
asserting that slaves were happier and in better condition
than free laborers. He called forth pride in many
Northerners:

Why, who are the laboring people of the North? They
are the North. They are the people who cultivate their
own farms with their own hands; free holders, educated
men, independent men. If they are not free holders,
they earn wages; these wages accumulate, are turned
into capital, into new free holds, and small
capitalists are formed. They provide the means of
independence.

He complained of "free colored men" being seized from
Northern ships in Southern ports, an unconstitutional act.
Finally, he suggested that the South, like the North, had
constitutional obligations to perform. Completing the
symmetry of his appeal, Webster said: "[So] far as any of
these grievances have their foundation in matters of law,
they can be redressed . . . and so far as they have their
foundation in matters of opinion . . . all that we can do is
to allay the agitation, and cultivate a better feeling and
more fraternal sentiments between the North and the
South."[21]

Politicians and historians, such as Henry Cabot Lodge
and John F. Kennedy, have often relied on the reaction of
Abolitionists to this speech to assess its worth.
Certainly, the response of philosophical leaders in the
North was hostile. These same men had much direct influence
on newspapers. John Greenleaf Whittier, Ralph Waldo
Emerson, James Russell Lowell, George Washington Julian,
Horace Mann, Henry Longfellow, William Cullen Bryant, Edmund
Quincy, and Henry David Thoreau all attacked Webster for his
Seventh of March Speech.[22] Whittier wrote this of Webster:

> All else is gone; from those great eyes
>   The soul has fled:
> When faith is lost, when honor dies,
>   The man is dead!
> Then, pay the reverence of old days
>   To his dead fame;
> Walk backward, with averted gaze,
>   And hide the shame!

Abolitionists such as William Lloyd Garrison, Wendell Phillips, Theodore Parker, and Frederick Douglass, viewed slavery as a moral rather than political question and were especially vicious in attacking Webster both in print and at public meetings. On March 25, Phillips, Douglass, and Parker spoke to a mass meeting at Faneuil Hall in Boston.[23] Reverend Parker started with the accusation that Webster's stand could only be viewed as a "bid for the Presidency."[24]

Among the prominent and hostile Northern politicians, Charles Sumner placed Webster in "the dark list of apostates," and William H. Seward pronounced him a "traitor to the cause of freedom."[25] "Not one of my colleagues from New England," Webster acknowledged, "would publicly support the speech."[26]

A portion of the Northern press was less than enthusiastic about the speech. The Boston Atlas said, "His sentiments are not our sentiments. They are not, we venture to say, the sentiments of the Whigs of New England."[27] The New York Tribune considered it "unequal to the occasion and unworthy of its author." The New York Evening Post described the speech as a "traitorous retreat" and Webster as "a man who deserted the cause which he lately defended." The Abolitionist Liberator called the speech "the scarlet infamy of Daniel Webster . . . an indescribably base and wicked speech."[28]

The effect of Webster's speech in the North cannot be measured accurately by relying on the commentary of abolitionists. Several press reactions, legislative acts, and even votes reveal considerable positive influence of Webster's words. On March 12, the Daily Advertiser said: "So far as we can tell, the Boston public fully support Mr. Webster, not with an enthusiastic rush of blind admiration, but with a calm belief that he has placed a vexed question in a position in which it can and must be fairly settled."[29] "As a constitutional argument to be applied to the existing dispute between the North and the South, it is impregnable, unassailable, irrefutable," the Boston Courier said on March 13.[30] The Philadelphia Evening Bulletin remarked that "the speech . . . was an able and patriotic effort." The editorial praised the "practical" and "candid" nature of Webster's argument.[31]

Furthermore, there were several measures of success. In the South, Whig papers applauded it. For example, the Charleston Mercury called it a "great speech." These sentiments would help win Southern senators open to compromise. In the Massachusetts General Court a motion was introduced that read:

> The Hon. Daniel Webster, in his recent speech in the Senate of the United States, has not faithfully represented the sentiments of the people of Massachusetts.

The resolution was rejected by a vote of 19 to 10. Two more resolutions were introduced directing Webster to support the Wilmot Proviso and to oppose Mason's Fugitive Slave Bill. They too were rejected. Between six and eight hundred businessmen from New York sent Webster a letter and a gold watch thanking him for his speech.32 Close to a thousand leading Bostonians followed suit; the Boston Courier published their names and their letter. A majority of the faculty at Harvard voted to support Webster's stand. Bonds, a crucial indicator of compromise chances, were falling in price before the speech and rose dramatically just after it.33

The North's reaction to Webster's Seventh of March Address cannot accurately be deduced from selective commentary--often of an elite group--that occurred after the speech. The most reliable way to determine the North's reaction is to analyze all available evidence in light of the varied Northern attitudes on slavery. Then one can evaluate how well Webster utilized those attitudes in his speeches to create an atmosphere of compromise in the North. These attitudes were set into a complicated political context.

Abolitionist, Whig, and Democratic groups represented the major factions on the slavery question. But even these factions were fractured. First, there was the American Anti-Slavery Society (AAS) whose motto was "No Union With Slave Holders." William Lloyd Garrison's condemnation of the Constitution and his refusal to use political means to end slavery caused the Society to split unevenly in 1840. By 1850, the AAS had lost about 110,000 members, reducing its membership to only 40,000.34

After 1840, the American and Foreign Anti-Slavery Society, splintering with the AAS while trying to gain political power to implement their policy, evolved into the Free Soil Party. Their candidate in 1848, former President Martin Van Buren, polled only 291,263 votes.35

However, the vast majority of Northerners were caught between their prejudice against blacks and the conviction that there was a "Slave Power" conspiracy attempting to capture political power.36 The Abolitionists contributed to this conviction by arguing: "Slavery produced a ruling caste, a minority group of large slaveholders, who, through the constitutional provision for counting three-fifths of the slaves in computing the basis of congressional representation, controlled the destinies of the South and the nation."37

Slaveholders contributed to Northern fears by aggressively trying to force slavery into the territories. Acts of violence and inflammatory remarks by a few Southerners heightened the belief of many Northerners that the Southern oligarchy was trying to destroy the Union. The Abolitionist press blew these acts and remarks out of proportion and invented others. These reports concerned Northerners who were considering migrating westward. Conservative Northerners were more influenced by the fear of "Slave Power" pushing into the territories than by any argument concerning the sin of slavery in the Southern states.38

The Free Soil Party was not immune to this conservatism. The majority of Free Soilers were anti-slavery not because they wanted to change the system radically, but because they wanted to preserve their political, social, and economic institutions and extend them westward.[39]   Votes for Van Buren were likely to be reactions against the choice of Lewis Cass, a popular sovereignty advocate, and General Zachary Taylor, a Southern slave owner.

The Whig and Democratic parties were also split. "Conscience" Whigs held many of the same views as Free Soilers, but avoided identification with the latter's many radical Abolitionists. Northern "Cotton" Whigs were mainly bankers and businessmen concerned with a new tariff in 1850.

The Democratic Party in the North had a pro-slavery faction and a Free Soil faction. (Hard core members of the pro-slavery faction would become the "Copperheads" during the Civil War who so violently opposed Lincoln.) Most of the Free Soil Democrats voted for Van Buren in 1848. What is important to remember in evaluating Webster's use of attitudes is that the Democrats and Whigs polled a sizeable majority in the North by running men like Cass and Taylor. In his home state, New York, where the Liberty League and Free Soil Party were founded, former President Van Buren polled only 120,000 against Cass' 114,000 and Taylor's 218,000. The Free Soil-Abolitionist coalition was rejected; the conservatives carried the day, indicating a public preference for pragmatic rather than moralistic approaches to the slave problem.

This analysis of Northern attitudes indicates that Daniel Webster's Seventh of March Address was effective in creating an atmosphere of compromise in the North.[40]   The crucial strategy for Webster was his appeal to the pragmatic majority in the North to preserve the Union.

Daniel Webster was successful in helping to create an atmosphere of compromise in the North by appealing to prevalent pragmatic attitudes. Contrary to the commentary after the speech, the majority of the North reacted favorably to the speech. After Webster's address, senators began to ridicule the idea of secession for the first time on the floor of the Senate.[41] Over three thousand persons at Boston's Faneuil Hall signed their names in support of the Compromise. Webster's effectiveness is all the more remarkable when we note that Webster's freedom to speak out on Northern attitudes was limited by the fact that he could not affront Southern senators essential to compromise.

The speech was only the beginning of Webster's campaign for the North's acceptance of the Compromise. The speech was rewritten into a pamphlet dropping out only a few positions that might prove controversial. One hundred thousand copies were mailed by Webster's office alone and requests continued to come in.[42] But momentum for compromise was interrupted by the death of Calhoun on March 31, an event that coalesced Southern obstinacy. Undaunted, Webster toured the North in April to campaign for the Compromise. He talked to legislators and judges, wrote letters that were published in the newspapers and gave speeches at mass meetings. In his private letters, Webster continued to campaign for compromise. He wrote to Peter

Harvey in May that Southern Whigs "will not give a single vote for the tariff until this slavery business is settled. The Lowell mills might stop unless the North quit this violence of abuse -- and showed a disposition to be reasonable in the present existing questions."[43]   Northern businessmen needed a new tariff and Webster was telling them that there would be no consideration of one until the crisis was settled.   No wonder over ten thousand New York businessmen pledged themselves to aid in the rendition of fugitive slaves.   The speech, along with everything else he did and said from March seventh to September twelfth, has to be considered in making a full evaluation of Webster's effort to rally support for the Compromise.

Webster wrote to his son, Fletcher, in 1848 that the best strategy for maintaining the Union would be to isolate extremists on each side of the slavery question.[44]   In the Seventh of March speech, Webster separated the extremists, North and South, from the pragmatic majority by attacking their legislative proposals, radical methods, and strident rhetoric.   He knew they would never favor compromise and were of use to him only as examples of what over-moralization could cause.   Then he made positive overtures to moderates on each side, while reconceptualizing the problem from a philosophical confrontation into a pragmatic deliberation.   Whigs, essentially conservative, were told that prosperity came only with Union.   Businessmen were promised a settlement of the bond issue and a tariff reform in the future.   Free Soilers, who Webster knew to be more fearful of the closing of the frontier than affronted by the immorality of slavery, were told that the forces of nature would preclude development of cash crops in the territories, which would thereby stop the expansion of slavery; thus, they need not worry about Southern expansionism.   Southerners were promised peace at home and return of their slaves.   In short, Webster created an audience amenable to compromise, particularly among Whigs, because he was able to recognize a pervasive conservative sentiment and articulate it in pragmatic rhetoric acceptable to self-interested segments in the North and South.

But while the address was persuasive to the public,[45] the speech was less influential in the Senate.   First, events beyond Webster's control hampered his efforts. William Seward had been in contact with President Taylor from the outset.   On March 11, Seward rose to present the Northern case.   His speech neatly balanced Calhoun's.   He appealed to "higher law" and split the Whig Party.   The first half of Seward's speech concentrated on the question of statehood for California.   Seward, like the president, wanted California admitted for strategic as well as economic reasons.   He talked at length about how California had grown from a "Mexican province" to a major population center.   Recognizing California's vote for free status, Seward concluded one early section of the speech this way: "California, the youthful Queen of the Pacific, in her robes of freedom, gorgeously inlaid with gold. . . . There are silver and gold in the mountains and ravines of California; the granite of New England and New York is

barren."   He went on to answer charges that California had
been organized too quickly.   Defending the president's
action, Seward opposed any compromise, arguing that if
California was not admitted, it would become an independent
republic and take Oregon with it.   Webster was so disturbed
by Seward's address that he interrupted it at one point to
remind Seward that Texas had the right to divide itself into
four slave states if it saw fit!
      Sentiment for compromise was also stalled by John C.
Calhoun's call for states' rights in the lengthy speech read
for him on March 4; and his death on March 31 only
strengthened Southern resistance.   Between them, Seward and
Calhoun had eaten away at Webster's moderate coalition.   And
throughout this period, President Taylor obstinately opposed
compromise.
      Second, Webster probably spoke too early to have much
impact in the Senate.   His speech followed Clay's of
February 5 and 6, and Calhoun's of March 4.   The young
lions--Foote, Davis, Root, Douglas--had not had their chance
to speak out on the issues.   Furthermore, to them, Webster
seemed to be merely mirroring Clay's position.   Webster had
had less than two weeks to prepare the speech, and probably
relied too much on Clay's legislative suggestions.[46]   In
fact, even Webster doubted the merits of his address.   On
March 17, he wrote that if the fate of the speech "should be
to go to the bottom, it has no cargo of value, and only one
passenger to be drowned."[47]   Perhaps this explains why he
revised the speech so extensively before releasing it to the
public.   On May 18, more than two months after the address,
Webster wrote to Franklin Haven that his influence had
ebbed: "If more than six Southern senators refuse their
support, the compromise bill will fail in the Senate."[48]
Webster's address failed to create an atmosphere of
compromise in the Senate, though with the public it had more
success.[49]

THE LEGISLATIVE INTERREGNUM

      Congressional debate remained acrimonious and cynical
through May and June; the necessary elements of legislative
compromise failed to make any headway.   For example, Douglas
tried to have California statehood voted on separately but
was defeated by a vote of 28 to 24.   Webster rarely spoke
during this period, but was present to keep an eye on the
maneuvering.   The speeches he gave were short and
conciliatory.   On April 1, 1850, he gave the obligatory
eulogy honoring Calhoun.   On June 3, he spoke briefly on
the Fugitive Slave Bill, reaffirming his position that
slavery was impractical in the territories.   On June 13 and
again on June 17, Webster addressed the Compromise Bill only
to clarify legalistic arguments.
      On June 27 and 28, Webster engaged in more lengthy
debate.   The question concerned an amendment by Senator
Pierre Soule of Louisiana on "California Public Lands and
Boundaries."   Webster spoke against the amendment.   In
marked contrast with the Seventh of March Address, it was
legalistic, filled with facts, and almost entirely
refutative in nature.   The speech demonstrates Webster's

intimate knowledge of documents, facts, and strategies surrounding the Compromise, a point many historians overlook. The amendment was defeated 36 to 19, and Webster deserves a good deal of the credit. His effectiveness with his colleagues and his impact on the legislative process are quite clear.

When not watching over the Senate, he was busy writing public letters and editorials, and bringing political pressure to bear on vacillating senators. Through this whole period he tried to avoid a confrontation with the president. By the end of June, Webster claimed that "the issue of union or disunion was still touch and go."[50] But he continued to monitor the situation and advise all who would listen, including Stephen A. Douglas (who some credit with passage of the Compromise), on how to solve the crisis.

THE SEVENTEENTH OF JULY ADDRESS

On July 4, 1850, under a hot Washington sun, President Zachary Taylor cooled himself by eating cherries soaked in bourbon. He contracted a violent stomach disorder, "cholera morbus," and died five days later.[51] Millard Fillmore, who actually had been born in a log cabin, succeeded Taylor, becoming the last Whig president of the United States. Not only was one of the major obstacles to compromise thus removed with the death of Taylor, but the new president had been put on the ticket to satisfy Webster's wing of the party. Moreover, Fillmore, as president of the Senate, had told Clay he would break a tie in favor of compromise should the opportunity present itself. Fillmore's admiration for Webster was unabashed, so it was not surprising that on July 12, Fillmore asked Webster to become Secretary of State and to head his cabinet. Webster agreed to return to the post he had held from 1841 to 1844 under Presidents Harrison and Tyler.

These events presented Webster with a remarkable opportunity to press home the Compromise. A farewell address to the Senate would receive special attention, enhance his credibility, and allow Webster to focus his remarks on the very body essential to compromise hopes. Webster rose on July 17 to make his last formal appeal for the Compromise.

Dressed in a blue waistcoat and black pants, Webster stared into the faces of the men with whom he had so long served and debated. He must have known that his success or failure with the national audience was not critical at this juncture: The Seventh of March speech had been for them. Now he must move his colleagues to act. This is not to say that the secondary audience was ignored, nor that the speech was incomplete. It is simply to argue that Webster knew where his emphasis should lie.

Because Webster's Seventeenth of July speech is complex and subtle, it is best to examine his strategies as they emerge from the progression of arguments in the text. Several tactics are worth noting.

First, Webster, understanding the tangle in which the Senate was caught, attempted to transcend rivalries wherever he could.   Second, Webster argued that his solution was better than the others offered, not that it was the <u>only</u> one possible.   This maneuver left him room to change positions when need be (as he would do in August when the Compromise was moved as separate legislation rather than as an omnibus bill).   Third, Webster explained specifically and vividly what legislative steps were necessary to achieve a compromise.   Fourth, throughout the address, he judiciously used evidence to put a unionist interpretation on history and geography that would support his portrait of the crisis. This last tactic was important because it provided a coherent conceptualization that allowed the senators to rationalize their acceptance of the Compromise while transcending their differences.

In an apparent attempt to court ideological Whigs, Webster began his address with a tribute to the dead president, which diverted attention from divisive issues. At the same time, Webster argued that the Union had survived the crisis of the president's death; it had ascended the trouble: credit was unaffected, no disturbances arose, and the legislative body continued to function.   The Union works, claimed Webster, and it is our duty to the dead president to keep it working.

Throughout his introduction, Webster avoided any mention of Taylor's presidential policies; instead he concentrated on what Taylor, the war hero, achieved for Union.   By avoiding the alienating policies of the president and concentrating on the qualities of the general, he was able to identify the deceased Taylor with the cause of Union. And Union benefiting the whole nation was the picture Webster wanted his colleagues to accept.   Later, Webster would use himself to symbolize Union in an effort to reinforce the transcendent attitude he sought in the Senate.

Next, Webster proceeded to do what had to be done <u>pro</u> <u>forma</u>.   As on March 7, Webster chastized the Abolitionists for their rigid moral stand and its consequences.   Once again, he offered businessmen economic rewards for support of compromise: Texas bonds would be paid off; the tariff could be raised.   Once again, he presented pragmatic alternatives to disunion: leave slavery where it was, return slaves to their rightful owners, and open the territories to new settlers.   Webster began to identify a coalition composed of moderates from the border states, the undecideds, and those senators favoring various popular sovereignty remedies.   Once the audience that could be persuaded was formed, he focused his attention on the Compromise proposals and how to get them through the Senate.

What seems most remarkable about the Seventeenth of July speech is Webster's judicious shifting from the philosophical to the pragmatic, and back again, to suit his purpose.   If the issue was divisive, Webster treated it pragmatically, as legislation necessary to the workings of the nation.   He asked his colleagues to accept a few bitter pills so that the Compromise might pass and all might benefit.   If the issue had broad support, he elevated it to the ideal level, thus giving it more importance than the divisive issues.

As he had on many other occasions, Webster emphasized union.   From beginning to end, he supported the thesis he

uttered in his last line: "No man can suffer too much, and
no man can fall too soon, if he suffer or if he fall in
defense of the liberties and constitution of his country."[52]
The power of this Unionist appeal in this particular address
lay in the fact that Webster had stood for Union in speeches
dating back to his famous debate with Hayne in the Senate in
1830 and his celebrated addresses on the landing at Plymouth
and the ground breaking for the Bunker Hill monument, in
1820 and 1825, respectively. If he could provide an example
for enough senators, compromise would be achieved. Here,
personal credibility became part of the consensus-building
process.

At this juncture, not only was Webster trying to advance
the Compromise, he was trying to identify it and himself
with the survival of the Union, thereby allowing his
colleagues a way to transcend their petty differences: "I
wish, Sir, so far as I can, to harmonize opinions. I wish
to facilitate some measure of conciliation. I wish to
consummate some proposition or other, that shall bring
opponents' sentiments together." This appeal led to
Webster's consistent argumentative synthesis: all
responsible members of Congress wanted the Union to survive
and the current crisis to end. But Webster not only gave
his colleagues a rationale for voting for compromise, he
also showed them the way to achieve it.

To accomplish this feat under these difficult
circumstances, Webster based his plea for the Compromise on
its comparative advantage over the alternative. The
legislative proposals were not right nor wrong, one course
was simply more advantageous than another. Compromise,
Webster consistently argued, was simply a better road to
travel than the ideological sundering advocated by
extremists.

To support his case, Webster put the issues in
perspective. He interpreted history in a way that would
build his argumentative synthesis: the expansion of slavery
into the territories was an economic impossibility, so open
the territories to all who wanted to go into them; admit
California as a free state; the Union of states would expand
to the Pacific and all parties would benefit. Furthermore,
all of these advantages could be obtained through the
legislative process.

On several occasions, Webster went into great detail to
prove just how simple a compromise could be. Webster's
discussion of California is a case in point. It was
connected to questions of prosperity and preservation of the
Union, as it had been in the Seventh of March Address. In
this section, Webster articulated the strategy Douglas
eventually used to pass the Compromise: the essential bills
need not be seen as an omnibus. Here is one exchange that
took place during Webster's speech; it reveals just how
ready Webster was to engineer the legislative process in
order to achieve consensus:

Mr. Webster: The honorable member from Illinois, who is
at the head of that committee, sits near me, and I take
it for granted that he can say whether I am right or not
in the opinion, that, if we should this day admit
California alone, he would to-morrow feel it his duty to

bring in a bill for the government of the Territories,
or to make some disposition of them. . . .
Mr. Douglas: Mr. President, if California should be
admitted by herself, I should certainly feel it my duty,
as the Chairman of the Committee on Territories, to move
to take up the subject of the Territories at once, and
put them through, and also the Texas boundary question,
and to settle them by detail if they are not settled in
the aggregate. . . .
Mr. Webster: Then, Sir, it is as I supposed. We should
not get rid of the subject, even for the present, by
admitting California alone. Now, Sir, it is not wise to
conceal our condition from ourselves. Suppose we admit
California alone. My honorable friend from Illinois
brings in, then, a bill for territorial government for
New Mexico and Utah. We must open our eyes to the state
of opinion in the two houses respectively, and endeavor
to forsee what would be the probable fate of such a
bill. If it be a bill containing a prohibition of
slavery, we know it could not pass this house. If it be
a bill without such prohibition, we know what
difficulty it would encounter elsewhere. So that we
very little relieve ourselves from the embarrassing
circumstances in which we are placed by taking up
California and acting upon it alone.[53]

These paragraphs read like an in-house memorandum and give
the clearest evidence that Webster was concerned not only
with persuading his colleagues but with showing them the
legislative path to compromise. The same strategy was
employed when Webster moved to a discussion of the New
Mexico and Utah territories. Even the transition tended
toward the pragmatic. Said Webster, "What is next to be
done?" Webster then placated Southern senators by admitting
that he had "the strongest objection to a premature creation
of states." This bit of parliamentary maneuvering is
typical of the legislative cast of the address.
Continuing to balance interest against interest, and
continuing to argue that no crisis had so unnecessarily tied
up Congress, Webster then took up the questions surrounding
Texas. Could the border dispute with the New Mexico
Territory be settled? Should the federal government assume
Texas' debt? Again, sounding much like a legislative
manager, Webster explained how Texas was central to the
complex deliberations. Unless the Texas boundary was set,
New Mexico could not be organized as a territory. If
Texas's debt were not paid, then there would be no trade-off
for California's entry, nor any way to pay off Texas bonds.
Perhaps at no point was Webster more pragmatic. The money
that would come to the Texas bondholders in the North was
never far from Webster's rhetorical focus, nor, as it turned
out, from his own pocketbook.

Having moved from the admission of California, a
Northern bill, to the Texas questions, a Southern bill,
Webster had reduced the debate to a question of proper
management of legislation. At that point he once again
characterized the motivations of those who opposed the
Compromise. As in the Seventh of March speech, he described
as irrational those "directly opposed to each other in every
matter connected with the subject under consideration." He

disassociated himself and compromise legislation from those
who would "fight it to the last." Even more strongly than
in the March address, Webster asserted that the enemies of
the Compromise had become allied because of a desire to see
the Compromise destroyed for their own sectional advantage.
His sarcastic attack on "the consistency of the opposition
to this measure" once again carved away extremists from the
majority he wished to coalesce. Extremists from North and
South threatened not only the Compromise, but the Union as
well. They would destroy the system of government that had
worked so well to serve so many--the Whig banker, the
Southern cotton merchant, the Free Soil farmer, the New
England textile owner, and the Northern industrialist.
Thus, Webster established a dialectic between union, the
transcendent value that meant work and prosperity, and
disunion, the course that led to destruction. On the side
of union, he lined up the elements he needed for his
compromise majority. On the side of disunion, he placed the
extremists.
     Having attacked ideological intransigence, Webster made
an appeal for all senators to re-examine the procedure
whereby they voted according to instructions from their
state legislatures. Again, the rhetorical focus was on a
pragmatic, parliamentary point. Webster knew that if the
Compromise was to succeed, some senators would have to
violate their instructions. (In fact, Senator Foote of
Mississippi would do just that.) If instructions were to be
followed, then no debate was necessary, no flexible
representation possible. Webster identified senators who
were voting against their conscience because of instructions
from home. And while discussing this dilemma, he
sympathized with these men and avoided impugning their
motives:

     I cannot but regret, certainly, that gentlemen who sit
     around me . . . and my friends from Massachusetts in the
     other house, are obliged, by the sense of duty, to
     oppose a measure which I feel bound by conscience to
     support to the utmost of my ability. They are just as
     high minded, as patriotic, as pure, and every way as
     well intentioned as I am. . . .
But Webster asked them to make a sacrifice nonetheless. He
compared voting on instructions with "involuntary
servitude," thus reducing senators who followed
instructions to slaves of their states whereas he knew that
most of these men were from states opposed to slavery. He
equated voting independently with conscience, freedom, and
transcendent values that few could resist. Webster was able
to elevate this pragmatic issue of voting on instructions to
a question of conscience where it worked to his advantage.
The mechanics of achieving legislative compromise were to
Webster the issues of conscience, while the questions of
regional loyalty became the tools of destruction. He turned
Calhoun's view of the Compromise upside down!
     Then Webster proceeded to discuss the value of the
Compromise to the moderates. Webster used a powerful form
of progressive argument. It began with a single example,
the state of Massachusetts, then expanded in implication to
include the whole of the North, and eventually the entire

Union.   In counterpoint, he showed at each level of expansion what gain would occur with compromise.   Next he repeated the argumentative strategy showing what loss would occur in each case without compromise.   The parallel structure of this argument from consequences is compelling and at times overwhelming.

The Massachusetts example was sustained by twelve paragraphs that frankly discussed what the Compromise would mean to the North.   This section of the speech rehearsed again the issues of the debate, as Webster embellished them by showing how each piece of the Compromise benefited Northern interests: "She gains the quiet of New Mexico, and she gains the settlement of the Texas boundary . . . . More than that, Sir, she gains . . . and the whole country gains, the final adjustment of by far the greater part of all the slavery questions."   The "final adjustment" would result in the "greatest of all possible benefits . . . the restoration of this government to the ordinary exercise of its functions."   Once again, Webster had merged preservation of the Union with the pragmatic operation of Congress but had developed that theme by linking passage of the bills first to the benefit of Massachusetts, then to the North, and finally to the entire country.   Webster used the same strategy of progression in the very next passage when he showed what Massachusetts, the North, and the nation, would lose if the bills failed.

The strategy of progression-and-gain versus dissolution-and- loss is employed again in the section of the speech devoted to gaining Southern adherence to the Compromise.   But before Webster embarked on this most delicate persuasion, he once again reminded his audience, in vivid and pragmatic terms, of the problem confronting the nation: "Men must live; to live, they must work.   And how is this to be done, if . . . all the business of society is stopped, and everything is placed in a state of stagnation."   Thus, before reinforcing the comparative advantage of his position, Webster painted the picture of the crisis he wanted his colleagues to perceive.

As Webster turned to southern senators to explain why they should support the Compromise, his transition reinforced the dramatic nature of the crisis: the government was "hardly able to keep . . . alive . . . all is paralysis . . . everything is suspended upon this one topic."

Having gained the attention of Southern moderates, Webster argued that the North had given up the Wilmot Proviso, would enforce the Fugitive Slave Act, would absorb the Texas debt, and allow free choice in the territories. These concessions were generous enough to warrant a quid pro quo from Southern senators.   Throughout this portion of his address, Webster maintained a delicate balance between seducing the South into compromise and retaining Northern support for bills that might benefit the South.   But most important, he again achieved transcendence by arguing from the parts (legislative concessions) to the whole (Southern support for the Compromise).

As Webster had used Massachusetts to actualize the benefits of the Compromise to the North, he used Maryland to demonstrate advantages to the South.   The selection of Maryland was materially significant to moderates because it

was a border state. Webster appealed for calm, deliberate
consideration of the issues upon which compromise depended
and asked that the more patriotic Southern senators prevail
on those "not as wise." He compared those who used the
Nashville Convention on secession "as a syllabus of Southern
sentiment" to those Northerners who were "tinctured with
abolitionism." Thus, Webster renewed his pragmatic
argument, appealed to the better nature of moderates, and
once again isolated the extremists, who refused to support
the Compromise in any case.

Webster ended this section of the speech with a plea to
all moderates to "come together as brethren, enjoying one
renown, one destiny, and expecting one and the same destiny
hereafter." He recounted his privilege at having served in
Congress "with good union men from the South." Much more
than in the March address did Webster court Southern favor.
He spoke of the valor of Southern military leaders in the
war with Mexico. He praised Southern sentiment and values.
He concluded by claiming that he separated himself from
those who questioned the loyalty of his Southern colleagues.
As he had with Northern senators, Webster sought
identification with moderate senators from the South
through an appeal to conscience based on unionist motives.
In short, he praised where he could afford to praise, moved
away from the divisive and emotional questions, and
obviously hoped these appeals would raise southern
consciences to the transcendent compromise he endorsed.

Webster began his summation by calling for the
preservation of the Union. Again, Massachusetts was used as
an example of a state with close ties to the Union and the
Constitution. But union transcended statehood; it was "the
law which determines the destiny" of us all: "Like that
column which...perpetuates the memory of the first great
battle of the Revolution." Suddenly, Webster's pragmatic
address, which aimed at opening as many Senators as possible
to the Compromise, attempted to seal that persuasion with an
emotional and florid conclusion. Into that highly charged
moment, Webster once again asserted his own credibility:

> I shall stand by the Union, and by all who stand by it.
> I shall do justice to the whole country . . . in all I
> say . . . and mean to stand upon the constitution . . .
> . The ends I aim at shall be my country's, my God's, and
> Truth's. I was born an American; I will live an
> American; I shall die an American; and I intend to
> perform the duties incumbent upon me in that character
> to the end of my career.

Taylor and Webster, symbolic exponents of union, served
as terminals for the speech. In the same way, Massachusetts
and Maryland served as synecdoches for the beneficial
consequences of compromise in the North, the South, and
hence to the whole Union. In between, an argumentative net
was woven that used history to justify compromise, and
pragmatic suggestions to achieve consensus. If any part of
the portrait were neglected, his coalition would remain
unconvinced that the picture was a coherent one. The way he
painted the picture demonstrated that the Compromise was
essential to national survival. Webster fashioned his
appeal with colorful phrasing and a favorable

interpretation of historical fact. The credibility of this perspective worked to prevent the dissidents from reducing the deliberative body to quarrelsome disarray.

As in every other speech cited here, Webster grounded all of his strategies in detailed audience analysis. He knew what interests were most salient to each of his listeners. These interests guided his selection of words, phrases, arguments, and values. This ability to master his subject, to understand his audience, and to fashion his speech worked well in a free Republic. Like Pericles in Athens, Cicero in Rome, and Burke in the English Parliament, Webster was able to rouse his colleagues to action because his government gave him the freedom to make his case.

Evidence is strong that Webster was successful in moving the Senate toward compromise. The non-Abolitionist press of the North praised the speech as they had Webster's Seventh of March Address.[54] Samuel Eliot, a Whig and Webster's candidate for Congress, defeated Abolitionist Charles Sumner in Boston on August 22, and Webster claimed vindication for his support of compromise.

Perhaps the best measure of Webster's effectiveness came in the Senate in the weeks following his speech on July 17. The earlier confusion diminished and an aura of business-as-usual replaced it.[55] On July 18, a motion by Foote to split California was defeated 34 to 20. Clay, who had left the Senate early in the summer pronouncing the situation hopeless, returned for Webster's address and on July 22 gave a three-hour speech for compromise. The thirty-plus vote coalition for compromise held again on July 24 when a Southern attempt to change the Texas border failed. It held together against Northern extremists on July 25.

Throughout this period, Webster's colleagues, particularly some of his most ardent critics, praised the Seventeenth of July speech. Senator Hale, a New Hampshire extremist, referred to Webster's "graphic powers of delineation." Senator Foote of Mississippi said he was inspired to a new "spirit of concord" and would not press divisive amendments. Senator Dawson said it was time to restore harmony "to this country again." For others it provided the perfect opportunity to save face.

As soon as the new administration was organized, Webster began to work with Senator Douglas to move the crucial bills through the Senate. As Secretary of State, Webster wrote a message to Congress for President Fillmore that spelled out how the Compromise legislation should be passed. The message focused on the Texas boundary question but several lines inserted by Webster gave a clear signal that the president wanted the Compromise passed. For example, unlike his predecessor, Fillmore told the Congress that it "is the sole judge of the time and manner of creating" a territorial government. After creating a conciliatory mood, he wrote, "I express my deep and earnest conviction of the importance of an immediate decision or arrangement or settlement of the question of boundary between Texas and the Territory of New Mexico." Fillmore further argued that all other questions flowed from the settlement of the boundary:

I think no event would be hailed with more gratification by the people of the United States than the amicable adjustment of questions of difficulty which have now for a long time agitated the country and occupied to the exclusion of other subjects, the time and attention of Congress. . . .   In the train of such an adjustment we may well hope that there will follow a return of harmony and good will, an increased attachment to the Union, and the general satisfaction of the country.

Thus Webster used Fillmore to complete his strategy. Within a week after receiving this message, the Senate passed the boundary legislation and set the stage for Douglas to then present the remaining parts of the Compromise as separate bills.   Throughout this period, Webster dominated the president and the cabinet.   Edward Curtis, a visitor to Washington, observed in August of 1850 that "Mr. Webster appears among [the cabinet members] like a father teaching his listening children."   The Secretary of the Navy claimed that Webster brought "light" to the Congress "after chaos and dissension" had dominated for so long.   These statements give weight to the thesis that Webster was much more the innovator of strategy at this point in the proceedings than was Douglas.

In September, the various Compromise bills passed the Senate, and when the House passed them, joyous Washingtonians took to the streets in wild celebration.   As much in relief as in joy, the citizens of the nation's capital paraded with torches and lit huge bonfires that illuminated the public buildings.

The legislation admitted California as a free state, organized the Utah and New Mexico Territory, had Texas relinquish its claim to New Mexico Territory in return for a ten million dollar payment, abolished the slave trade in the District of Columbia, and established a system by which the federal government could enforce the return of fugitive slaves to their owners.

Some historians have praised Douglas for separating Clay's omnibus bill into separate parts.   But as we have seen, many others, including Webster in his Seventeenth of July Address and as Secretary of State when he penned the Texas boundary message for Fillmore, had thought of the same strategy.   Even Clay came out for it on August 1.   Douglas realized this when he spoke on September 16 to thank his colleagues for their cooperation:

The particular form of the proceeding was a matter of small   moment.   I supported [the bills] as a joint measure, and when they failed I supported each as a separate measure. . . . The decision of that point involved no principle; it was purely a matter of policy. . . . No men and no party has acquired a triumph, except the party to the Union triumphing over abolition and disunion.[56]

Few men worked harder for that triumph than Daniel Webster, culminating in his Seventeenth of July Address. Nevertheless, Webster would have to suffer the vilification of former friends like Emerson and, later, historians like Henry Cabot Lodge.

He would not live to see the revision of his compromise into "popular sovereignty," a legislative maneuver that forced the citizens of the territories to determine how

their states would enter the Union--slave or free.   It was a
decision by which the Congress arrogated its responsibility
to the states and territories and thereby caused a civil war
in the Kansas-Nebraska Territory by 1854.

But the night the Compromise passed, Webster, in ill
health, had to be carried to his doorstep to wave at parade
goers and to speak to unruly gangs of admirers because they
refused to disperse until he came out to receive their
adulation. Webster had the satisfaction of knowing that his
last deliberative speech in the Senate had helped shape the
strategy that would preserve the Union beyond his lifetime.
More important, his legend would reinforce the virtues of
freedom of expression in a democratic republic.

5

A Gauge of Greatness

Webster's leadership of the cabinet and the passage of the 1850 Compromise gave him renewed stature across the country. He underwent a renaissance of spirit that energized his life. He served as Secretary of State with great distinction and in 1851 began planning ways by which he could capture the Whig presidential nomination. Webster had sought the prize before only to be denied by his narrow base of support or the ambition of Clay. In 1851, many in New England believed it was Webster's turn. Clay was too old and sickly; Fillmore was an accidental president, presumed to be loyal to Webster. Seward was too uncompromising and regionally oriented. The only man who stood in Webster's way was General Winfield Scott.

But many in the party saw Webster as an effective, bright legislator who could not translate his assets into large numbers of votes. This perception ignored Webster's popular ceremonial speeches and the effective campaign he had waged on behalf of the Whig ticket in 1840. Nonetheless, the Whigs had won only when they ran war heroes for the presidency--William Henry "Tippecanoe" Harrison in 1840 and Zachary "Old Rough and Ready" Taylor in 1848.

Webster's ceremonial speeches kept him in the public limelight. In May of 1851, he toured New York with President Fillmore defending the Compromise and Union. In late May in Buffalo he asserted that a "house divided" could not stand; it would not be the first time he borrowed from the New Testament, nor the first time he uttered a phrase that would later appear in Lincoln's speeches.[1] He then left the president and travelled on to Syracuse and back to Washington, D.C.

In June he went into the South trying to broad his base of support within the party. After all, most southern Whigs had supported the Compromise of 1850 and Webster was the mastermind behind its passage. Late in June in Winchester, Virginia, Webster said, "I am as ready to fight and fall for the Constitutional rights of Virginia as I am for those of Massachusetts." The speech was printed in the Washington press and seemed a clear indication that Webster was seeking the Presidency.[2] On the Fourth of July, 1851, Webster dedicated the addition to the Capitol (see chapter two) while President Fillmore listened attentively. There was little question among those listening that Webster was the more presidential of the two men.

But Webster and the president could not control growing Free Soil and Democratic sentiment. In Webster's Massachusetts they took control of the legislature, threw the Whigs out, elevated Sumner to the Senate, and vilified Webster. On May 25, 1852, a few days after falling from a carriage and three weeks before the Whig Convention in Baltimore, Webster spoke at Faneuil Hall for the last time. He was seventy years old. Either due to his injuries or alcohol, he gave a disjointed, rambling address that often fell into incoherency. The speech stunned the audience and rumors about Webster's mental and physical health plagued his managers at the Convention.[3]

The Democrats had already nominated Franklin Pierce of New Hampshire when the Whig convention commenced on June 16, 1852. Seward, with the help of Thurlow Weed, advanced the candidacy of the sixty-six year old General Scott. They were blocked in their home state of New York by Fillmore, who left his hat in the ring even though some saw him as a stalking horse for Webster. Fillmore's managers argued that the president was a serious candidate and that only Fillmore could defeat Pierce in New York. The first ballot showed the effect of this argument and must have devastated the hopes of Webster:

Fillmore......133
Scott.........131
Webster........29

One hundred and forty-seven votes were needed for nomination. Webster and Fillmore together had that majority. But Webster's managers could not guarantee that all of his votes would go to Fillmore. And Fillmore's people knew that all their votes, especially in New York, would not necessarily be cast for Webster should Fillmore withdraw. Forty-six ballots followed during which southern Whigs pledged to switch their support from Fillmore to Webster if he could manage to get his total up to 41. But Webster's total never exceeded 32.[4]

The next morning a heart-broken Webster sent a mesage to his managers to throw his support to Fillmore. Ironically, Fillmore had sent a messenger to his managers instructing them to throw their support to Webster. But Fillmore's managers had no confidence that his delegates would be loyal to Webster. So they held fast for Fillmore. On the forty-eighth ballot, three Missouri delegates switched to Scott and the tension on the floor of the convention heightened. On the forty-ninth ballot, the New Hampshire delegation deserted Webster and shifted to Scott. He was declared the winner on the fifty-third ballot.[5]

As if to punctuate the rejection of the old guard, Clay died on June 29. After Clay's funeral and some reflection, Webster refused to endorse Scott, claiming his nomination would be the downfall of the party.[6] Webster's supporters formed a "Union Whig" ticket but it did not generate any enthusiasm outside of New England and the project was soon abandoned. The realization that he had no national following broke Webster's health. He sought medical attention in Boston on September 20. Doctors told him he did not have long to live.

He quietly retired to his home at Marshfield and began preparations for his death. On October 10, he dictated plans for his funeral and an epitaph for his tombstone. He requested the same ceremony that would be accorded a simple farmer. On October 18, he revised his will. On October 23, he signed a new will while propped up in his bed beside a first floor window that overlooked a field and pond. He asked that his favorite ox be brought to the window so he could pet her. That night he gave a talk on the life of Jesus to those assembled around the bed. Daniel Webster died at 2:37 AM on Sunday, October 24, 1852. His funeral was attended by ten thousand people.

Webster's legacy has long outlived his life of service. His ability to use available means of persuasion to advance his policies was supported by his intimate and sophisticated use of rhetorical form. When pleading a case, he not only understood the importance of evidence and argument, he appreciated the good will of associates on the bench, the scene of the crime, and the imagination of the jury. When speaking at a ceremony, he knew that the audience needed to feel that they were a part of the occasion if they were to be persuaded to the values he endorsed. And when addressing the Senate, he knew that the issues had to be re-configured so that his colleagues could transcend their division and unite behind his pragmatic proposals.

His understanding of organizational strategies and audience adaptation matched his mastery over the elements of style. The French essayist Buffon wrote that "Style is the man himself." Webster was truly a self-made man who constructed an enormously effective persona through his rhetorical style. His artistic use of tropes and figures, particularly metaphor, irony, and wit, made him a man of letters in his own time. His ability to bring scenes alive before an audience reinforced the logical thrust of his narration and produced some of the most effective discourse in U.S. history.

Like the best speakers in ancient Greece, Webster recognized that the stronger argument would prevail over the weaker and that the more he approximated the truth as it was perceived by the listener, the more he was likely to gain the adherence of that person. Like a Romantic composer, Webster did not back away from innovative form, nor did he abandon established methods. He was equally at home using the fugal form of narrative development or the progressive form of argumentation. Like few other speakers in American history, Daniel Webster was able to appeal to the actual consciousness of the audience in terms of their needs and desires while at the same time appealing to their innate potential consciousness in the spiritual values he espoused. Perhaps that is why he played such a large role for such a long time; his speeches are ever ingrained in this country's rhetorical literature, and through them, as his last recorded words warranted, "I still live."[7]

Notes

INTRODUCTION

1. Irving H. Bartlett, _Daniel Webster_ (New York: W. W. Norton, 1978), pp. 18-19.
2. This Haddock is not be confused with Webster's nephew Charles B. Haddock, who also became a professor of rhetoric at Dartmouth. See Bibliography. See also, Merrill D. Peterson, _The Great Triumvirate: Webster, Clay and Calhoun_ (New York: Oxford University Press, 1987), p. 181.
3. Merrill Peterson, _The Great Triumvirate_, pp. 30-31.
4. See Bartlett, _Daniel Webster_, pp. 26-27.
5. See Bartlett, _Daniel Webster_, pp. 28-30.
6. See Peterson, _The Great Triumvirate_, pp. 38-39.
7. See Peterson, _The Great Triumvirate_, pp. 34, 39.
8. Maurice G. Baxter, _Daniel Webster and the Supreme Court_ (Amherst: University of Massachusetts Press, 1966), p. v.
9. See Richard Current, _Daniel Webster and the Rise of National Conservatism_ (Boston: Little, Brown, and Co., 1955), p. 2.
10. Wirt opposed Webster in the _Dartmouth_ case and in _Ogden v. Saunders_; he joined Webster in _Gibbons v. Ogden_ and _McCulloch v. Maryland_.
11. Claude Fuess, _Daniel Webster_ (Boston: Little, Brown and Co., 1930), vol. 1, pp. 273-80.
12. See Peterson, _The Great Triumvirate_, pp. 492-93.
13. Aristotle, _Rhetoric_, trans. W. Rhys Roberts (New York: Random House, 1954). See particularly Book One, Chapter Three.
14. Aristotle, _Rhetoric_, 1358a ff., 1408b ff.
15. Craig Smith, "Actuality and Potentiality: The Essence of Criticism," _Philosophy and Rhetoric_, 3 (1970), pp. 133-40.
16. Aristotle, _Rhetoric_, 1358b24-25; 1391b8-20; 1414b ff.

CHAPTER 1: FORENSIC SPEAKING

1. See Irving Bartlett, _Daniel Webster_ (New York: W. W. Norton, 1978), pp. 75, 79, 80.
2. See, for example, the opening to the Reply to Hayne and the Seventh of March Address in Part II.

3. See Merrill D. Peterson, The Great Triumvirate: Webster, Clay and Calhoun (New York: Oxford University Press, 1987), pp. 338, 396.
4. Dictionary of American Biography (hereafter DAB), eds. Allen Johnson and Dumas Malone (New York: Charles Scribners' Sons, 1960), vol. 6, p. 318.
5. Biographical Dictionary of the Federal Judiciary (hereafter BDFJ), eds. Harold Chase, Samuel Krislov, Keith Boyum, Jerry Clark (Detroit: Gale Research Co., 1976), p. 176.
6. BDFJ, p. 291.
7. DAB, vol. 6, p. 313.
8. Gustavus Myert, The History of the Supreme Court of the United States (New York: Bert Franklin, 1968 reprint of 1912 edition), p. 252.
9. DAB, vol. 5, p. 129; BDFJ, p. 102.
10. Myert, The History of the Supreme Court, p. 290; DAB, vol. 9, pp. 103-106; Peterson, The Great Triumvirate, pp. 104, 156, 223.
11. BDFJ, p. 79.
12. DAB, vol. 9, p. 472; BDFJ, p. 275.
13. Claude Fuess, Daniel Webster (Boston: Little, Brown and Co., 1930), vol. 1, pp. 220-21.
14. The record of this speech is from the recollection of Chauncey Goodrich, a Yale Professor who specialized in British public address. See The Writings and Speeches of Daniel Webster, (hereafter Writings), ed. James W. McIntyre, (New York: National Edition, 1903), vol. 10, pp. 194-233.
15. DAB, vol. 6, p. 313.
16. Peterson, The Great Triumvirate, p. 102.
17. DAB, vol. 10, p. 588.
18. See Writings, vol. 15, pp. 261-67.
19. See Baxter, Daniel Webster and the Supreme Court, pp. 173-75. Justice Story believed Pinkney's speech to be better than any he had ever heard before the Court. When Pinkney died three years later, Webster was left as the preeminent spokesman for national conservatism before the Court.
20. 9 Wheaton 738.
21. One of the cases Webster took opposing the Bank was Etting v. Bank of the U.S. Webster was joined by Taney. The Court split evenly thereby allowing the lower court's decision to stand. It had ruled that the loan of Webster's client had to be paid even though the Bank had been operated improperly.
22. 9 Wheaton 1.
23. See Federalist No. 32.
24. 12 Wheaton 213.
25. Baxter, Daniel Webster and the Supreme Court, pp. 114-15.
26. Letter to Jeremiah Mason, February 13, 1837.
27. DAB, vol. 9, p. 291; BDFJ, p. 270.
28. Peterson, The Great Triumvirate, pp. 180-82.
29. Bartlett, Daniel Webster, pp. 126-27.
30. Writings, vol. 13, p. 582.

CHAPTER 2: CEREMONIAL SPEAKING

1. See Richard Current, Daniel Webster and the Rise of National Conservatism (Boston: Little, Brown, and Co., 1955).
2. Howell and Hudson begin their discussion of legislative speeches with this remark, "Turning now to Webster's deliberative oratory, as Aristotle would have classified speeches in Congress . . ." William S. Howell and Hoyt H. Hudson, "Daniel Webster," in History and Criticism of American Public Address, vol. 11, ed. William N. Brigance (New York: McGraw- Hill, 1943), p. 692; Glenn Mills, "Daniel Webster's Principles of Rhetoric," Speech Monographs, 9 (1942), 124-40.
3. Claude Fuess, Daniel Webster (Boston: Little, Brown, and Co., 1930), vol. 1, pp. 231-35.
4. Writings and Speeches of Daniel Webster, ed. James W. McIntyre, (New York: National Edition, 1903), vol. 1, p. 183.
5. Howell and Hudson, "Daniel Webster," p. 681.
6. Dictionary of American Biography, eds. Allen Johnson and Dumas Malone (New York: Charles Scribners' Sons, 1960) p. 588.
7. Irving Bartlett, Daniel Webster, (New York: W. W. Norton, 1978), p. 196; Merrill Peterson, The Great Triumvirate: Webster, Clay and Calhoun (New York: Oxford University Press, 1987), pp. 355-56.
8. Peterson, The Great Triumvirate, p. 268.
9. Robert T. Oliver and Eugene White, Selected Speeches from American History (Boston: Allyn and Bacon, 1966), p. 45.
10. Current, Daniel Webster, p. 109.
11. Aristotle, Rhetoric, trans. Rhys Roberts (New York: Random House, 1954), 1367b37 to 1368a10. At 1368b10-20, Aristotle explains how forensic judgments of past action are useful in epideictic discourse.
12. Peterson, The Great Triumvirate, pp. 110-11.
13. Howell and Hudson, Daniel Webster, p. 682.
14. Aristotle, Rhetoric, 1358b28.
15. Aristotle, Rhetoric, 1417b32-34.
16. Aristotle, Rhetoric, 1414b25-29, 1416b15-16, 1418b33-34.
17. Aristotle, Rhetoric, 1415b28-29, 1414a12-16.
18. Lloyd Bitzer, "The Rhetorical Situation," Philosophy and Rhetoric, 1 (1968), p. 13. Bitzer claims that persistent situations lead to the creation of "rhetorical literature." The epideictic speech is most likely to fulfill Bitzer's hypotheses. In fact, Bitzer's example is mainly epideictic.
19. Howell and Hudson, "Daniel Webster," p. 684.
20. Writings, ed. James W. McIntrye, vol. 17, pp. 463-65.

CHAPTER 3: DELIBERATIVE SPEAKING TO 1845

1. Irving Bartlett, Daniel Webster (New York: W. W. Norton, 1978), pp. 54-68.
2. Dictionary of American Biography, eds. Allen Johnson and Dumas Mallone (New York: Charles Scribners' Sons, 1960), p. 587.

3. Richard Current, Daniel Webster and the Rise of National Conservativism (Boston: Little, Brown and Co., 1955), p. 27.
4. Merrill Peterson, The Great Triumvirate: Webster, Clay and Calhoun (New York: Oxford University Press, 1987), pp. 43-44.
5. Peterson, The Great Triumvirate, pp. 72, 96-97.
6. Current, Daniel Webster, p. 35.
7. Claude Fuess, Daniel Webster (Boston: Little, Brown and Co., 1930), vol. 1, pp. 273-80.
8. Current, Daniel Webster, pp. 51-54.
9. Bartlett, Daniel Webster, pp. 114-16; Current, Daniel Webster, p. 52.
10. Current, Daniel Webster, p. 59.
11. Current, Daniel Webster, p. 60.
12. Current, Daniel Webster, pp. 60-61; The Writings and Speeches of Daniel Webster, ed. James W. McIntyre (New York: National Edition, 1903), vol. 5, pp. 248-69 and vol. 6, pp. 3-75.
13. Bartlett, Daniel Webster, p. 117; Fuess, Daniel Webster, vol. 1, p. 372.
14. Peterson, The Great Triumvirate, pp. 172-80.
15. Bartlett, Daniel Webster, p. 120.
16. Bartlett, Daniel Webster, p. 117.
17. Joseph Gales retold this story in the National Intelligencer of March 20, 1841. It is available on microfilm at the Library of Congress in Washington, D.C.
18. Current, Daniel Webster, p. 54.
19. Current, Daniel Webster, p. 67; Peterson, The Great Triumvirate, pp. 214-15, 222-24, 228-30, 232-33, 238.
20. See discussion of McCulloch v. Maryland in chapter one.
21. Current, Daniel Webster, p. 78. Dictionary of American Biography, p. 589.
22. Current, Daniel Webster, p. 100-6.
23. Current, Daniel Webster, p. 107.
24. Current, Daniel Webster, pp. 110-12.
25. New York Herald, August 24, 28, September 24, 25, 26, 30, 1840. See also Writings, ed. James W. McIntyre, vol. 3, pp. 3-37 and vol. 13, pp. 114-42.
26. These newspapers are available on microfilm at the Library of Congress in Washington, D.C.
27. Current, Daniel Webster, p. 136; Bartlett, Daniel Webster, pp. 193, 200, 201. Over the next few years, Webster invested $90,000 in his country home at Marshfield. His retainers were very high for the time.
28. Current, Daniel Webster, p. 136. Former President Tyler helped Webster on this occasion by making clear he had authorized Webster's use of the Secret Service Fund. Webster was cleared of all wrong-doing by a select House Committee.

CHAPTER 4: THE COMPROMISE OF 1850

1. Irving Bartlett writes, "In an age of great orators, few of Webster's contemporaries challenged his pre-eminence. . . . Later generations of American orators were brought up on Webster's speeches the way writers fed on Shakespeare." Daniel Webster (New York: W. W. Norton, 1978), pp. 3-4. See

also, pp. 78, 82, 99, and 108.
2. A sampling of this analysis can be found in the bibliography.
3. See Paul Arntson and Craig R. Smith, "The Seventh of March Address: A Mediating Influence," Southern Speech Communication Journal, 40 (1975), 288-301. See also Craig R. Smith, "Daniel Webster's July 17th Address: Deliberative Oratory as a Mediating Influence in Conflict Situations," Quarterly Journal of Speech, 71 (August, 1985), pp. 349-61.
4. Recent revisions and an examination of primary documents and contemporary newspapers have revealed past studies to be incorrect. The following sources, to varying degrees, hold to the traditional but outdated view: Robert F. Dalzell, Daniel Webster and the Trial of American Nationalism: 1843-1852 (Boston: Houghton Mifflin, 1973), pp. 191-216. Roy F. Nichols, The Stakes of Power (New York: Hill and Wang, 1961), p. 27. Elbert B. Smith, The Death of Slavery (Chicago: University of Chicago Press, 1967), pp. 107-14. Robert H. Jones, Disrupted Decades: The Civil War and Reconstruction Years (New York: Scribner, 1973), pp. 89-90. James Ford Rhodes, The History of the United States from the Compromise of 1850, ed. Allan Nevins (Chicago: University of Chicago Press, 1966), pp. 60, 64, 65.   Paul I. Wellman, The House Divides (Garden City, New York: Doubleday, 1966), pp. 330-31. See the bibliographic section at the end of this volume for the most reliable sources now available.
5. The percentages in this section were calculated using the figures provided by Holman Hamilton, Prologue to Conflict: The Crisis and Compromise of 1850 (New York: W. W. Norton, 1964), p. 34.
6. Merrill Peterson, The Great Triumvirate: Webster, Clay, and Calhoun (New York: Oxford University Press, 1987), pp. 452-56.
7. It is possible that Calhoun wrote the message in such a provocative style to defeat the treaty. He believed the acquisitions would exacerbate the slave question. See Peterson, The Great Triumvirate, p. 436.
8. Bartlett, Daniel Webster, pp. 235-36
9. Peterson, The Great Triumvirate, p. 454.
10. Zachary Taylor, "Message to Senate," (January 23, 1850) in A Compilation of the Messages and Papers of the Presidents, 1789-1902, ed. James D. Richardson (Washington, D.C.: Bureau of National Literature and Art, 1902), vol. 5, p. 27.
11. Holman Hamilton, "Democratic Senate Leadership and the Compromise of 1850," The Mississippi Valley Historical Review, vol. 41, pp. 403-18, and "Texas Bonds and Northern Profits," vol. 43, pp. 579-94.
12. The Brown pamphlet is reprinted in Slavery Attacked: The Abolitionist Crusade, ed. John L. Thomas (Englewood Cliffs, New Jersey: Prentice-Hall, 1965), pp. 100-102. The response to Clay appears in A Defense of Southern Slavery and other Pamphlets (New York: Negro University Press, 1969), p. 6.
13. Richard Current, T. Harry Williams, and Frank Freidel, American History: A Survey (New York: Alfred A. Knopf, 1963), p. 325.
14. Bartlett, Daniel Webster, p. 250.
15. Bartlett, Daniel Webster, p. 121.

16. Samuel M. Smucker, The Life, Speeches, and Memorials of Daniel Webster (Philadelphia: Duane Rulison, 1861), p. 254. If one doubts that Webster adapted in the face of crisis, one need only examine Webster's letters of mid-February which indicate little fear of crisis. Then after several signs of Southern intransigence Webster shows concern. See Daniel Webster, The Writings and Speeches of Daniel Webster, ed. James W. McIntyre (New York: National Edition, 1903), vol. 16, pp. 533-34; vol. 18, p. 355. See edited version of text in the appendix.
17. Henry Cabot Lodge, Daniel Webster (Boston: Houghton Mifflin, 1884), p. 301.
18. Webster's passage on the splits in the Methodist and Episcopal churches is yet another example of how artificial the differences over slavery were. The implied identification is with Northern and Southern interests.
19. Van Buren, in a published letter to Webster, 20 March 1850, is particularly upset with Webster's attack on Abolitionists. Early in the letter the former president and Free Soil candidate of 1848 calls the speech "Sophistical Argumentation." Smucker, The Life, Speeches, p. 293-94.
20. Lorman Ratner, Powder Keg Northern Opposition to the Anti-Slavery Movement (New York: Basic Books, 1968), p. 138.
21. This argument was added to the speech for its publication in the North. Smucker, The Life, Speeches, p. 297-98.
22. Lawrence Lader, The Bold Brahmins (New York: E.P. Dutton, 1961), pp. 150-53. John F. Kennedy, Profiles in Courage (New York: Pocket Books, 1957) pp. 63-66. Claude Fuess, Daniel Webster (Boston: Little, Brown and Co., 1930), vol. 2, pp. 221-25. H. D. Foster, "Webster's Seventh of March Speech and the Secessionist Movement, 1850" American Historical Review, 27 (1922), p. 245.
23. Fuess, Daniel Webster, vol. 2, p. 198.
24. Bartlett, Daniel Webster, p. 269.
25. Kennedy, Profiles in Courage, p. 62.
26. Letter from Daniel Webster to A. Huntington, December 21, 1850. Writings, ed. James W. McIntyre, vol. 16, p. 582.
27. Boston Atlas, 11 March 1850, p. 1.
28. Kennedy, Profiles in Courage, pp. 62, 65.
29. The Albany Argos does an admirable job of abstracting the speech for its readers, with instant analysis provided on the same page. The editor compliments Webster for being conciliatory. March 9, 1850, p. 2.
30. The Whig press in the South sought at times to point out agreement between Webster's stance and Calhoun's. See, for example, the Vicksburg Weekly Whig, 20 March 1850, p. 1, or the New Orleans Picayune, 10-20 March 1850, pp. 1-2. The Vicksburg Weekly Whig (March 27, p. 1) wrote, "Webster's speeches seem to be made not for a day only, but for all time; and they will be read and studied in future generations as the orations of Grecian and Roman orators now are."
31. The Philadelphia Evening Bulletin, March 8, 1850, p. 2.
32. Current, Daniel Webster, p. 168. Foster cites many examples of success, "Webster's Seventh of March," pp. 264-65.

33. Fuess, <u>Daniel Webster</u>, vol. 2, p. 241.   Later, even those who had loudly condemned the speech as pro-Southern, men like Edward Everett, Issac Hill, and Mayor Huntington of Salem admitted that the speech was effective in turning sentiment away from the extremes and toward compromise. Foster, "Webster's Seventh of March Address," pp. 265-66. Webster's "vindication" was diminished in the next election when the anti-slavery Whigs combined with the Free Soil Democrats to win from the Whigs the election of Governor and Senator, with Sumner taking Webster's old seat.
34. Arthur Young Lloyd, <u>The Slavery Controversy 1831-1860</u> (Chapel Hill: University of North Carolina Press, 1939), pp. 55, 63.   The figure of 40,000 was based on the amount of money the society made.   In 1840, there were 150,000 members and the society made $47,000.   During the next fifteen years, the income failed to go over $12,000 a year.
35. Lloyd, <u>The Slavery Controversy</u>, p. 281.   The Albany <u>Argos</u>, a supporter of Van Buren's Free Soil bid, was calling the party a "decaying hybrid," 6 March 1850, p. 2.   The paper analyzes the party structure in several states, including Massachusetts and Connecticut, where it was once strong.
36. Lorman Ratner, <u>Powder Keg</u>, p. 140.
37. Lloyd, <u>The Slavery Controversy</u>, p. 65.
38. Ratner, <u>Powder Keg</u>, p. 68; Lloyd, <u>The Slavery Controversy</u>, pp. 66-67.
39. Major L. Wilson argues that Free Soilers in general were conservative due to nationalistic and expansionist sentiment.   "The slogan 'freedom national' and 'slavery local' precisely expressed this position. . . . They attributed to the founding fathers the geopolitical idea . . . that when slavery ceased to spread out into new and unsettled areas it would in time die out." Major L. Wilson, "The Free Soil Concept of Progress and the Irrepressible Conflict," <u>American Quarterly</u>, 22, (1970), p. 76.   See also Rowland Berthoff, "The American Social Order: A Conservative Hypothesis," <u>American Historical Review</u>, 65 (1960), pp. 498-504.
40. The speech Webster gave on the Senate floor was not the exact speech that was circulated in the North.   In the printed speech Webster struck out the passage about the money collected by Abolitionists being sufficient to have purchased the freedom of every slave in Maryland.   He added to the list of "Northern Grievances" the item concerning the imprisonment of "free colored sea men."   By March 31, 120,000 copies had been distributed.   Foster argues that the pressure for secession reached a peak just before Webster's speech (in "Webster's Seventh of March," pp. 242, 260).   He continues that "Webster's conciliatory Union policy, in harmony with that of border state leaders, enabled Maryland, Kentucky, and Missouri to stand by the Union and refuse to send delegates to the Nashville Convention," p. 252.   Many argue that Webster's speech deflated the Nashville Convention.   In any case, when it resumed its business after the Compromise was passed, only one-third of the delegates returned.
41. Foster, "Webster's Seventh of March Address," p. 261.

No such speeches had been given before Webster's Address.
42. Lodge, Daniel Webster, p. 307. A reading of Southern papers shows moderate to strong support for Webster's speech. The Charleston Courier, 12 March 1850, p. 2, reacted typically: "Mr. Webster's speech has poured oil on troubled waters. . . . The anti-slavery men will never forgive his heresy." Obviously, Whig papers were more enthusiastic than Democratic, but even radical secessionist papers reflected a shift to Webster. For a survey of them, see Herman V. Ames, "John C. Calhoun and the Secessionist Movement of 1850," Proceedings of the American Antiquarian Society, 28 (April 10, 1918-October 16, 1918), pp. 41-43.
43. Current, Daniel Webster, p. 169.
44. Bartlett, Daniel Webster, p. 231.
45. Arntson and Smith, "The Seventh of March Address," p. 299-301. The response Webster received from the national audience was stunning. As late as mid-April, Webster wrote that "from the South, the West, and some parts of the middle states, addresses, letters and calls for speeches continue to come in. . . . It is evident there is a milder feeling in the country [than in the Congress]." Fletcher Webster, The Private Correspondence of Daniel Webster (Boston: Little, Brown, and Co., 1857), vol 2, p. 365-66. In the Senate, Webster seemed to have quieted the calls for secession. See Foster, "Webster's Seventh of March Address," p. 261; Bartlett, Daniel Webster, pp. 246-50.
46. On January 21, 1850, Clay had visited Webster for an hour. Webster agreed with Clay's plans, but did not perceive the crisis to be critical. As late as February 13, 1850, Webster wrote to Peter Harvey: "Things will cool off." A day later he wrote: "There is no serious danger." Walker Lewis, Speak for Yourself, Daniel: A Life of Webster in His Own Words (Boston: Houghton-Mifflin Co., 1969), p. 399. Not until February 24, after a meeting with Southerners, did Webster's optimism fail: "I am nearly broken down with labor and anxiety. I know not how to meet the present emergency, or with what weapons to beat down the Northern and Southern follies, now raging in equal extremes." See also, p. 400.
47. Fletcher Webster, The Private Correspondence, vol. 2, p. 359.
48. Fletcher Webster, The Private Correspondence, vol. 2, p. 369.
49. See Current, Daniel Webster, p. 162; Fuess, Daniel Webster, vol. 2, p. 241; Foster, "Webster's Seventh of March Address," pp. 265-66.
50. Lewis, Speak for Yourself, p. 413. In a letter to Samuel Lawrence in mid-June, Webster said he would fight for compromise to the end. It is an early indication that Webster saw the need to speak again.
51. Webster delivered a tribute to the dead President on July 10, 1850. He said: "Unfortunately, his career at the head of this government was short. . . . The circumstances under which he conducted the government for the short time he was the head of it have been such as perhaps not to give him a very favorable opportunity of developing his principles." Writings, vol. 10, p. 142. On July 16 Webster rose to call for the erection of a monument to Taylor. See Fletcher Webster, The Private Correspondence, vol.2, pp. 360-400. For text see Writings, ed. James W.

McIntyre, vol. 10, pp. 144-70.
52. Writings, ed. James W. McIntyre, vol. 10, p. 170.
53. Writings, ed. James W. McIntyre, vol. 10, pp. 147-48;
Bartlett, Daniel Webster, p. 252.   David Potter, in Chapter
5 of The Impending Crisis: 1848-1861 (New York: Harper and
Row, 1976), pp. 110-11, touches on the role of Douglas and
Webster.   Potter appears to have missed the exchange I
quote, Webster's later memos to Douglas, Webster's enormous
influence over President Fillmore, and his role in getting
legislation passed.
54. The New York Herald said that "on the whole, Mr.
Webster's speech yesterday is a credit to him, and we will
be much mistaken if it does not exercise a very great
influence on the settlement of the slavery question."   New
York Herald, July 18, 1850, p. 1-2.   The Philadelphia
Evening Bulletin was even more generous, calling the speech
the "most conclusive argument he has attempted during the
present session."   18 July, 1850, p. 1.   See also: The
Quawka (Illinois) Spectator, July 24, 1850, pp. 1-2; the
Washington Union, July 18, 1850,   p. 3.   Benjamin Tefft
claims, "never was Webster so praised," in Life of Daniel
Webster (Philadelphia: Henry T. Coates and Co., 1899), p.
431.   The Vicksburg Weekly Whig articulated Southern
moderates' sentiment when it wrote, "Daniel Webster has
acted so independently that upon the slavery question he
might now be classed as a supporter of our institutions."
July 31, 1850, p. 3.   This is not to say that Webster had
high credibility among Abolitionists or southern extremists,
but even arch-foe Ralph Waldo Emerson called Webster the
greatest orator of the time. Complete Works of Ralph Waldo
Emerson, (New York: William H. Wise, 1929), vol. 7, p. 369
and vol. 11, pp. 202, 221.   Webster's credibility was
highest with those elements of his audience who were most
essential to the Compromise, that is, Whigs and border
Democrats.
55. The transition is documented by a reading of Hamilton,
Prologue to Conflict, p. 115; Avery Craven, The Coming of
the Civil War (Chicago: University of Chicago Press, 1963),
p. 271, and the record of debate in the Senate from which
this description is drawn.
56.   Hamilton, Prologue to Conflict, p. 147.   The eventual
failure of the Compromise ten years later is analyzed by
Walter R. Fisher, "The Failure of Compromise in 1860-1861: A
Rhetorical   View," Speech Monographs, 33, (1966), p.
364-71. Just as the death of Taylor in July of 1850 helped
make the Compromise possible, the election of Lincoln
precluded it continuing beyond 1860.

CHAPTER 5: A GAUGE OF GREATNESS

1. See The Writings and Speeches of Daniel Webster, ed.
James W. McIntyre (New York: National Edition, 1903), vol.
4, pp. 242-62.
2. Writings, ed. James W. McIntyre, vol. 13, pp. 237-41.
3. Merrill Peterson, The Great Triumvirate: Webster, Clay
and Calhoun (New York: Oxford University Press, 1987), pp.
485-86.

4. Irving Bartlett, <u>Daniel Webster</u>, (New York: W. W. Norton, 1978), p. 274.
5. Peterson, <u>The Great Triumvirate</u>, pp. 486-87.
6. <u>Dictionary of American Biography</u>, eds. Allen Johnson and Dumas Malone (New York: Charles Scribners' Sons, 1960), vol. 10, p. 592.
7. Robert T. Oliver, <u>History of Public Speaking in America</u> (Boston: Allyn and Bacon, 1964), p. 154.

II

COLLECTED
SPEECHES

McCulloch v. Maryland (1819)

[This text is taken from the Supreme Court report; it is, therefore, a summary of Webster's remarks, not the full text. It is reproduced here because it so clearly lays out his argumentative framework.]

[T]he question whether Congress constitutionally possesses the power to incorporate a bank, might be raised upon this record; and it was in the discretion of the defendant's counsel to agitate it. But it might have been hoped that it was not now to be considered as an open question. It is a question of the utmost magnitude, deeply interesting to the government itself, as well as to individuals. The mere discussion of such a question may most essentially affect the value of a vast amount of private property. We are bound to suppose that defendant in error is well aware of these consequences, and would not have intimated an intention to agitate such a question, but with a real design to make it a topic of serious discussion, and with a view of demanding upon it the solemn judgment of this court. This question arose early after the adoption of the constitution, and was discussed, and settled, as far as legislative decision could settle it, in the first Congress. The arguments drawn from the constitution in favor of this power, were stated and exhausted, in that discussion. They were exhibited, with characteristic perspicuity and force, by the first Secretary of the Treasury, in his report to the President of the United States. The first Congress created and incorporated a bank. Nearly each succeeding Congress, if not every one, has acted and legislated on the presumption of the legal existence of such power in the government. Individuals, it is true, have doubted, or thought otherwise; but it cannot be shown that either branch of the legislature has, at any time, expressed an opinion against the existence of the power. The executive government has acted upon it; and the courts of law have acted upon it. Many of those who doubted or denied the existence of the power, when first attempted to be exercised, have yielded to the first decision, and acquiesced in it, as a settled question. When all branches of the government have thus been acting on the existence of this power nearly thirty years, it would seem almost too late to call it in question, unless its repugnancy with the

constitution were plain and manifest. Congress, by the
Constitution, is invested with certain powers; and, as to
the objects, and within the scope of these powers, it is
sovereign. Even without the aid of the general clause in
the constitution, empowering Congress to pass all necessary
and proper laws for carrying its powers into execution, the
grant of powers itself necessarily implies the grant of all
usual and suitable means for the execution of the powers
granted.

Congress may declare war; it may consequently carry on
war, by armies and navies, and other suitable means and
methods of warfare. So it has the power to raise a revenue,
and to apply it in the support of the government, and
defense of the country. It may, of course, use all proper
and suitable means, not specially prohibited, in the raising
and disbursement of the revenue. And if, in the progress of
society and the arts, new means arise, either of carrying on
war or of raising revenue, these new means doubtless would
be properly considered as within the grant. Steam frigates,
for example, were not in the minds of those who framed the
Constitution, as among the means of naval warfare; but no
one doubts the power of Congress to use them, as means to an
authorized end. It is not enough to say, that it does not
appear that a bank was in the contemplation of the framers
of the Constitution. It was not their intention, in these
cases, to enumerate particulars. The true view of the
subject is, that if it be a fit instrument to an authorized
purpose, it may be used, not being specially prohibited.

Congress is authorized to pass all laws "necessary and
proper" to carry into execution the powers conferred on it.
These words "necessary and proper," in such an instrument,
are probably to be considered as synonymous. Necessary
powers must here intend such powers as are suitable and
"fitted to the object"; such as are best and most useful in
relation to the end proposed. If this be not so, and if
Congress could use no means but such as were absolutely
indispensable to the existence of a granted power, the
government would hardly exist; at least, it would be wholly
inadequate to the purposes of its formation.

A bank is a proper and suitable instrument to assist
the operations of the government in the collection and
disbursement of the revenue; in the occasional anticipations
of taxes and imposts; and in the regulation of the actual
currency, as being a part of the trade and exchange between
the states. It is not for this court to decide whether a
bank, or such a bank as this, be the best possible means to
aid these purposes of government. Such topics must be left
to that discussion which belongs to them in the two houses
of Congress. Here, the only question is, whether a bank, in
its known and ordinary operations, is capable of being so
connected with the finances and revenues of the government
as to be fairly within the discretion of Congress, when
selecting means and instruments to execute its powers and
perform its duties.

A bank is not less the proper subject for the choice of
Congress, nor the less constitutional, because it requires
to be executed by granting a charter of incorporation. It
is not of itself unconstitutional in Congress to create a
corporation. Corporations are but means. They are not ends

and objects of government. No government exists for the purpose of creating corporations as one of the ends of its being. They are institutions established to effect certain beneficial purposes; and, as means, take their character generally from their end and object. They are civil or eleemosynary, public or private, according to the object intended by their creation. They are common means, such as all governments use. The state governments create corporations to execute powers confided to their trust, without any specific authority in the state constitutions for that purpose. There is the same reason that Congress should exercise its discretion as to the means by which it must execute the powers conferred upon it. Congress has duties to perform and powers to execute. It has a right to the means by which these duties can be properly and most usefully performed, and these powers executed. Among other means, it has established a bank; and before the act establishing it can be pronounced unconstitutional and void, it must be shown that a bank has no fair connection with the execution of any power or duty of the national government, and that its creation is consequently a manifest usurpation.

The second question is, whether, if the bank be constitutionally created, the state governments have power to tax it. The people of the United States have seen fit to divide sovereignty, and to establish a complex system. They have conferred certain powers on the state governments, and certain other powers on the national government. As it was easy to foresee that questions must arise between these governments thus constituted, it became of great moment to determine upon what principle these questions should be decided, and who should decide them. The constitution, therefore, declares, that the constitution itself, and the laws passed in pursuance of its provisions, shall be the supreme law of the land, and shall control all state legislation and state constitutions which may be incompatible therewith; and it confides to this court the ultimate power of deciding all questions arising under the constitution and laws of the United States. The laws of the United States, then, made in pursuance of the constitution, are to be the supreme law of the land, anything in the laws of any state to the contrary notwithstanding.

The only inquiry, therefore, in this case is, whether the law of the state of Maryland imposing this tax be consistent with the free operation of the law establishing the bank, and the full enjoyment of the privileges conferred by it. If it be not, then it is void; if it be, then it may be valid.

Upon the supposition that the bank is constitutionally created, this is the only question; and this question seems answered as soon as it is stated. If the states may tax the bank, to what extent shall they tax it, and where shall they stop?

An unlimited power to tax involves, necessarily, a power to destroy; because there is a limit beyond which no institution and no property can bear taxation. A question of constitutional power can hardly be made to depend on a question of more or less. If the states may tax, they have no limit but their discretion; and the bank, therefore, must depend on the discretion of the state governments for its existence. This consequence is inevitable. The object in laying this tax may have been revenue to the state. In the next case, the object may be to expel the bank from the state; but how is this object to be ascertained, or who is to judge the motives of legislative acts? The government of the United States has itself a great pecuniary interest in this corporation. Can the states tax this property? Under the confederation, when the national government, not having the power of direct legislation, could not protect its own property by its own laws, it was expressly stipulated, that "no impositions, duties, or restrictions, should be laid by any state on the property of the United States." Is it supposed that property of the United States is now subject to the power of the state governments, in a greater degree than under the confederation? If this power of taxation be admitted, what is to be its limit? The United States have, and must have, property locally existing in all the states; and may the states impose on this property, whether real or personal, such taxes as they please? Can they tax proceedings in the federal courts? If so, they can expel those judicatures from the states.

As Maryland has undertaken to impose a stamp tax on the notes of this bank, what hinders her from imposing a stamp tax also on permits, clearances, registers, and all other documents connected with imposts and navigation? If by one she can suspend the operations of the bank, by the other she can equally well shut up the custom-house. The law of Maryland, in question, makes a requisition. The sum called for is not assessed on property, nor deducted from profits or income. It is a direct imposition on the power, privilege, or franchise of the corporation. The act purports, also, to restrain the circulation of the paper of the bank to bills of certain descriptions. It narrows and abridges the powers of the bank in a manner which, it would seem, even Congress could not do.

This law of Maryland cannot be sustained but upon principles and reasoning which would subject every important measure of the national government to the revision and control of the state legislatures. By the charter, the bank is authorized to issue bills of any denomination above five dollars. The act of Maryland purports to restrain and limit their powers in this respect. The charter, as well as the laws of the United States, makes it the duty of all collectors and receivers to receive the notes of the bank in payment of all debts due the government. The act of Maryland makes it penal, both on the person paying and the person receiving such bills, until stamped by the authority of Maryland. This is a direct interference with the revenue. The legislature of Maryland might, with as much propriety, tax treasury notes. This is either an attempt to expel the bank from the state, or it is an attempt to raise a revenue for state purposes by an imposition on property and franchises holden under the national government, and created by that government for purposes connected with its own administration. In either view there cannot be a clearer case of interference. The bank cannot exist, nor can any bank established by Congress exist, if this right to tax it exists in the state governments. One or the other

must be surrendered; and a surrender on the part of the
government of the United States would be a giving up of
those fundamental and essential powers without which the
government cannot be maintained. A bank may not be, and is
not, absolutely essential to the existence and preservation
of the government. But it is essential to the existence and
preservation of the government that Congress should be able
to exercise its constitutional powers at its own discretion,
without being subject to the control of state legislation.
The question is not whether a bank be necessary, or useful,
but whether Congress may not constitutionally judge of that
necessity or utility; and whether, having so judged and
decided, and having adopted measures to carry its decision
into effect, the state governments may interfere with that
decision, and defeat the operation of its measures. Nothing
can be plainer than that, if the law of Congress
establishing the bank be a constitutional act, it must have
its full and complete effects. Its operations cannot be
either defeated or impeded by acts of state legislation. To
hold otherwise, would be to declare that Congress can only
exercise its constitutional powers subject to the
controlling discretion, and under the sufferance of the
state governments.

The Knapp-White Murder Case (1830)

I am little accustomed, gentlemen, to the part which I am now attempting to perform. Hardly more than once or twice has it happened to me to be concerned on the side of the government in any criminal prosecution whatever; and never, until the present occasion, in any case affecting life.

But I very much regret that it should have been thought necessary to suggest to you that I am brought here to "hurry you against the law and beyond the evidence." [Webster is making a sarcastic reference to the defense lawyer's claim.] I hope I have too much regard for justice, and too much respect for my own character, to attempt either; and were I to make such an attempt, I am sure that in this court nothing can be carried against the law, and that gentlemen, intelligent and just as you are, are not, by any power, to be hurried beyond the evidence. Though I could well have wished to shun this occasion, I have not felt at liberty to withhold my professional assistance, when it is supposed that I may be in some degree useful in investigating and discovering the truth respecting this most extraordinary murder. It has seemed to be a duty incumbent on me, as on every other citizen, to do my best and my utmost to bring to light the perpetrators of this crime. Against the prisoner at the bar, as an individual, I cannot have the slightest prejudice. I would not do him the smallest injury or injustice. But I do not affect to be indifferent to the discovery and the punishment of this deep guilt. I cheerfully share in the opprobrium, how so-ever great it may be, which is cast on those who feel and manifest an anxious concern that all who had a part in planning, or a hand in executing, this deed of midnight assassination, may be brought to answer for their enormous crime at the bar of public justice.

Gentlemen, it is a most extraordinary case. In some respects, it has hardly a precedent anywhere; certainly none in our New England history. This bloody drama exhibited no suddenly excited, ungovernable rage. The actors in it were not surprised by a lion-like temptation springing upon their virtue, and overcoming it, before resistance could begin. Nor did they do the deed to glut savage vengeance, or satiate long-settled and deadly hate. It was a cool, calculating, money-making murder. It was all "hire and salary, not revenge." It was the weighing of money against life; the counting out of so many pieces of silver against so many ounces of blood.

An aged man, without an enemy in the world, in his own house, and in his own bed, is made the victim of a butcherly murder, for mere pay. Truly, here is a new lesson for painters and poets. Whoever shall hereafter draw the portrait of murder, if he will show it as it has been exhibited, where such example was last to have been looked for, in the very bosom of our New England society, let him not give it the grim visage of Moloch, the brow knitted by revenge, the face black with settled hate, and the bloodshot eye emitting livid fires of malice. Let him draw, rather, a decorous, smooth-faced, bloodless demon; a picture in repose, rather than in action; not so much an example of human nature in its depravity, and in its paroxysms of crime, as an infernal being, a fiend, in the ordinary display and development of his character.

The deed was executed with a degree of self-possession and steadiness equal to the wickedness with which it was planned. The circumstances now clearly in evidence spread out the whole scene before us. Deep sleep had fallen on the destined victim, and on all beneath his roof. A healthful old man, to whom sleep was sweet, the first sound slumbers of the night held him in their soft but strong embrace. The assassin enters, through the window already prepared, into an unoccupied apartment. With noiseless foot he paces the lonely hall, half lighted by the moon; he winds up the ascent of the stairs, and reaches the door of the chamber. Of this, he moves the lock, by soft and continued pressure, till it turns on its hinges without noise; and he enters, and beholds his victim before him. The room is uncommonly open to the admission of light. The face of the innocent sleeper is turned from the murderer, and the beams of the moon, resting on the gray locks of his aged temple, show him where to strike. The fatal blow is given! and the victim passes, without a struggle or a motion, from the repose of sleep to the repose of death! It is the assassin's purpose to make sure work; and he plies the dagger, though it is obvious that life has been destroyed by the blow of the bludgeon. He even raises the aged arm, that he may not fail in his aim at the heart, and replaces it again over the wounds of the poniard! To finish the picture, he explores the wrist for the pulse! He feels for it, and ascertains that it beats no longer! It is accomplished. The deed is done. He retreats, retraces his steps to the window, passes out through it as he came in, and escapes. He has done the murder. No eye has seen him, no ear has heard him. The secret is his own, and it is safe!

Ah! gentlemen, that was a dreadful mistake. Such a secret can be safe nowhere. The whole creation of God has neither nook nor corner where the guilty can bestow it, and say it is safe. Not to speak of that Eye which pierces through all disguises, and beholds everything as in the splendor of noon, such secrets of guilt are never safe from detection, even by men. True it is, generally speaking, that "murder will out." True it is, that Providence hath so ordained, and doth so govern things, that those who break the great law of Heaven by shedding man's blood seldom succeed in avoiding discovery. Especially, in a case exciting so much attention as this, discovery must come, and will come, sooner or later. A thousand eyes turn at once to explore every man, everything, every circumstance, connected with the time and place; a thousand ears catch every whisper; a thousand excited minds intensely dwell on the scene, shedding all their light, and ready to kindle the slightest circumstance into a blaze of discovery. Meantime the guilty soul cannot keep its own secret. It is false to itself; or rather it feels an irresistible impulse of conscience to be true to itself. It labors under its guilty possession, and knows not what to do with it. The human heart was not made for the residence of such an inhabitant. It finds itself preyed on by a torment, which it dares not acknowledge to God or man. A vulture is devouring it, and it can ask no sympathy or assistance, either from heaven or earth. The secret which the murderer possesses soon comes to possess him; and, like the evil spirits of which we read, it overcomes him, and leads him whithersoever it will. He feels it beating at his heart, rising to his throat, and demanding disclosure. He thinks the whole world sees it in his face, reads it in his eyes, and almost hears its workings in the very silence of his thoughts. It has become his master. It betrays his discretion, it breaks down his courage, it conquers his prudence. When suspicions from without begin to embarrass him, and the net of circumstance to entangle him, the fatal secret struggles with still greater violence to burst forth. It must be confessed, it will be confessed; there is no refuge from confession but suicide, and suicide is confession.

Much has been said, on this occasion, of the excitement which has existed, and still exists, and of the extraordinary measures taken to discover and punish the guilty. No doubt there has been, and is, much excitement, and strange indeed it would be had it been otherwise. Should not all the peaceable and well-disposed naturally feel concerned, and naturally exert themselves to bring to punishment the authors of this secret assassination? Was it a thing to be slept upon or forgotten? Did you, gentlemen, sleep quite as quietly in your beds after this murder as before? Was it not a case for rewards, for meetings, for committees, for the united efforts of all the good, to find out a band of murderous conspirators, of midnight ruffians, and to bring them to the bar of justice and law? If this be excitement, is it an unnatural or an improper excitement?

It seems to me, gentlemen, that there are appearances of another feeling, of a very different nature and character; not very extensive, I would hope, but still there is too much evidence of its existence. Such is human nature, that some persons lose their abhorrence of crime in their admiration of its magnificent exhibitions. Ordinary vice is reprobated by them, but extraordinary guilt, exquisite wickedness, the high flights and poetry of crime, seize on the imagination, and lead them to forget the depths of the guilt, in admiration of the excellence of the performance, or the unequalled atrocity of the purpose. There are those in our day who have made great use of this

infirmity of our nature, and by means of it done infinite
injury to the cause of good morals. They have affected not
only the taste, but I fear also the principles, of the
young, the heedless, and the imaginative, by the exhibition
of interesting and beautiful monsters. They render
depravity attractive, sometimes by the polish of its
manners, and sometimes by its very extravagance; and study
to show off crime under all the advantages of cleverness and
dexterity. Gentlemen, this is an extraordinary murder, but
it is still a murder. We are not to lose ourselves in
wonder at its origin, or in gazing on its cool and skillful
execution. We are to detect and to punish it; and while we
proceed with caution against the prisoner, and are to be
sure that we do not visit on his head the offences of
others, we are yet to consider that we are dealing with a
case of most atrocious crime, which has not the slightest
circumstance about it to soften its enormity. It is
murder; deliberate, concerted, malicious murder. . . .

It is said, that "laws are made, not for the
punishment of the guilty, but for the protection of the
innocent." This is not quite accurate, perhaps, but if so,
we hope they will be so administered as to give that
protection. But who are the innocent whom the law would
protect? Gentlemen, Joseph White was innocent. They are
innocent who, having lived in the fear of God through the
day, wish to sleep in his peace through the night, in their
own beds. The law is established that those who live
quietly may sleep quietly; that they who do no harm may feel
none. The gentlemen can think of none that are innocent
except the prisoner at the bar, not yet convicted. Is a
proved conspirator to murder innocent? Are the
Crowninshields and the Knapps innocent? What is innocence?
How deep stained with blood, how reckless in crime, how deep
in depravity may it be, and yet retain innocence? The law
is made, if we would speak with entire accuracy, to protect
the innocent by punishing the guilty. But there are those
innocent out of a court, as well as in; innocent citizens
not suspected of crime, as well as innocent prisoners at the
bar.

The criminal law is not founded in a principle of
vengeance: it does not punish that it may inflict
suffering. The humanity of the law feels and regrets every
pain it causes, every hour of restraint it imposes, and more
deeply still every life it forfeits. But it uses evil as
the means of preventing greater evil. It seeks to deter
from crime by the example of punishment. This is its true,
and only true main object. It restrains the liberty of the
few offenders, that the many who do not offend may enjoy
their liberty. It takes the life of the murderer, that
other murders may not be committed. . . . The law . . .
punishes, not to satisfy any desire to inflict pain, but
simply to prevent the repetition of crimes. When the
guilty, therefore, are not punished, the law has so far
failed of its purpose; the safety of the innocent is so far
endangered. Every unpunished murder takes away something
from the security of every man's life. Whenever a jury,
through whimsical and ill-founded scruples, suffer the
guilty to escape, they make themselves answerable for the
augmented danger of the innocent. . . .

Gentlemen, let us now come to the case. Your first inquiry, on the evidence, will be, Was Captain White murdered in pursuance of a conspiracy, and was the defendant one of this conspiracy? If so, the second inquiry is, Was he so connected with the murder itself as that he is liable to be convicted as a principal. The defendant is indicted as a principal. If not guilty as such, you cannot convict him. The indictment contains three distinct classes of counts. In the first, he is charged as having done the deed with his own hand; in the second, as an aider and abettor to Richard Crowninshield, Jr., who did the deed; in the third, as an aider and abettor to some person unknown. If you believe him guilty on either of these counts, or in either of these ways, you must convict him.

It may be proper to say, as a preliminary remark, that there are two extraordinary circumstances attending this trial. One is, that Richard Crowninshield, Jr., the supposed immediate perpetrator of the murder, since his arrest, has committed suicide. He has gone to answer before a tribunal of perfect infallibility. The other is, that Joseph Knapp, the supposed originator and planner of the murder, having once made a full disclosure of the facts, under a promise of indemnity, is, nevertheless, not now a witness. Notwithstanding his disclosure and his promise of indemnity, he now refuses to testify. He chooses to return to his original state, and now stands answerable himself, when the time shall come for his trial. These circumstances it is fit you should remember, in your investigation of the case.

Your decision may affect more than the life of this defendant. If he be not convicted as principal, no one can be. Nor can any one be convicted of a participation in the crime as accessory. The Knapps and George Crowninshield will be again on the community. This shows the importance of the duty you have to perform, and serves to remind you of the care and wisdom necessary to be exercised in its performance. But certainly these considerations do not render the prisoner's guilt any clearer, nor enhance the weight of the evidence against him. No one desires you to regard consequences in that light. No one wishes anything to be strained, or too far pressed against the prisoner. Still, it is fit you should see the full importance of the duty which devolves upon you.

And now, gentlemen, in examining this evidence, let us begin at the beginning, and see first what we know independent of the disputed testimony. This is a case of circumstantial evidence. And these circumstances, we think, are full and satisfactory. The case mainly depends upon them, and it is common that offences of this kind must be proved in this way. Midnight assassins take no witnesses. The evidence of the facts relied on has been somewhat sneeringly denominated, by the learned counsel, "circumstantial stuff," but it is not such stuff as dreams are made of. Why does he not rend this stuff? Why does he not scatter it to the winds? He dismisses it a little too summarily. It shall be my business to examine this stuff, and try its cohesion.

The letter from Palmer at Belfast, is that no more than

flimsy stuff?

The fabricated letters from Knapp to the committee and to Mr. White, are they nothing but stuff?

The circumstance, that the housekeeper was away at the time the murder was committed, as it was agreed she would be, is that, too, a useless piece of the same stuff?

The facts, that the key of the chamber door was taken out and secreted; that the window was unbarred and unbolted; are these to be so slightly and so easily disposed of?

It is necessary, gentlemen, to settle now, at the commencement, the great question of a conspiracy. If there was none, or the defendant was not a party, then there is no evidence here to convict him. If there was a conspiracy, and he is proved to have been a party, then these two facts have a strong bearing on others, and all the great points of inquiry. The defendant's counsel take no distinct ground, as I have already said, on this point, either to admit or to deny. They choose to confine themselves to a hypothetical mode of speech. They say, supposing there was a conspiracy, non sequitur that the prisoner is guilty as principal. Be it so. But still, if there was a conspiracy, and if he was a conspirator, and helped to plan the murder, this may shed much light on the evidence which goes to charge him with the execution of that plan.

We mean to make out the conspiracy; and that the defendant was a party to it; and then to draw all just inferences from these facts.

Let me ask your attention, then, in the first place, to those appearances, on the morning after the murder, which have a tendency to show that it was done in pursuance of a preconcerted plan of operation. What are they? A man was found murdered in his bed. No stranger had done the deed, no one unacquainted with the house had done it. It was apparent that somebody within had opened, and that somebody without had entered. There had obviously and certainly been concert and co-operation. The inmates of the house were not alarmed when the murder was perpetrated. The assassin had entered without any riot or any violence. He had found the way prepared for him. The house had been previously opened. The window was unbarred from within, and its fastening unscrewed. There was a lock on the door of the chamber in which Mr. White slept, but the key was gone. It had been taken away and secreted. The footsteps of the murderer were visible, outdoors, tending toward the window. The plank by which he entered the window still remained. The road he pursued had been thus prepared for him. The victim was slain, and the murderer escaped. Everything indicated that somebody within had co-operated with somebody without. Everything proclaimed that some of the inmates, or somebody having access to the house, had had a hand in the murder. On the face of the circumstances, it was apparent, therefore, that this was a premeditated, concerted murder; that there had been a conspiracy to commit it. Who, then, were the conspirators? If not now found out, we are still groping in the dark, and the whole tragedy is still a mystery.

If the Knapps and the Crowninshields were not the conspirators in this murder, then there is a whole set of conspirators not yet discovered. Because, independent of the testimony of Palmer and Leighton, independent of all disputed evidence, we know, from uncontroverted facts, that this murder was, and must have been, the result of concert and co-operation between two or more. We know it was not done without plan and deliberation; we see, that whoever entered the house to strike the blow was favored and aided by some one who had been previously in the house, without suspicion, and who had prepared the way. This is concert, this is co-operation, this is conspiracy. If the Knapps and the Crowninshields, then, were not the conspirators, who were? Joseph Knapp had a motive to desire the death of Mr. White, and that motive has been shown.

He was connected by marriage with the family of Mr. White. His wife was the daughter of Mrs. Beckford, who was the only child of a sister of the deceased. The deceased was more than eighty years old, and had no children. His only heirs were nephews and nieces. He was supposed to be possessed of a very large fortune, which would have descended, by law, to his several nephews and nieces in equal shares; or, if there was a will, then according to the will. But as he had but two branches of heirs, the children of his brother, Henry White, and of Mrs. Beckford, each of these branches, according to the common idea, would have shared one-half of his property....

When we look back, then, to the state of things immediately on the discovery of the murder, we see that suspicion would naturally turn at once, not to the heirs at law, but to those principally benefited by the will. They, and they alone, would be supposed or seem to have a direct object for wishing Mr. White's life to be terminated. And, strange as it may seem, we find counsel now insisting, that, if no apology, it is yet mitigation of the atrocity of the Knapps' conduct in attempting to charge this foul murder on Mr. White, the nephew and principal devisee, that public suspicion was already so directed! As if assassination of character were excusable in proportion as circumstances may render it easy. Their endeavors, when they knew they were suspected themselves, to fix the charge on others, by foul means and by falsehood, are fair and strong proof of their own guilt. . . .

What, then, was this conspiracy? J. J. Knapp, Jr., desirous of destroying the will, and of taking the life of the deceased, hired a ruffian, who, with the aid of other ruffians, was to enter the house, and murder him in his bed. . . .

Gentlemen, I shall dwell no longer on the evidence which tends to prove that there was a conspiracy, and that the prisoner was a conspirator. All the circumstances concur to make out this point. Not only Palmer swears to it, in effect, and Leighton, but Allen mainly supports Palmer, and Osborn's books lend confirmation, so far as possible from such a source. Palmer is contradicted in nothing, either by any other witness, or any proved circumstance or occurrence. Whatever could be expected to support him does support him. All the evidence clearly manifests, I think, that there was a conspiracy; that it originated with Joseph Knapp; that defendant became a party to it, and was one of its conductors, from first to last.

One of the most powerful circumstances is Palmer's letter from Belfast. The amount of this is a direct charge on the Knapps of the authorship of this murder. How did they treat this charge; like honest men, or like guilty men? We have seen how it was treated. Joseph Knapp fabricated letters, charging another person, and caused them to be put into the post-office.

I shall now proceed on the supposition, that it is proved that there was a conspiracy to murder Mr. White, and that the prisoner was a party to it.

The second and the material inquiry is--Was the prisoner present at the murder, aiding and abetting therein?. . . .

There are two sorts of murder; the distinction between them it is of essential importance to bear in mind: 1. Murder in an affray, or upon sudden and unexpected provocation.   2. Murder secretly, with a deliberate, predetermined intention to commit the crime.   Under the first class, the question usually is, whether the offence be murder or manslaughter, in the person who commits the deed. Under the second class, it is often a question whether others than he who actually did the deed were present, aiding and assisting therein. Offences of this kind ordinarily happen when there is nobody present except those who go on the same design. If a riot should happen in the court-house, and one should kill another, this may be murder, or it may not, according to the intention with which it was done; which is always matter of fact, to be collected from the circumstances at the time.   But in secret murders, premeditated and determined on, there can be no doubt of the murderous intention; there can be no doubt, if a person be present, knowing a murder is to be done, of his concurring in the act. His being there is a proof of his intent to aid and abet; else, why is he there?

It has been contended, that proof must be given that the person accused did actually afford aid, did lend a hand in the murder itself; and without this proof, although he may be nearby, he may be presumed to be there for an innocent purpose; he may have crept silently there to hear the news, or from mere curiosity to see what was going on. Preposterous, absurd!   Such an idea shocks all common-sense. A man is found to be a conspirator to commit a murder; he has planned it; he has assisted in arranging the time, the place, and the means; and he is found in the place, and at the time, and yet it is suggested that he might have been there, not for co-operation and concurrence, but from curiosity!   Such an argument deserves no answer. It would be difficult to give it one, in decorous terms. Is it not to be taken for granted, that a man seeks to accomplish his own purposes?   When he has planned a murder, and is present at its execution, is he there to forward or to thwart his own design?   is he there to assist, or to prevent?   But "Curiosity!"   He may be there from mere "curiosity!" Curiosity to witness the success of the execution of his own plan of murder!   The very walls of a court-house ought not to stand, the ploughshare should run through the ground it stands on, where such an argument could find toler- ation. . . .

Now as to the facts.   Frank Knapp knew that the murder

was that night to be committed; he was one of the
conspirators, he knew the object, he knew the time. He had
that day been to Wenham to see Joseph, and probably to
Danvers to see Richard Crowninshield, for he kept his
motions secret. He had that day hired a horse and chaise of
Osborn, and attempted to conceal the purpose for which it
was used; he had intentionally left the <u>place</u> and the <u>price</u>
blank on Osborn's books. He went to Wenham by the way of
Danvers; he had been told the week before to hasten Dick; he
had seen the Crowninshields several times within a few days;
he had a saddle-horse the Saturday night before; he had seen
Mrs. Beckford at Wenham and knew she would not return that
night. She had not been away before for six weeks, and
probably would not soon be again. He had just come from
Wenham. Every day, for the week previous, he had visited
one or another of these conspirators, save Sunday, and then
probably he saw them in town. When he saw Joseph on the 6th,
Joseph had prepared the house, and would naturally tell him
of it; there were constant communications between them;
daily and nightly visitation; too much knowledge of these
parties and this transaction, to leave a particle of doubt
on the mind of any one, that Frank Knapp knew the murder was
to be committed this night. The hour was come, and he knew
it; if so, and he was in Brown Street, without explaining
why he was there, can the jury for a moment doubt whether he
was there to countenance, aid, or support; or for curiosity
alone; or to learn how the wages of sin and death were
earned by the perpetrator?. . . .
     The prisoner has attempted to prove an alibi in two
ways. In the first place, by four young men with whom he
says he was in company, on the evening of the murder, from
seven o'clock till near ten o'clock. This depends upon the
certainty of the night. In the second place, by his family,
from ten o'clock afterward. This depends upon the certainty
of the time of the night. These two classes of proof have
no connection with each other. One may be true, and the
other false, or they may both be true, or both be false. I
shall examine this testimony with some attention, because,
on a former trial, it made more impression on the minds of
the court than on my own mind. I think, when carefully
sifted and compared, it will be found to have in it more of
plausibility than reality. . . .
     Suppose, gentlemen, you were either of you asked where
you were, or what you were doing, on the fifteenth day of
June; you could not answer this question without calling to
mind some events to make it certain. Just as well may you
remember on what you dined each day of the year past. Time
is identical. Its subdivisions are all alike. No man
knows one day from another, or one hour from another, but by
some fact connected with it. Days and hours are not visible
to the senses, nor to be apprehended and distinguished by
the understanding. The flow of time is known only by
something which marks it; and he who speaks of the date of
occurrences with nothing to guide his recollection speaks at
random, and is not to be relied on. This young gentleman
remembers the facts and occurrences; he knows nothing why
they should not have happened on the evening of the 6th;
but he knows no more. All the rest is evidently conjecture

or impression. . . .

This fearful concatenation of circumstances puts him to an account. He was a conspirator. He had entered into this plan of murder. The murder is committed, and he is known to have been within three minutes' walk of the place. He must account for himself. He has attempted this, and failed....

I think you will be of opinion, that Brown Street was a probable place for the conspirators to assemble, and for an aid to be stationed. If we knew their whole plan, and if we were skilled to judge in such a case, then we could perhaps determine on this point better. But it is a retired place, and still commands a full view of the house; a lonely place, but still a place of observation. Not so lonely that a person would excite suspicion to be seen walking there in an ordinary manner; not so public as to be noticed by many. It is near enough to the scene of the action in point of law. It was their point of centrality. The club was found near the spot, in a place provided for it, in a place that had been previously hunted out, in a concerted place of concealment. <u>Here was their point of rendezvous</u>. Here might the lights be seen. Here might an aid be secreted. Here was he within call. Here might he be aroused by the sound of the whistle. Here might he carry the weapon. Here might he receive the murderer after the murder. . . .

Gentlemen, I have gone through with the evidence in this case, and have endeavored to state it plainly and fairly before you. I think there are conclusions to be drawn from it, the accuracy of which you cannot doubt. I think you cannot doubt that there was a conspiracy formed for the purpose of committing this murder, and who the conspirators were:

That you cannot doubt that the Crowninshields and the Knapps were the parties in this conspiracy:

That you cannot doubt that the prisoner at the bar knew that the murder was to be done on the night of the 6th of April:

That you cannot doubt that the murderers of Captain White were the suspicious persons seen in and about Brown Street on that night:

That you cannot doubt that Richard Crowninshield was the perpetrator of that crime:

That you cannot doubt that the prisoner at the bar was in Brown Street on that night.

If there, then it must be by agreement, to countenance, to aid the perpetrator. And if so, then he is guilty as PRINCIPAL.

Gentlemen, your whole concern should be to do your duty, and leave consequences to take care of themselves. You will receive the law from the court. Your verdict, it is true, may endanger the prisoner's life, but then it is to save other lives. If the prisoner's guilt has been shown and proved beyond all reasonable doubt, you will convict him. If such reasonable doubts of guilt still remain, you will acquit him. You are the judges of the whole case. You owe a duty to the public, as well as to the prisoner at the bar. You cannot presume to be wiser than the law. Your duty is a plain, straightforward one. Doubtless we would all judge him in mercy. Toward him, as an individual, the law inculcates no hostility; but toward him, if proved to be

a murderer, the law, and the oaths you have taken, and
public justice, demand that you do your duty.

   With consciences satisfied with the discharge of duty,
no consequences can harm you. There is no evil that we
cannot either face or fly from, but the consciousness of
duty disregarded. A sense of duty pursues us ever. It is
omnipresent, like the Deity. If we take to ourselves the
wings of the morning, and dwell in the uttermost parts of
the sea, duty performed, or duty violated, is still with us,
for our happiness or our misery. If we say the darkness
shall cover us, in the darkness as in the light our
obligations are yet with us. We cannot escape their power,
nor fly from their presence. They are with us in this life,
will be with us at its close; and in that scene of
inconceivable solemnity, which lies yet further onward, we
shall still find ourselves surrounded by the consciousness
of duty, to pain us wherever it has been violated, and to
console us so far as God may have given us grace to perform
it.

The First Bunker Hill Address (1825)

This uncounted multitude before me, and around me, proves the feeling which the occasion has excited. These thousands of human faces, glowing with sympathy and joy, and, from the impulses of a common gratitude, turned reverently to heaven, in this spacious temple of the firmament, proclaim that the day, the place, and the purpose of our assembling have made a deep impression on our hearts.

If, indeed, there be anything in local association fit to affect the mind of man, we need not strive to repress the emotions which agitate us here. We are among the sepulchres of our fathers. We are on ground distinguished by their valor, their constancy, and the shedding of their blood. We are here, not to fix an uncertain date in our annals, nor to draw into notice an obscure and unknown spot. If our humble purpose had never been born, the seventeenth of June, 1775, would have been a day on which all subsequent history would have poured its light, and the eminence where we stand, a point of attraction to the eyes of successive generations. But we are Americans. We live in what may be called the early age of this great continent; and we know that our posterity, through all time, are here to suffer and enjoy the allotments of humanity. We see before us a probable train of great events; we know that our own fortunes have been happily cast; and it is natural, therefore, that we should be moved by the contemplation of occurrences which have guided our destiny before many of us were born, and settled the condition in which we should pass that portion of our existence which God allows to men on earth.

We do not read even of the discovery of this continent without feeling something of a personal interest in the event; without being reminded how much it has affected our own fortunes and our own existence. It is more impossible for us, therefore, than for others, to contemplate with unaffected minds that interesting, I may say, that most touching and pathetic scene, when the great discoverer of America stood on the deck of his shattered bark, the shades of night falling on the sea, yet no man sleeping; tossed on the billows of an unknown ocean, yet the stronger billows of alternate hope and despair tossing his own troubled thoughts; extending forward his harassed frame, straining westward his anxious and eager eyes, till Heaven at last granted him a moment of rapture and ecstasy, in blessing his vision with the sight of the unknown world.

Nearer to our times, more closely connected with our fates, and therefore still more interested to our feelings and affections, is the settlement of our own country by colonists from England. We cherish every memorial of these worthy ancestors; we celebrate their patience and fortitude; we admire their daring enterprise; we teach our children to venerate their piety; and we are justly proud of being descended from men who have set the world an example of founding civil institutions on the great and united principles of human freedom and human knowledge. To us, their children, the story of their labors and sufferings can never be without its interest. We shall not stand unmoved on the shore of Plymouth, while the sea continues to wash it; nor will our brethren, in another early and ancient colony, forget the place of its first establishment, till their river shall cease to flow by it. No vigor of youth, no maturity of manhood, will lead the nation to forget the spots where its infancy was cradled and defended.

But the great event, in the history of the continent, which we are now met here to commemorate; that prodigy of modern times, at once the wonder and the blessing of the world, is the American Revolution. In a day of extraordinary prosperity and happiness, of high national honor, distinction, and power, we are brought together, in this place, by our love of country, by our admiration of exalted character, by our gratitude for signal services and patriotic devotion.

The society, whose organ I am, was formed for the purpose of rearing some honorable and durable monument to the memory of the early friends of American Independence. They have thought that for this object no time could be more propitious than the present prosperous and peaceful period; that no place could claim preference over this memorable spot; and that no day could be more auspicious to the undertaking than the anniversary of the battle which was here fought. The foundation of that monument we have now laid. With solemnities suited to the occasion, with prayers to Almighty God for his blessing, and in the midst of this cloud of witnesses, we have begun the work. We trust it will be prosecuted, and that springing from a broad foundation rising high in massive solidity and unadorned grandeur it may remain as long as Heaven permits the works of man to last, a fit emblem, both of the events in memory of which it is raised and of the gratitude of those who have reared it.

We know, indeed, that the record of illustrious actions is most safely deposited in the universal remembrance of mankind. We know that if we could cause this structure to ascend, not only till it reached the skies, but till it pierced them, its broad surfaces could still contain but part of that which, in an age of knowledge, hath already been spread over the earth, and which history charges itself with making known to all future times. We know that no inscription on entablatures less broad than the earth itself can carry information of the events we commemorate where it has not already gone; and that no structure which shall not outlive the duration of letters and knowledge among men, can prolong the memorial. But our object is by this edifice to show our own deep sense of the value and importance of the achievements of our ancestors; and by presenting this work of gratitude to the eye to keep alive similar sentiments and to foster a constant regard for the principles of the Revolution. Human beings are composed not of reason only, but of imagination also, and sentiment; and that is neither wasted nor misapplied which is appropriated to the purpose of giving right direction to sentiments and opening proper springs of feeling in the heart. Let it not be supposed that our object is to perpetuate national hostility, or even to cherish a mere military spirit. It is higher, purer, nobler. We consecrate our work to the spirit of national independence, and we wish that the light of peace may rest upon it forever. We rear a memorial of our conviction of that unmeasured benefit which has been conferred on our own land, and of the happy influences which have been produced by the same events on the general interests of mankind. We come as Americans to mark a spot which must forever be dear to us and our posterity. We wish that whosoever, in all coming time, shall turn his eye higher, may behold that the place is not undistinguished where the first great battle of the Revolution was fought. We wish that this structure may proclaim the magnitude and importance of that event to every class and every age. We wish that infancy may learn the purpose of its erection from maternal lips and that weary and withered age may behold it and be solaced by the recollections which it suggests. We wish that labor may look up here and be proud in the midst of its toil. We wish in those days of disaster which, as they come on all nations, must be expected to come on us also, desponding patriotism may turn its eyes hitherward and be assured that the foundations of our national power still stand strong.

We wish that this column rising toward heaven among the pointed spires of so many temples dedicated to God may contribute also to produce in all minds a pious feeling of dependence and gratitude. We wish, finally, that the last object on the sight of him who leaves his native shore, and the first to gladden his who revisits it, may be something which shall remind him of the liberty and the glory of his country. Let it rise till it meet the sun in his coming; let the earlier light of the morning gild it, and parting day linger and play on its summit.

We live in a most extraordinary age. Events so various and so important that they might crowd and distinguish centuries are in our times compressed within the compass of a single life. When has it happened that history has had so much to record in the same term of years as since the seventeenth of June, 1775? Our own Revolution, which under other circumstances might itself have been expected to occasion a war of half a century, has been achieved; twenty-four sovereign and independent States erected; and a general government established over them, so safe, so wise, so free, so practical, that we might well wonder its establishment should have been accomplished so soon were it not for the greater wonder that it should have been

established at all.   Two or three millions of people have
been augmented to twelve; and the great forests of the West
prostrated beneath the arm of successful industry; and the
dwellers on the banks of the Ohio and the Mississippi become
the fellow-citizens and neighbors of those who cultivate the
hills of New England.   We have a commerce that leaves no sea
unexplored; navies which take no law from superior force;
revenues adequate to all the exigencies of government,
almost without taxation; and peace with all nations,
founded on equal rights and mutual respect.

Europe, within the same period, has been agitated by a
mighty revolution, which, while it has been felt in the
individual condition and happiness of almost every man, has
shaken to the center her political fabric, and dashed
against one another thrones which had stood tranquil for
ages.   On this, our continent, our own example has been
followed; and colonies have sprung up to be nations.
Unaccustomed sounds of liberty and free government have
reached us from beyond the track of the sun; and at this
moment the dominion of European power in this continent,
from the place where we stand to the South Pole, is
annihilated forever.

In the meantime, both in Europe and America, such has
been the general progress of knowledge; such the
improvements in legislation, in commerce, in the arts, in
letters, and, above all, in liberal ideas and the general
spirit of the age, that the whole world seems changed.

Yet, notwithstanding that this is but a faint abstract
of the things which have happened since the day of the
battle of Bunker Hill, we are but fifty years removed from
it; and we now stand here to enjoy all the blessings of our
own condition, and to look abroad on the brightened
prospects of the world, while we hold still among us some of
those who were active agents in the scenes of 1775, and who
are now here from every quarter of New England to visit once
more, and under circumstances so affecting, I had almost
said so overwhelming, this renowned theatre of their courage
and patriotism.

Venerable men, you have come down to us from a former
generation.   Heaven has bounteously lengthened out your
lives that you might behold this joyous day.   You are now
where you stood fifty years ago this very hour, with your
brothers and your neighbors, shoulder to shoulder, in the
strife for your country.   Behold, how altered!   The same
heavens are, indeed, over your heads; the same ocean rolls
at your feet; but all else, how changed!   You hear now no
roar of hostile cannon, you see no mixed volumes of smoke
and flame rising from burning Charlestown.   The ground
strewed with the dead and the dying; the impetuous charge;
the steady and successful repulse; the loud call to
repeated assault; the summoning of all that is manly to
repeated resistance; a thousand bosoms freely and
fearlessly bared in an instant to whatever of terror there
may be in war and death; all these you have witnessed, but
you witness them no more.   All is peace.   The heights of
yonder metropolis, its towers and roofs which you then saw
filled with wives and children and countrymen in distress
and terror, and looking with unutterable emotions for the
issue of the combat, have presented you to-day with the

sight of its whole happy population come out to welcome and
greet you with a universal jubilee. Yonder proud ships by a
felicity of position appropriately lying at the foot of this
mount, and seeming fondly to cling around it, are not means
of annoyance to you, but your country's own means of
distinction and defence. All is peace; and God has granted
you this sight of your country's happiness ere you slumber
in the grave forever. He has allowed you to behold and to
partake the reward of your patriotic toils; and he has
allowed us, your sons and countrymen, to meet you here, and
in the name of the present generation, in the name of your
country, in the name of liberty, to thank you!

But, alas! you are not all here! Time and the sword
have thinned your ranks. Prescott, Putnam, Stark, Brooks,
Read, Pomeroy, Bridge! our eyes seek for you in vain amid
this broken band. You are gathered to your fathers, and
live only to your country in her grateful remembrance and
your own bright example. But let us not too much grieve
that you have met the common fate of men. You lived at
least long enough to know that your work had been nobly and
successfully accomplished. You lived to see your country's
independence established and to sheathe your swords from
war. On the light of Liberty you saw arise the light of
Peace, like "Another morn, Risen on mid-noon," and the sky
on which you closed your eyes was cloudless.

But--ah!--Him! the first great martyr in this great
cause! Him! the premature victim of his own self-devoting
heart! Him! the head of our civil councils and the destined
leader of our military bands, whom nothing brought hither
but the unquenchable fire of his own spirit; him! cut off by
Providence in the hour of overwhelming anxiety and thick
gloom; falling ere he saw the star of his country rise;
pouring out his generous blood like water before he knew
whether it would fertilize a land of freedom or of bondage!
how shall I struggle with the emotions that stifle the
utterance of thy name! Our poor work may perish, but thine
shall endure! This monument may moulder away; the solid
ground it rests upon may sink down to a level with the sea,
but thy memory shall not fail! Wheresoever among men a
heart shall be found that beats to the transports of
patriotism and liberty, its aspirations shall be to claim
kindred with thy spirit!

But the scene amid which we stand does not permit us to
confine our thoughts or our sympathies to those fearless
spirits who hazarded or lost their lives on this consecrated
spot. We have the happiness to rejoice here in the presence
of a most worthy representation of the survivors of the
whole Revolutionary army.

Veterans, you are the remnant of many a well-fought
field. You bring with you marks of honor from Trenton and
Monmouth, from Yorktown, Camden, Bennington, and Saratoga.
Veterans of half a century, when in your youthful days you
put everything at hazard in your country's cause, good as
that cause was, and sanguine as youth is, still your
fondest hopes did not stretch onward to an hour like this!
At a period to which you could not reasonably have expected
to arrive; at a moment of national prosperity, such as you
could never have forseen, you are now met here to enjoy the

fellowship of old soldiers and to receive the overflowings of a universal gratitude.

But your agitated countenances and your heaving breasts inform me that even this is not an unmixed joy. I perceive that a tumult of contending feelings rushes upon you. The images of the dead, as well as the persons of the living, throng to your embraces. The scene overwhelms you, and I turn from it. May the Father of all mercies smile upon your declining years and bless them! And when you shall here have exchanged your embraces; when you shall once more have pressed the hands which have been so often extended to give succor in adversity, or grasped in the exultation of victory; then look abroad into this lovely land, which your young valor defended, and mark the happiness with which it is filled; yea, look abroad into the whole earth and see what a name you have contributed to give to your country, and what a praise you have added to freedom, and then rejoice in the sympathy and gratitude which beam upon your last days from the improved condition of mankind.

The occasion does not require of me any particular account of the battle of the seventeenth of June, nor any detailed narrative of the events which immediately preceded it. These are familiarly known to all. In the progress of the great and interesting controversy, Massachusetts and the town of Boston had become early and marked objects of the displeasure of the British Parliament. This had been manifested in the act for altering the government of the Province, and in that for shutting up the port of Boston. Nothing sheds more honor on our early history, and nothing better shows how little the feelings and sentiments of the Colonies were known or regarded in England, than the impression which these measures everywhere produced in America. It had been anticipated that while the other Colonies would be terrified by the severity of the punishment inflicted on Massachusetts, the other seaports would be governed by a mere spirit of gain; and that, as Boston was now cut off from all commerce, the unexpected advantage which this blow on her was calculated to confer on other towns would be greedily enjoyed. How miserably such reasoners deceived themselves! How little they knew of the depth, and the strength, and the intenseness of that feeling of resistance to illegal acts of power which possessed the whole American people! Everywhere the unworthy boon was rejected with scorn. The fortunate occasion was seized everywhere to show to the whole world that the Colonies were swayed by no local interest, no partial interest, no selfish interest. The temptation to profit by the punishment of Boston was strongest to our neighbors of Salem. Yet Salem was precisely the place where this miserable proffer was spurned in a tone of the most lofty self-respect and the most indignant patriotism. "We are deeply affected," said its inhabitants, "with the sense of our public calamities; but the miseries that are now rapidly hastening on our brethren in the capital of the Province greatly excite our commiseration. By shutting up the port of Boston some imagine that the course of trade might be turned hither, and to our benefit; but we must be dead to every idea of justice, lost to all feelings of humanity, could we indulge

a thought to seize on wealth and raise our fortunes on the
ruin of our suffering neighbors." These noble sentiments
were not confined to our immediate vicinity. In that day of
general affection and brotherhood, the blow given to Boston
smote on every patriotic heart, from one end of the country
to the other. Virginia and the Carolinas, as well as
Connecticut and New Hampshire, felt and proclaimed the cause
to be their own. The Continental Congress, then holding its
first session in Philadelphia, expressed its sympathy for
the suffering inhabitants of Boston, and addresses were
received from all quarters assuring them that the cause was
a common one, and should be met by common efforts and common
sacrifices. The Congress of Massachusetts responded to
these assurances; and in an address to the Congress at
Philadelphia, bearing the official signature, perhaps among
the last of the immortal Warren, notwithstanding the
severity of its suffering and the magnitude of the dangers
which threatened it, it was declared that this Colony "is
ready, at all times, to spend and to be spent in the cause
of America."

But the hour drew nigh which was to put professions to
the proof and to determine whether the authors of these
mutual pledges were ready to seal them in blood. The
tidings of Lexington and Concord had no sooner spread than
it was universally felt that the time was at last come for
action. A spirit pervaded all ranks, not transient, not
boisterous, but deep, solemn, determined--"Totamque infusa
per artus/ Mens agitat molem, et magno se corpore miscet."

War, on their own soil and at their own doors, was,
indeed, a strange work to the yeomanry of New England; but
their consciences were convinced of its necessity, their
country called them to it and they did not withhold
themselves from the perilous trail. The ordinary
occupations of life were abandoned; the plow was stayed in
the unfinished furrow; wives gave up their husbands, and
mothers gave up their sons to the battles of a civil war.
Death might come, in honor, on the field; it might come, in
disgrace, on the scaffold. For either and for both they
were prepared. The sentiment of Quincy was full in their
hearts. "Blandishments," said that distinguished son of
genius and patriotism, "will not fascinate us, nor will
threats of a halter intimidate; for, under God, we are
determined that wheresoever, whensoever, or howsoever we
shall be called to make our exit, we will die free men."

The seventeenth of June saw the four New England
Colonies standing here, side by side, to triumph or to fall
together; and there was with them from that moment to the
end of the war, what I hope will remain with them
forever--one cause, one country, one heart.

The battle of Bunker Hill was attended with the most
important effects beyond its immediate result as a military
engagement. It created at once a state of open, public war.
There could now be no longer a question of proceeding
against individuals as guilty of treason or rebellion. That
fearful crisis was past. The appeal now lay to the sword,
and the only question was whether the spirit and the
resources of the people would hold out till the object
should be accomplished. Nor were its general consequences

confined to our own country.   The previous proceedings of
the Colonies, their appeals, resolutions, and addresses had
made their cause known to Europe.   Without boasting, we may
say that in no age or country has the public cause been
maintained with more force of argument, more power of
illustration, or more of that persuasion which excited
feeling and elevated principle can alone bestow, than the
Revolutionary State papers exhibit.   These papers will
forever deserve to be studied, not only for the spirit which
they breathe, but for the ability with which they were
written.

To this able vindication of their cause, the Colonies
had now added a practical and severe proof of their own true
devotion to it, and evidence also of the power which they
could bring to its support.   All now saw that if America
fell, she would not fall without a struggle.   Men felt
sympathy and regard as well as surprise when they beheld
these infant States, remote, unknown, unaided, encounter the
power of England, and in the first considerable battle leave
more of their enemies dead on the field, in proportion to
the number of combatants, than they had recently known in
the wars of Europe.

Information of these events circulating through Europe
at length reached the ears of one who now hears me.   He had
not forgotten the emotion which the fame of Bunker Hill and
the name of Warren excited in his youthful breast.

Sir, we are assembled to commemorate the establishment
of great public principles of liberty, and to do honor to
the distinguished dead.   The occasion is too severe for
eulogy to the living.   But, sir, your interesting relation
to this country, the peculiar circumstances which surround
you and surround us, call on me to express the happiness
which we derive from your presence and aid in this solemn
commemoration.

Fortunate, fortunate man! with what measure of
devotion will you not thank God for the circumstances of
your extraordinary life!   You are connected with both
hemispheres and with two generations.   Heaven saw fit to
ordain that the electric spark of liberty should be
conducted, through you, from the New World to the Old; and
we, who are now here to perform this duty of patriotism,
have all of us long ago received it in charge from our
fathers to cherish your name and your virtues.   You will
account it an instance of your good fortune, sir, that you
crossed the seas to visit us at a time which enables you to
be present at this solemnity.   You now behold the field, the
renown of which reached you in the heart of France, and
caused a thrill in your ardent bosom.   You see the lines of
the little redoubt thrown up by the incredible diligence of
Prescott; defended to the last extremity, by his
lion-hearted valor; and within which the cornerstone of our
monument has now taken its position.   You see where Warren
fell, and where Parker, Gardner, McCleary, Moore, and other
early patriots fell with him.   Those who survived that day,
and whose lives have been prolonged to the present hour, are
now around you.   Some of them you have known in the trying
scenes of the war.   Behold! they now stretch forth their
feeble arms to embrace you.   Behold! they raise their
trembling voices to invoke the blessing of God on you and

yours forever.

Sir, you have assisted us in laying the foundation of this edifice. You have heard us rehearse, with our feeble commendation, the names of departed patriots. Sir, monuments and eulogy belong to the dead. We give them this day to Warren and his associates. On other occasions they have been given to your more immediate companions in arms, to Washington, to Greene, to Gates, Sullivan, and Lincoln. Sir, we have become reluctant to grant these, our highest and last honors, further. We would gladly hold them yet back from the little remnant of that immortal band. "Serus in coelum redeas." Illustrious as are your merits, yet far, oh, very far distant be the day when any inscription shall bear your name, or any tongue pronounce its eulogy!

The leading reflection to which this occasion seems to invite us respects the great changes which have happened in the fifty years since the battle of Bunker Hill was fought. And it peculiarly marks the character of the present age that, in looking at these changes and in estimating their effect on our condition, we are obliged to consider, not what has been done in our own country only, but in others also. In these interesting times, while nations are making separate and individual advances in improvement, they make, too, a common progress; like vessels on a common tide, propelled by the gales at different rates, according to their several structure and management, but all moved forward by one mighty current beneath, strong enough to bear onward whatever does not sink beneath it.

A chief distinction of the present day is a community of opinions and knowledge among men, in different nations, existing in a degree heretofore unknown. Knowledge has, in our time, triumphed, and is triumphing over distance, over difference of languages, over diversity of habits, over prejudice, and over bigotry. The civilized and Christian world is fast learning the great lesson, that difference of nation does not imply necessary hostility, and that all contact need not be war. The whole world is becoming a common field for intellect to act in. Energy of mind, genius, power, wheresoever it exists, may speak out in any tongue, and the world will hear it. A great chord of sentiment and feeling runs through two continents, and vibrates over both. Every breeze wafts intelligence from country to country; every wave rolls it; all give it forth, and all in turn receive it. There is a vast commerce of ideas; there are marts and exchanges for intellectual discoveries, and a wonderful fellowship of those individual intelligences which make up the mind and opinion of the age. Mind is the great lever of all things; human thought is the process by which human ends are ultimately answered; and the diffusion of knowledge, so astonishing in the last half century, has rendered innumerable minds, variously gifted by nature, competent to be competitors, or fellow-workers, on the theatre of intellectual operation.

From these causes, important improvements have taken place in the personal condition of individuals. Generally speaking, mankind are not only better fed and better clothed, but they are able also to enjoy more leisure; they possess more refinement and more self-respect. A superior

tone of education, manners, and habits prevails.   This
remark, most true in its application to our own country, is
also partly true when applied elsewhere.   It is proved by
the vastly augmented consumption of those articles of
manufacture and of commerce which contribute to the
comforts and the decencies of life--an augmentation which
has far outrun the progress of population.   And while the
unexampled and almost incredible use of machinery would seem
to supply the place of labor, labor still finds its
occupation and its reward; so wisely has Providence adjusted
men's wants and desires to their condition and their
capacity.
     Any adequate survey, however, of the progress made in
the last half century, in the polite and the mechanic arts,
in machinery and manufactures, in commerce and agriculture,
in letters and in science, would require volumes.   I must
abstain wholly from these subjects, and turn, for a moment,
to the contemplation of what has been done on the great
question of politics and government.   This is the master
topic of the age; and during the whole fifty years, it has
intensely occupied the thoughts of men.   The nature of civil
government, its ends and uses, have been canvassed and
investigated; ancient opinions attacked and defended; new
ideas recommended and resisted by whatever power the mind
could bring to the controversy.   From the closet and the
public halls the debate has been transferred to the field;
and the world has been shaken by wars of unexampled
magnitude, and the greatest variety of fortune.   A day of
peace has at length succeeded; and now that the strife has
subsided, and the smoke cleared away, we may begin to see
what has actually been done, permanently changing the state
and condition of human society.   And without dwelling on
particular circumstances, it is most apparent that, from the
before-mentioned causes of augmented knowledge and improved
individual condition, a real, substantial, and important
change has taken place, and is taking place, greatly
beneficial, on the whole, to human liberty and human
happiness.
     The great wheel of political revolution began to move
in America.   Here its rotation was guarded, regular, and
safe.   Transferred to the other continent, from unfortunate
but natural causes, it received an irregular and violent
impulse; it whirled along with a fearful celerity, till at
length, like the chariot wheels in the races of antiquity,
it took fire from the rapidity of its own motion, and blazed
onward, spreading conflagration and terror around.
     We learn from the result of this experiment how
fortunate was our own condition, and how admirably the
character of our people was calculated for making the great
example of popular governments.   The possession of power did
not turn the heads of the American people, for they had long
been in the habit of exercising a great portion of
self-control.   Although the paramount authority of the
parent State existed over them, yet a large field of
legislation had always been open to our Colonial assemblies.
They were accustomed to representative bodies and the forms
of free government; they understood the doctrine of the
division of power among different branches and the necessity
of checks on each.   The character of our countrymen,

moreover, was sober, moral, and religious; and there was little in the change to shock their feelings of justice and humanity, or even to disturb an honest prejudice. We had no domestic throne to overturn, no privileged orders to cast down, no violent changes of property to encounter. In the American Revolution, no man sought or wished for more than to defend and enjoy his own. None hoped for plunder or for spoil. Rapacity was unknown to it; the axe was not among the instruments of its accomplishment; and we all know that it could not have lived a single day under any well-founded imputation of possessing a tendency adverse to the Christian religion.

It need not surprise us that, under circumstances less auspicious, political revolutions elsewhere, even when well intended, have terminated differently. It is, indeed, a great achievement, it is the master-work of the world, to establish governments entirely popular, on lasting foundations; nor is it easy, indeed, to introduce the popular principle at all into governments to which it has been altogether a stranger. It cannot be doubted, however, that Europe has come out of the contest, in which she has been so long engaged, with greatly superior knowledge, and, in many respects, a highly improved condition. Whatever benefit has been acquired is likely to be retained, for it consists mainly in the acquisition of more enlightened ideas. And although kingdoms and provinces may be wrested from the hands that hold them, in the same manner they were obtained; although ordinary and vulgar power may, in human affairs, be lost as it has been won, yet it is the glorious prerogative of the empire of knowledge, that what it gains it never loses. On the contrary, it increases by the multiple of its own power; all its ends become means; all its attainments help to new conquests. Its whole abundant harvest is but so much seed wheat, and nothing has ascertained, and nothing can ascertain, the amount of ultimate product.

Under the influence of this rapidly increasing knowledge, the people have begun, in all forms of government, to think and to reason on affairs of state. Regarding government as an institution for the public good, they demand a knowledge of its operations and a participation in its exercise. A call for the representative system, wherever it is not enjoyed, and where there is already intelligence enough to estimate its value, is perseveringly made. Where men may speak out, they demand it; where the bayonet is at their throats, they pray for it.

When Louis XIV said: "I am the State," he expressed the essence of the doctrine of unlimited power. By the rules of that system, the people are disconnected from the State; they are its subjects; it is their lord. These ideas, founded in the love of power, and long supported by the excess and the abuse of it, are yielding in our age to other opinions; and the civilized world seems at last to be proceeding to the conviction of that fundamental and manifest truth, that the powers of government are but a trust, and that they cannot be lawfully exercised but for the good of the community. As knowledge is more and more extended, this conviction becomes more and more general.

Knowledge, in truth, is the great sun in the firmament.
Life and power are scattered with all its beams. The prayer
of the Grecian combatant, when enveloped in unnatural clouds
and darkness, is the appropriate political supplication for
the people of every country not yet blessed with free
institutions:

"Dispel this cloud, the light of heaven restore;
  Give me to see--and Ajax asks no more."

We may hope that the growing influence of enlightened
sentiments will promote the permanent peace of the world.
Wars, to maintain family alliances, to uphold or to cast
down dynasties, to regulate successions to thrones, which
have occupied so much room in the history of modern times,
if not less likely to happen at all, will be less likely to
become general and involve many nations, as the great
principle shall be more and more established, that the
interest of the world is peace, and its first great statute,
that every nation possesses the power of establishing a
government for itself. But public opinion has attained also
an influence over governments which do not admit the popular
principle into their organization. A necessary respect for
the judgement of the world operates, in some measure, as a
control over the most unlimited forms of authority. It is
owing, perhaps, to this truth, that the interesting struggle
of the Greeks has been suffered to go on so long, without a
direct interference, either to wrest that country from its
present masters, and add it to other powers, or to execute
the system of pacification by force, and, with united
strength, lay the neck of Christian and civilized Greece at
the foot of the barbarian Turk. Let us thank God that we
live in an age when something has influence besides the
bayonet, and when the sternest authority does not venture to
encounter the scorching power of public reproach. Any
attempt of the kind I have mentioned should be met by one
universal burst of indignation; the air of the civilized
world ought to be made too warm to be comfortably breathed
by any who would hazard it.

It is, indeed, a touching reflection, that while, in
the fulness of our country's happiness, we rear this
monument to her honor, we look for instruction in our
undertaking, to a country which is now in fearful contest,
not for works of art or memorials of glory, but for her own
existence. Let her be assured that she is not forgotten in
the world; that her efforts are applauded, and that
constant prayers ascend for her success. And let us
cherish a confident hope for her final triumph. If the true
spark of religious and civil liberty be kindled, it will
burn. Human agency cannot extinguish it. Like the earth's
central fire, it may be smothered for a time; the ocean may
overwhelm it; mountains may press it down; but its inherent
and unconquerable force will heave both the ocean and the
land, and at some time or another, in some place or
another, the volcano will break out and flame up to heaven.

Among the great events of the half-century, we must
reckon, certainly, the revolution of South America; and we
are not likely to overrate the importance of that
revolution, either to the people of the country itself or to
the rest of the world. The late Spanish Colonies, now
independent States, under circumstances less favorable,

doubtless, than attended our own Revolution, have yet
successfully commenced their national existence. They have
accomplished the great object of establishing their
independence; they are known and acknowledged in the world;
and, although in regard to their systems of government,
their sentiments on religious toleration, and their
provisions for public instruction, they may have yet much to
learn, it must be admitted that they have risen to the
condition of settled and established States more rapidly
than could have been reasonably anticipated. They already
furnish an exhilarating example of the difference between
free governments and despotic misrule. Their commerce at
this moment creates a new activity in all the great marts of
the world. They show themselves able by an exchange of
commodities to bear a useful part in the intercourse of
nations. A new spirit of enterprise and industry begins to
prevail; all the great interests of society receive a
salutary impulse; and the progress of information not only
testifies to an improved condition, but constitutes itself
the highest and most essential improvement.
      When the battle of Bunker Hill was fought, the
existence of South America was scarcely felt in the
civilized world. The thirteen little Colonies of North
America habitually called themselves the "Continent." Borne
down by Colonial subjugation, monopoly, and bigotry, these
vast regions of the South were hardly visible above the
horizon. But in our day there hath been, as it were, a new
creation. The Southern Hemisphere emerges from the sea.
Its lofty mountains begin to lift themselves into the light
of heaven; its broad and fertile plains stretch out in
beauty to the eye of civilized man and at the mighty being
of the voice of political liberty, the waters of darkness
retire.
      And now let us indulge an honest exultation in the
conviction of the benefit which the example of our country
has produced and is likely to produce on human freedom and
human happiness. And let us endeavor to comprehend in all
its magnitude and to feel in all its importance the part
assigned to us in the great drama of human affairs. We are
placed at the head of the system of representative and
popular governments. Thus far our example shows that such
governments are compatible, not only with respectability and
power, but with repose, with peace, with security of
personal rights, with good laws, and a just administration.
      We are not propagandists. Whatever other systems are
preferred, either as being thought better in themselves or
as better suited to existing conditions, we leave the
preference to be enjoyed. Our history hitherto proves,
however, that the popular form is practicable and that, with
wisdom and knowledge, men may govern themselves; and the
duty incumbent on us is to preserve the consistency of this
cheering example and take care that nothing may weaken its
authority with the world. If in our case the representative
system ultimately fail, popular governments must be
pronounced impossible. No combination of circumstances more
favorable to the experiment can ever be expected to occur.
The last hopes of mankind, therefore, rest with us; and if
it should be proclaimed that our example has become an

argument against the experiment, the knell of popular
liberty would be sounded throughout the earth.

These are incitements to duty; but they are not
suggestions of doubt. Our history and our condition, all
that is gone before us and all that surrounds us, authorize
the belief that popular governments, though subject to
occasional variations, perhaps not always for the better in
form, may yet in their general character be as durable and
permanent as other systems. We know, indeed, that in our
country any other is impossible. The principle of free
governments adheres to the American soil. It is bedded in
it--immovable as its mountains.

And let the sacred obligations which have devolved on
this generation and on us sink deep into our hearts. Those
are daily dropping from among us who established our liberty
and our government. The great trust now descends to new
hands. Let us apply ourselves to that which is presented to
us as our appropriate object. We can win no laurels in a
war for independence. Earlier and worthier hands have
gathered them all. Nor are there places for us by the side
of Solon, and Alfred, and other founders of States. Our
fathers have filled them. But there remains to us a great
duty of defence and preservation; and there is opened to us
also a noble pursuit to which the spirit of the times
strongly invites us. Our proper business is improvement.
Let our age be the age of improvement. In a day of peace
let us advance the arts of peace and the works of peace.
Let us develop the resources of our land, call forth its
powers, build up its institutions, promote all its great
interests, and see whether we also, in our day and
generation, may not perform something worthy to be
remembered. Let us cultivate a true spirit of union and
harmony. In pursuing the great objects which our condition
points out to us, let us act under a settled conviction, and
a habitual feeling that these twenty-four States are one
country. Let our conceptions be enlarged to the circle of
our duties. Let us extend our ideas over the whole of the
vast field in which we are called to act. Let our object be
our country, our whole country, and nothing but our country.
And by the blessing of God may that country itself become a
vast and splendid monument, not of oppression and terror,
but of wisdom, of peace, and of liberty, upon which the
world may gaze with admiration, forever.

Eulogy to Adams and Jefferson (1826)

This is an unaccustomed spectacle. For the first time, fellow-citizens, badges of mourning shroud the columns and overhang the arches of this hall. These walls, which were consecrated, so long ago, to the cause of American liberty, which witnessed her infant struggles, and rung with the shouts of her earliest victories, proclaim, now, that distinguished friends and champions of that great cause have fallen. It is right that it should be thus. The tears which flow, and the honors that are paid, when the founders of the Republic die, give hope that the Republic itself may be immortal. It is fit that, by public assembly and solemn observance, by anthem and by eulogy, we commemorate the services of national benefactors, extol their virtues, and render thanks to God for eminent blessings, early given and long continued, through their agency, to our favored country.

Adams and Jefferson are no more; and we are assembled, fellow-citizens, the aged, the middle-aged, and the young, by the spontaneous impulse of all, under the authority of the municipal government, with the presence of the Chief Magistrate of the commonwealth, and others its official representatives, the University, and the learned societies, to bear our part in those manifestations of respect and gratitude which pervade the whole land. Adams and Jefferson are no more. On our fiftieth anniversary, the great day of national jubilee, in the very hour of public rejoicing, in the midst of echoing and re-echoing voices of thanksgiving, while their own names were on all tongues, they took their flight together to the world of spirits. . . .

Neither of these great men, fellow-citizens, could have died, at any time, without leaving an immense void in our American society. They have been so intimately, and for so long a time, blended with the history of the country, and especially so united, in our thoughts and recollections, with the events of the Revolution, that the death of either would have touched the chords of public sympathy. We should have felt that one great link, connecting us with former times, was broken; that we had lost something more, as it were, of the presence of the Revolution itself, and of the act of independence, and were driven on, by another great

remove from the days of our country's early distinction, to
meet posterity, and to mix with the future.   Like the
mariner, whom the currents of the ocean and the winds carry
along, till he sees the stars which have directed his
course and lighted his pathless way descend, one by one,
beneath the rising horizon, we should have felt that the
stream of time had borne us onward till another great
luminary, whose light had cheered us and whose guidance we
had followed, had sunk away from our sight.
     But the concurrence of their death on the anniversary
of Independence has naturally awakened stronger emotions.
Both had been Presidents, both had lived to great age, both
were early patriots, and both were distinguished and ever
honored by their immediate agency in the act of
independence.   It cannot but seem striking and
extraordinary, that these two should live to see the
fiftieth year from the date of that act; that they should
complete that year; and that then, on the day which had fast
linked forever their own fame with their country's glory,
the heavens should open to receive them both at once.   As
their lives themselves were the gifts of Providence, who is
not willing to recognize in their happy termination, as well
as in their long continuance, proofs that our country and
its benefactors are objects of His care?
     Adams and Jefferson, I have said, are no more.   As
human beings, indeed, they are no more.   They are no more,
as in 1776, bold and fearless advocates of independence; no
more, as at subsequent periods, the head of the government;
no more, as we have recently seen them, aged and venerable
objects of admiration and regard.   They are no more.   They
are dead.   But how little is there of the great and good
which can die!   To their country they yet live, and live
forever.   They live in all that perpetuates the remembrance
of men on earth; in the recorded proofs of their own great
actions, in the offspring of their intellect, in the
deep-engraved lines of public gratitude, and in the respect
and homage of mankind.   They live in their example; and they
live, emphatically, and will live, in the influence which
their lives and efforts, their principles and opinions, now
exercise, and will continue to exercise, on the affairs of
men, not only in their own country, but throughout the
civilized world.   A superior and commanding human intellect,
a truly great man, when Heaven vouchsafes so rare a gift, is
not a temporary flame, burning brightly for a while, and
then giving place to returning darkness.   It is rather a
spark of fervent heat, as well as radiant light, with power
to enkindle the common mass of human mind; so that when it
glimmers in its own decay, and finally goes out in death, no
night follows, but it leaves the world all light, all on
fire, from the potent contact of its own spirit.   Bacon
died; but the human understanding, roused by the touch of
his miraculous wand to a perception of the true philosophy
and the just mode of inquiring after truth, has kept on its
course successfully and gloriously.   Newton died; yet the
courses of the spheres are still known, and they yet move on
by the laws which he discovered, and in the orbits which he
saw, and described for them, in the infinity of space.
     No two men now live, fellow-citizens, perhaps it may be
doubted whether any two men have ever lived in one age, who,

more than those we now commemorate, have impressed on
mankind their own sentiments in regard to politics and
government, infused their own opinions more deeply into the
opinions of others, or given a more lasting direction to the
current of human thought. Their work doth not perish with
them. The tree which they assisted to plant will flourish,
although they water it and protect it no longer; for it has
struck its roots deep, it has sent them to the very centre;
no storm, not of force to burst the orb, can overturn it;
its branches spread wide; they stretch their protecting arms
broader and broader, and its top is destined to reach the
heavens. We are not deceived. There is no delusion here.
No age will come in which the American Revolution will
appear less than it is, one of the greatest events in human
history. No age will come in which it shall cease to be
seen and felt, on either continent, that a mighty step, a
great advance, not only in American affairs, but in human
affairs, was made on the 4th of July, 1776. And no age will
come, we trust, so ignorant or so unjust as not to see and
acknowledge the efficient agency of those we now honor in
producing that momentous event.
     We are not assembled, therefore, fellow-citizens, as
men overwhelmed with calamity by the sudden disruption of
the ties of friendship or affection, or as in despair for
the Republic by the untimely blighting of its hopes. Death
has not surprised us by an unseasonable blow. We have,
indeed, seen the tomb close, but it has closed only over
mature years, over long-protracted public service, over the
weakness of age, and over life itself only when the ends of
living had been fulfilled. These suns, as they rose slowly
and steadily, amid clouds and storms, in their ascendant,
so they have not rushed from their meridian to sink
suddenly in the west. Like the mildness, the serenity, the
continuing benignity of a summer's day, they have gone down
with slow-descending, grateful, long-lingering light; and
now that they are beyond the visible margin of the world,
good omens cheer us from "the bright track of their fiery
car"!
     There were many points of similarity in the lives and
fortunes of these great men. They belonged to the same
profession, and had pursued its studies and its practice,
for unequal lengths of time indeed, but with diligence and
effect. Both were learned and able lawyers. They were
natives and inhabitants, respectively, of those two of the
Colonies which at the Revolution were the largest and most
powerful, and which naturally had a lead in the political
affairs of the times. When the Colonies became in some
degree united, by the assembling of a general Congress, they
were brought to act together in its deliberations, not
indeed at the same time, but both at early periods. Each
had already manifested his attachment to the cause of the
country, as well as his ability to maintain it, by printed
addresses, public speeches, extensive correspondence, and
whatever other mode could be adopted for the purpose of
exposing the encroachments of the British Parliament, and
animating the people to a manly resistance. Both were not
only decided, but early, friends of Independence. While
others yet doubted, they were resolved; where others

hesitated, they pressed forward.   They were both members of
the committee for preparing the Declaration of
Independence, and they constituted the sub-committee
appointed by the other members to make the draft.   They left
their seats in Congress, being called to other public
employments, at periods not remote from each other, although
one of them returned to it afterward for a short time.
Neither of them was of the assembly of great men which
formed the present Constitution, and neither was at any time
a member of Congress under its provisions.   Both have been
public ministers abroad, both Vice-Presidents and both
Presidents of the United States.   These coincidences are now
singularly crowned and completed.   They have died together;
and they died on the anniversary of liberty....
     John Adams was born at Quincy, then part of the
ancient town of Braintree, on the 19th day of October, 1735.
He was a descendant of the Puritans, his ancestors having
early emigrated from England, and settled in Massachusetts.
. . .   Having been admitted, in 1751, a member of Harvard
College, Mr. Adams was graduated, in course, in 1755; and on
the catalogue of that institution, his name, at the time of
his death, was second among the living Alumni, being
preceded only by that of the venerable Holyoke. . . .   In
1758 he was admitted to the bar, and entered upon the
practice of the law in Braintree. . . .   In 1766 he removed
his residence to Boston, still continuing his attendance on
the neighboring circuits, and not infrequently called to
remote parts of the Province.   In 1770 his professional
firmness was brought to a test of some severity, on the
application of the British officers and soldiers to
undertake their defence, on the trial of the indictments
found against them on account of the transactions of the
memorable 5th of March.   He seems to have thought, on this
occasion, that a man can no more abandon the proper duties
of his profession, than he can abandon other duties.   The
event proved, that, as he judged well for the interest and
permanent fame of his country.   The result of that trial
proved that, notwithstanding the high degree of excitement
then existing in consequence of the measures of the British
Government, a jury of Massachusetts would not deprive the
most reckless enemies, even the officers of that standing
army quartered among them, which they so perfectly
abhorred, of any part of that protection which the law, in
its mildest and most indulgent interpretation, affords to
persons accused of crimes. . . .
     While still living at Quincy, and at the age of
twenty-four, Mr. Adams was present, in this town, at the
argument before the Supreme Court respecting Writs of
Assistance, and heard the celebrated and patriotic speech of
James Otis.   Unquestionably, that was a masterly
performance.   No flighty declamation about liberty, no
superficial discussion of popular topics, it was a learned,
penetrating, convincing, constitutional argument, expressed
in a strain of high and resolute patriotism.   He grasped the
question then pending between England and her Colonies with
the strength of a lion; and if he sometimes sported, if was
only because the lion himself is sometimes playful.   Its
success appears to have been as great as its merits, and its
impression widely felt.   Mr. Adams himself seems never to

have lost the feeling it produced, and to have entertained
constantly the fullest conviction of its important effects.
"I do say," he observes, "in the most solemn manner, that
Mr. Otis' Oration against the Writs of Assistance breathed
into this nation the breath of life."

In 1765 Mr. Adams laid before the public, anonymously,
a series of essays, afterward collected in a volume in
London, under the title of "A Dissertation on the Canon and
Feudal Law." The object of this work was to show that our
New England ancestors, in consenting to exile themselves
from their native land, were actuated mainly by the desire
of delivering themselves from the power of the hierarchy,
and from the monarchical and aristocratical systems of the
other continent; and to make this truth bear with effect on
the politics of the times. . . .

The citizens of this town conferred on Mr. Adams his
first political distinction, and clothed him with his first
political trust, by electing him one of their
representatives in 1770. Before this time he had become
extensively known throughout the Province, as well by the
part he had acted in relation to public affairs, as by the
exercise of his professional ability. He was among those
who took the deepest interest in the controversy with
England, and, whether in or out of the Legislature, his time
and talents were alike devoted to the cause. In the years
1773 and 1774 he was chosen a Councillor by the members of
the General Court, but rejected by Governor Hutchinson in
the former of those years, and by Governor Gage in the
latter.

The time was now at hand, however, when the affairs of
the Colonies urgently demanded united counsels throughout
the country. . . .

The proceedings of the first Congress are well known,
and have been universally admired. . . .

Mr. Adams was a constant attendant on the
deliberations of this body, and bore an active part in its
important measures. He was of the committee to state the
rights of the Colonies, and of that also which reported the
address to the king.

As it was in the Continental Congress,
fellow-citizens, that those whose deaths have given rise to
this occasion were first brought together, and called upon
to unite their industry and their ability in the service of
the country, let us now turn to the other of these
distinguished men, and take a brief notice of his life up to
the period when he appeared within the walls of Congress.

Thomas Jefferson, descended from ancestors who had been
settled in Virginia for some generations, was born near the
spot on which he died, in the County of Albemarle, on the 2d
of April, 1743. His youthful studies were pursued in the
neighborhood of his father's residence until he was removed
to the College of William and Mary, the highest honors of
which he in due time received. Having left the college with
reputation, he applied himself to the study of the law under
the tuition of George Wythe, one of the highest judicial
names of which that State can boast. At an early age he was
elected a member of the Legislature, in which he had no
sooner appeared than he distinguished himself by knowledge,

capacity, and promptitude. . . .

Entering with all his heart into the cause of liberty, his ability, patriotism, and power with the pen naturally drew upon him a large participation in the most important concerns. Wherever he was, there was found a soul devoted to the cause, power to defend and maintain it, and willingness to incur all its hazards. In 1774 he published a "Summary View of the Rights of British America," a valuable production among those intended to show the dangers which threatened the liberties of the country, and to encourage the people in their defence. In June, 1775, he was elected a member of the Continental Congress, as successor to Peyton Randolph, who had resigned his place on account of ill health, and took his seat in that body on the 21st of the same month.

And now, fellow citizens, without pursuing the biography of these illustrious men further, for the present, let us turn our attention to the most prominent act of their lives, their participation in the Declaration of Independence. . . .

It is usual, when committees are elected by ballot, that their members should be arranged in order, according to the number of votes which each has received. Mr. Jefferson, therefore, had received the highest, and Mr. Adams the next highest number of votes. The difference is said to have been but of a single vote. Mr. Jefferson and Mr. Adams, standing thus at the head of the committee, were requested by the other members to act as a sub-committee to prepare the draft; and Mr. Jefferson drew up the paper. . . .

It has sometimes been said, as if it were a derogation from the merits of this paper, that it contains nothing new; that it only states grounds of proceeding, and presses topics of argument, which had often been stated and pressed before. But it was not the object of the Declaration to produce anything new It was not to invent reasons for independence, but to state those which governed the Congress. For great and sufficient causes, it was proposed to declare independence; and the proper business of the paper to be drawn was to set forth those causes, and justify the authors of the measure, in any event of fortune, to the country and to posterity. The cause of American Independence, moreover, was now to be presented to the world in such manner, if it might so be, as to engage its sympathy, to command its respect, to attract its admiration; and in an assembly of most able and distinguished men, Thomas Jefferson had the high honor of being the selected advocate of this cause. To say that he performed his great work well, admirably well, would be inadequate and halting praise. Let us rather say, that he so discharged the duty assigned him, that all Americans may well rejoice that the work of drawing the title-deed of their liberties devolved upon him. . . .

The Declaration having been reported to Congress by the committee, the resolution itself was taken up and debated on the first day of July, and again on the second, on which last day it was agreed to and resolved, in these words:

"<u>Resolved</u>, That these united Colonies are, and of right ought to be, free and independent States; that they are absolved from all allegiance to the British crown, and that all political connection between them and the State of Great Britain is, and ought to be, totally dissolved. . . ."

The Congress of the Revolution, fellow citizens, sat with closed doors, and no report of its debates was ever made. The discussion, therefore, which accompanied this great measure, has never been preserved, except in memory and by tradition. But it is, I believe, doing no injustice to others to say, that the general opinion was, and uniformly has been, that in debate, on the side of independence, John Adams had no equal. . . .

Let us, then, bring before us the assembly, which was about to decide a question thus big with the fate of empire. Let us open their doors and look in upon their deliberations. Let us survey the anxious and careworn countenances, let us hear the firm-toned voices, of this band of patriots.

Hancock presides over the solemn sitting; and one of those not yet prepared to pronounce for absolute independence is on the floor, and is urging his reasons for dissenting from the Declaration. . . .

It was for Mr. Adams to reply to arguments like these. We know his opinions, and we know his character. He would commence with his accustomed directness and earnestness.

"Sink or swim, live or die, survive or perish, I give my hand and my heart to this vote. It is true, indeed, that in the beginning we aimed not at independence. But there's a Divinity which shapes our ends. The injustice of England has driven us to arms; and, blinded to her own interest for our good, she has obstinately persisted, till independence is now within our grasp. We have but to reach forth to it, and it is ours. Why, then, should we defer the Declaration? Is any man so weak as now to hope for a reconciliation with England, which shall leave either safety to the country and its liberties, or safety to his own life and his own honor? Are not you, sir, who sit in that chair--is not he, our venerable colleague near you--are you not both already the proscribed and predestined objects of punishment and vengeance? Cut off from all hope of royal clemency, what are you, what can you be, while the power of England remains, but outlaws? If we postpone independence, do we mean to carry on, or to give up, the war? Do we mean to submit to the measures of Parliament, Boston Port Bill and all? Do we mean to submit, and consent that we ourselves shall be ground to powder, and our country and its right trodden down in the dust? I know we do not mean to submit. We never shall submit. Do we intend to violate that most solemn obligation ever entered into by men, that plighting, before God, of our sacred honor to Washington, when, putting him forth to incur the dangers of war, as well as the political hazards of the times, we promised to adhere to him, in every extremity, with our fortunes and our lives? I know there is not a man here who would not rather see a general conflagration sweep over the land, or an earthquake sink it, than one jot or tittle of that plighted faith fall to the ground. For myself, having, twelve months ago, in this place, moved you, that George Washington be appointed commander of the forces raised, or to be raised, for defence of American liberty, may my right hand forget her cunning, and my tongue cleave to the roof of my mouth, if I hesitate or waver in the support I give him.

"The war, then, must go on. We must fight it through. And if the war must go on, why put off longer the Declaration of Independence? That measure will strengthen us. It will give us character abroad. The nations will then treat with us, which they never can do while we acknowledge ourselves subjects, in arms against our sovereign. Nay, I maintain that England herself will sooner treat for peace with us on the footing of independence, than consent, by repealing her acts, to acknowledge that her whole conduct toward us has been a course of injustice and oppression. Her pride will be less wounded by submitting to that course of things which now predestinates our independence, than by yielding the points in controversy to her rebellious subjects. The former she would regard as the result of fortune; the latter she would feel as her own deep disgrace. Why then, why then, sir, do we not as soon as possible change this from a civil to a national war? And since we must fight it through, why not put ourselves in a state to enjoy all the benefits of victory, if we gain the victory?

"If we fail it can be no worse for us. But we shall not fail. The cause will raise up armies; the cause will create navies. The people, the people, if we are true to them, will carry us, and will carry themselves, gloriously, through this struggle. I care not how fickle other people have been found. I know the people of these Colonies, and I know that resistance to British aggression is deep and settled in their hearts and cannot be eradicated. Every Colony, indeed, has expressed its willingness to follow, if we but take the lead. Sir, the Declaration will inspire the people with increased courage. Instead of a long and bloody war for the restoration of privileges, for redress of grievances, for chartered immunities, held under a British king, set before them the glorious object of entire independence, and it will breathe into them anew the breath of life. Read this Declaration at the head of the army; every sword will be drawn from its scabbard, and the solemn vow uttered, to maintain it, or to perish on the bed of honor. Publish it from the pulpit; religion will approve it, and the love of religious liberty will cling round it, resolved to stand with it, or fall with it. Send it to the public halls; proclaim it there; let them hear it who heard the first roar of the enemy's cannon; let them see it who saw their brothers and their sons fall on the field of Bunker Hill, and in the streets of Lexington and Concord, and the very walls will cry out in its support.

"Sir, I know the uncertainty of human affairs, but I see, I see clearly, through this day's business. You and I, indeed, may rue it. We may not live to the time when this Declaration shall be made good. We may die; die Colonists; die slaves; die, it may be, igniminiously and on the scaffold. Be it so. Be it so. If it be the pleasure of Heaven that my country shall require the poor offering of my life, the victim shall be ready, at the appointed hour of sacrifice, come when that hour may. But while I do live, let me have a country, or at least the hope of a country, and that a free country.

"But whatever may be our fate, be assured, be assured
that this Declaration will stand. It may cost treasure, and
it may cost blood; but it will stand, and it will richly
compensate for both. Through the thick gloom of the
present, I see the brightness of the future, as the sun in
heaven. We shall make this a glorious, an immortal day.
When we are in our graves, our children will honor it. They
will celebrate it with thanksgiving, with festivity, with
bonfires, and illuminations. On its annual return they will
shed tears, copious, gushing tears, not of subjection and
slavery, not of agony and distress, but of exultation, of
gratitude, and of joy. Sir, before God, I believe the hour
is come. My judgment approves this measure, and my whole
heart is in it. All that I have, and all that I am, and all
that I hope, in this life, I am now ready here to stake upon
it; and I leave off as I began, that live or die, survive or
perish, I am for the Declaration. It is my living
sentiment, and by the blessing of God it shall be my dying
sentiment, Independence now, and Independence forever."
    And so that day shall be honored, illustrious prophet
and patriot! so that day shall be honored, and as often as
it returns, thy renown shall come along with it, and the
glory of thy life, like the day of thy death, shall not fail
from the remembrance of men. . . .
    If anything yet remain to fill this cup of happiness,
let it be added, that he lived to see a great and
intelligent people bestow the highest honor in their gift
where he had bestowed his own kindest parental affections
and lodged his fondest hopes. Thus honored in life, thus
happy at death, he saw the jubilee, and he died; and with
the last prayers which trembled on his lips was the fervent
supplication for his country, "Independence forever!". . . .
    From the time of his final retirement from public life,
in 1809, Mr. Jefferson lived as became a wise man.
Surrounded by affectionate friends, his ardor in the pursuit
of knowledge undiminished, with uncommon health and unbroken
spirits, he was able to enjoy largely the rational pleasures
of life, and to partake in that public prosperity which he
had so much contributed to produce. His kindness and
hospitality, the charm of his conversation, the ease of his
manners, the extent of his acquirements, and, especially,
the full store of Revolutionary incidents which he had
treasured in his memory, and which he knew when and how to
dispense, rendered his abode in a high degree attractive to
his admiring countrymen, while his high public and
scientific character drew toward him every intelligent and
educated traveller from abroad. Both Mr. Adams and Mr.
Jefferson had the pleasure of knowing that the respect which
they so largely received was not paid to their official
stations. They were not men made great by office; but great
men, on whom the country for its own benefit had conferred
office. There was that in them which office did not give,
and which the relinquishment of office did not, and could
not, take away. In their retirement, in the midst of their
fellow citizens, themselves private citizens, they enjoyed
as high regard and esteem as when filling the most important
places of public trust. . . .
    Thus useful, and thus respected, passed the old age of

Thomas Jefferson. But time was on its ever ceaseless wing,
and was now bringing the last hour of this illustrious man.
He saw its approach with undisturbed serenity. He counted
the moments as they passed, and beheld that his last sands
were falling. That day, too, was at hand which he had
helped to make immortal. One wish, one hope, if it were not
presumptuous, beat in his fainting breast. Could it be so,
might it please God, he would desire once more to see the
sun, once more to look abroad on the scene around him, on
the great day of liberty. Heaven, in its mercy, fulfilled
that prayer. He saw that sun, he enjoyed its sacred light,
he thanked God for this mercy, and bowed his aged head to
the grave. _Felix, non vitae tantum claritate, sed etiam
opportunitate mortis._
   The last public labor of Mr. Jefferson naturally
suggests the expression of the high praise which is due,
both to him and to Mr. Adams, for their uniform and zealous
attachment to learning, and to the cause of general
knowledge. Of the advantages of learning, indeed, and of
literary accomplishments, their own characters were striking
recommendations and illustrations. They were scholars, ripe
and good scholars; widely acquainted with ancient, as well
as modern literature, and not altogether uninstructed in
the deeper sciences. Their acquirements, doubtless, were
different, and so were the particular objects of their
literary pursuits; as their tastes and characters, in these
respects, differed like those of other men. Being, also,
men of busy lives, with great objects requiring action
constantly before them, their attainments in letters did not
become showy or obtrusive. Yet I would hazard the opinion,
that, if we could now ascertain all the causes which gave
them eminence and distinction in the midst of the great men
with whom they acted, we should find not among the least
their early acquisitions in literature, the resources which
it furnished, the promptitude and facility which it
communicated, and the wide field it opened for analogy and
illustration; giving them thus, on every subject, a larger
view and a broader range, as well for discussion as for the
government of their own conduct. . . .
   But the cause of knowledge, in a more enlarged sense,
the cause of general knowledge and of popular education, had
no warmer friends, nor more powerful advocates, than Mr.
Adams and Mr. Jefferson. On this foundation they knew the
whole republican system rested; and this great and
all-important truth they strove to impress, by all the means
in their power. In the early publication already referred
to, Mr. Adams expresses the strong and just sentiment, that
the education of the poor is more important, even to the
rich themselves, than all their own riches. On this great
truth, indeed, is founded that unrivalled, that invaluable
political and moral institution, our own blessing and the
glory of our fathers, the New England system of free
schools.
   As the promotion of knowledge had been the object of
their regard through life, so these great men made it the
subject of their testamentary bounty. Mr. Jefferson is
understood to have bequeathed his library to the University
of Virginia, and that of Mr. Adams is bestowed on the
inhabitants of Quincy.

Mr. Adams and Mr. Jefferson, fellow citizens, were successively Presidents of the United States. The comparative merits of their respective administrations for a long time agitated and divided public opinion. They were rivals, each supported by numerous and powerful portions of the people, for the highest office. This contest, partly the cause and partly the consequence of the long existence of two great political parties in the country, is now part of the history of our government. We may naturally regret that anything should have occurred to create difference and discord between those who had acted harmoniously and efficiently in the great concerns of the Revolution. But this is not the time, nor this the occasion, for entering into the grounds of that difference, or for attempting to discuss the merits of the questions which it involves. As practical questions, they were canvassed when the measures which they regarded were acted on and adopted; and as belonging to history, the time has not come for their consideration. . . .

No men, fellow citizens, ever served their country with more entire exemption from every imputation of selfish and mercenary motives, than those to whose memory we are paying these proofs of respect. A suspicion of any disposition to enrich themselves or to profit by their public employments, never rested on either. No sordid motive approached them. The inheritance which they have left to their children is of their character and their fame.

Fellow citizens, I will detain you no longer by this faint and feeble tribute to the memory of the illustrious dead. Even in other hands, adequate justice could not be done to them, within the limits of this occasion. Their highest, their best praise, is your deep conviction of their merits, your affectionate gratitude for their labors and their services. It is not my voice, it is this cessation of ordinary pursuits, this arresting of all attention, these solemn ceremonies, and this crowded house, which speak their eulogy. Their fame, indeed, is safe. That is now treasured up beyond the reach of accident. Although no sculptured marble should rise to their memory, nor engraved stone bear record of their deeds, yet will their remembrance be as lasting as the land they honored. Marble columns may, indeed, moulder into dust, time may erase all impress from the crumbling stone, but their fame remains; for with American liberty it rose, and with American liberty only can it perish. It was the last swelling peal of yonder choir, "Their Bodies are Buried in Peace, but their Name Liveth Evermore." I catch that solemn song, I echo that lofty strain of funeral triumph, "Their name liveth evermore...."

And now, fellow citizens, let us not retire from this occasion without a deep and solemn conviction of the duties which have devolved upon us. This lovely land, this glorious liberty, these benign institutions, the dear purchase of our fathers, are ours; ours to enjoy, ours to preserve, ours to transmit. Generations past and generations to come hold us responsible for this sacred trust. Our fathers, from behind, admonish us, with their anxious paternal voices; posterity calls out to us from the bosom of the future; the world turns hither its solicitous eyes; all, all conjure us to act wisely, and faithfully, in the relation which we sustain. We can never, indeed, pay the debt which is upon us; but by virtue, by morality, by religion, by the cultivation of every good principle and every good habit, we may hope to enjoy the blessing, through our day, and to leave it unimpaired to our children. Let us feel deeply how much of what we are and of what we possess we owe to this liberty, and to these institutions of government. Nature has, indeed, given us a soil which yields bounteously to the hand of industry, the mighty fruitful ocean is before us, and the skies over our heads shed health and vigor. But what are lands, and seas, and skies to civilized man, without society, without knowledge, without morals, without religious culture; and how can these be enjoyed, in all their extent and all their excellence, but under the protection of wise institutions and a free government? Fellow citizens, there is not one of us, there is not one of us here present, who does not, at this moment, and at every moment, experience, in his own condition, and in the condition of those most near and dear to him, the influence and the benefits of this liberty and these institutions. Let us then acknowledge the blessing, let us feel it deeply and powerfully, let us cherish a strong affection for it, and resolve to maintain and perpetuate it. The blood of our fathers, let it not have been shed in vain; the great hope of posterity, let it not be blasted.

The striking attitude, too, in which we stand to the world around us, a topic to which, I fear, I advert too often, and dwell on too long, cannot be altogether omitted here. Neither individuals nor nations can perform their part well, until they understand and feel its importance, and comprehend and justly appreciate all the duties belonging to it. It is not to inflate national vanity, nor to swell a light and empty feeling of self-importance, but it is that we may judge justly of our situation, and of our own duties, that I earnestly urge upon you this consideration of our position and our character among the nations of the earth. It cannot be denied, but by those who would dispute against the sun, that with America, and in America, a new era commences in human affairs. This era is distinguished by free representative governments, by entire religious liberty, by improved systems of national intercourse, by a newly awakened and an unconquerable spirit of free inquiry, and by a diffusion of knowledge through the community, such as has been before altogether unknown and unheard of. America, America, our country, fellow citizens, our own dear and native land, is inseparably connected, fast bound up, in fortune and by fate, with these great interests. If they fall, we fall with them; if they stand, it will be because we have maintained them. Let us contemplate, then, this connection, which binds the prosperity of others to our own; and let us manfully discharge all the duties which it imposes. If we cherish the virtues and the principles of our fathers, Heaven will assist us to carry on the work of human liberty and human happiness. Auspicious omens cheer us. Great examples are before us. Our own firmament now shines brightly upon our path. Washington is in the clear, upper sky.   These other stars have now joined the American constellation; they circle round their centre, and the heavens beam with new light.   Beneath this illumination let us walk the course of life, and at its close devoutly commend our beloved country, the common parent of us all, to the Divine Benignity.

The Second Reply to Hayne (1830)

When the mariner has been tossed for many days, in thick weather, and on an unknown sea, he naturally avails himself of the first pause in the storm, the earliest glance of the sun, to take his latitude, and ascertain how far the elements have driven him from his true course. Let us imitate this prudence, and, before we float further on the waves of this debate, refer to the point from which we departed, that we may at least be able to conjecture where we now are. I ask for the reading of the resolution.

[The Secretary read the resolution, as follows:

Resolved, That the Committee on Public Lands be instructed to inquire and report the quantity of public lands remaining unsold within each State and Territory, and whether it be expedient to limit, for a certain period, the sales of the public lands to such lands only as have heretofore been offered for sale, and are now subject to entry at the minimum price. . . .]

We have thus heard, sir, what the resolution is, which is actually before us for consideration; and it will readily occur to every one that it is almost the only subject about which something has not been said in the speech, running through two days, by which the Senate has now been entertained by the gentleman from South Carolina. Every topic in the wide range of our public affairs, whether past or present--everything, general or local, whether belonging to national politics, or party politics, seems to have attracted more or less of the honorable member's attention, save only the resolution before the Senate. He has spoken of everything but the public lands. They have escaped his notice. To that subject, in all his excursions, he has not paid even the cold respect of a passing glance.

When this debate, sir, was to be resumed on Thursday morning, it so happened that it would have been convenient for me to be elsewhere. The honorable member, however, did not incline to put off the discussion to another day. He had a shot, he said, to return, and he wished to discharge it. That shot, sir, which it was kind thus to inform us was coming, that we might stand out of the way, or prepare ourselves to fall before it, and die with decency, has now been received. Under all advantages, and with expectation awakened by the tone which preceded it, it has been

discharged, and has spent its force. It may become me to
say no more of its effect than that if nobody is found,
after all, either killed or wounded by it, it is not the
first time, in the history of human affairs, that the vigor
and success of the war have not quite come up to the lofty
and sounding phrase of the manifesto. . . .

The honorable member complained that I had slept on his
speech. I must have slept on it, or not slept at all. The
moment the honorable member sat down, his friend from
Missouri rose, and, with much honeyed commendation of the
speech, suggested that the impressions which it had produced
were too charming and delightful to be disturbed by other
sentiments or other sounds, and proposed that the Senate
should adjourn. Would it have been quite amiable in me,
sir, to interrupt this excellent good feeling? Must I not
have been absolutely malicious, if I could have thrust
myself forward to destroy sensations thus pleasing? Was it
not much better and kinder, both to sleep upon them myself
and to allow others also the pleasure of sleeping upon
them?. . . . But the gentleman inquires why he was made the
object of such a reply? Why was he singled out? If an
attack has been made on the East, he, he assures us, did not
begin it--it was the gentleman from Missouri. Sir, I
answered the gentleman's speech because I happened to hear
it: and because, also, I chose to give an answer to that
speech which, if unanswered, I thought most likely to
produce injurious impressions. I did not stop to inquire
who was the original drawer of the bill. I found a
responsible indorser before me, and it was my purpose to
hold him liable, and to bring him to his just responsibility
without delay. But, sir, this interrogatory of the
honorable member was only introductory to another. He
proceeded to ask me whether I had turned upon him, in this
debate, from the consciousness that I should find an
overmatch if I ventured on a contest with his friend from
Missouri. If, sir, the honorable member, ex gratia
modestia, had chosen thus to defer to his friend and to pay
him a compliment, without intentional disparagement to
others, it would have been quite according to the friendly
courtesies of debate, and not at all ungrateful to my own
feelings. I am not one of those, sir, who esteem any
tribute of regard, whether light and occasional, or more
serious and deliberate, which may be bestowed on others, as
so much unjustly withholden from themselves. But the tone
and manner of the gentleman's question forbid me that I thus
interpret it. I am not at liberty to consider it as nothing
more than a civility to his friend. It had an air of taunt
and disparagement, something of the loftiness of asserted
superiority, which does not allow me to pass over it without
notice. It was put as a question for me to answer, and so
put as if it were difficult for me to answer: Whether I
deemed the member from Missouri an overmatch for myself in
debate here.   It seems to me, sir, that this is
extraordinary language, and an extraordinary tone, for the
discussions of this body.

Matches and overmatches! Those terms are more
applicable elsewhere than here, and fitter for other
assemblies than this. Sir, the gentleman seems to forget
where and what we are. This is a Senate; a Senate of

equals: of men of individual honor and personal character, and of absolute independence. We know no masters; we acknowledge no dictators. This is a hall for mutual consultation and discussion; not an arena for the exhibition of champions. I offer myself, sir, as a match for no man; I throw the challenge of debate at no man's feet. But then, sir, since the honorable member has put the question in a manner that calls for an answer, I will give him an answer; and I tell him that, holding myself to be the humblest of the members here, I yet know nothing in the arm of his friend from Missouri, either alone, or when aided by the arm of his friend from South Carolina, that need deter even me from espousing whatever opinions I may choose to espouse, from debating whatever I may choose to debate, or from speaking whatever I may see fit to say on the floor of the Senate. Sir, when uttered as matter of commendation or compliment, I should dissent from nothing which the honorable member might say of his friend. Still less do I put forth any pretensions of my own. But, when put to me as a matter of taunt, I throw it back, and say to the gentleman that he could possibly say nothing less likely than such a comparison to wound my pride of personal character. The anger of its tone rescued the remark from intentional irony, which otherwise probably would have been its general acceptation. But, sir, if it be imagined that by this mutual quotation and commendation; if it be supposed that, by casting the characters of the drama, assigning to each his part, to one the attack, to another the cry of onset; or if it be thought that by a loud and empty vaunt of anticipated victory any laurels are to be won here; if it be imagined, especially, that any or all these things will shake any purpose of mine, I can tell the honorable member, once for all, that he is greatly mistaken, and that he is dealing with one of whose temper and character he has yet much to learn. Sir, I shall not allow myself on this occasion, I hope on no occasion, to be betrayed into any loss of temper; but if provoked, as I trust I never shall be, into crimination and recrimination, the honorable member may perhaps find, that, in that contest, there will be blows to take as well as blows to give; that others can state comparisons as significant, at least, as his own; and that his impunity may possibly demand of him whatever powers of taunt and sarcasm he may possess. I commend him to be a prudent husbandry of his resources.

But, sir, the coalition! The coalition! Ay, "the murdered coalition"! The gentleman asks if I were led or frightened into this debate by the spectre of the coalition--"Was it the ghost of the murdered coalition," he exclaims, "which haunted the member from Massachusetts, and which, like the ghost of Banquo, would never down?" "The murdered coalition!" Sir, this charge of a coalition, in reference to the late administration, is not original with the honorable member. It did not spring up in the Senate. Whether as a fact, as an argument, or as an embellishment, it is all borrowed. He adopts it, indeed, from a very low origin and a still lower present condition. It is one of the thousand calumnies with which the press teemed during an excited political canvass. It was a charge of which there was not only no proof or probability, but which was, in itself, wholly impossible to be true. . . .

But, sir, the honorable member was not, for other reasons, entirely happy in his allusion to the story of Banquo's murder and Banquo's ghost. It was not, I think, the friends, but the enemies of the murdered Banquo, at whose bidding his spirit would not down. The honorable gentleman is fresh in his reading of the English classics, and can put me right if I am wrong; but, according to my poor recollection, it was at those who had begun with caresses, and ended with foul and treacherous murder, that the gory locks were shaken! The ghost of Banquo, like that of Hamlet, was an honest ghost. It disturbed no innocent man. It knew where its appearance would strike terror, and who would cry out, A ghost! It made itself visible in the right quarter, and compelled the guilty and the conscience-smitten, and none others, to start with--

"Pr'ythee, see there! behold!--look! lo!
If I stand here, I saw him!"

Their eyeballs were seared (was it not so, sir?) who had thought to shield themselves by concealing their own hand and laying the imputation of the crime on a low and hireling agency in wickedness; who had vainly attempted to stifle the workings of their own coward consciences by ejaculating, through white lips and chattering teeth: "Thou canst not say I did it!" I have misread the great poet if those who had in no way partaken in the deed of the death either found that they were, or feared that they should be, pushed from their stools by the ghost of the slain, or exclaimed to a spectre created by their own fears and their own remorse: "Avaunt! and quit our sight!"

There is another particular, sir, in which the honorable member's quick perception of resemblances might, I should think, have seen something in the story of Banquo, making it not altogether a subject of the most pleasant contemplation. Those who murdered Banquo, what did they win by it? Substantial good? Permanent power? Or disappointment, rather, and sore mortification--dust and ashes--the common fate of vaulting ambition, overleaping itself? Did not even-handed justice erelong commend the poisoned chalice to their own lips? Did they not soon find that for another they had "filed their mind"? that their ambition, though apparently for the moment successful, had but put a barren sceptre in their grasp? Ay, sir--

"A barren sceptre in their gripe,
Thence to be wrenched by an unlineal hand,
No son theirs succeeding."

Sir, I need pursue the allusion no further. I leave the honorable gentleman to run it out at his leisure, and to derive from it all the gratification it is calculated to administer. If he find himself pleased with the associations and prepared to be quite satisfied, though the parallel should be entirely completed, I had almost said, I am satisfied also--but that I shall think of. Yes, sir, I will think of that. . . .

I spoke, sir, of the Ordinance of 1787, which prohibited slavery in all future times, northwest of the Ohio, as a measure of great wisdom and foresight, and one which had been attended with highly beneficial and permanent

consequences.   I supposed that on this point no two
gentlemen in the Senate could entertain different opinions.
But the simple expression of this sentiment has led the
gentleman, not only into a labored defence of slavery, in
the abstract, and on principle, but, also, into a warm
accusation against me, as having attacked the system of
domestic slavery now existing in the Southern States.   For
all this there was not the slightest foundation in anything
said or intimated by me.   I did not utter a single word
which any ingenuity could torture into an attack on the
slavery of the South.   I said only that it was highly wise
and useful in legislating for the northwestern country,
while it was yet a wilderness, to prohibit the introduction
of slaves; and added that I presumed, in the neighboring
State of Kentucy, there was no reflecting and intelligent
gentleman who would doubt that if the same prohibition had
been extended at the same early period over that
Commonwealth, her strength and population would, at this
day, have been far greater than they are.   If these opinions
be thought doubtful, they are, nevertheless, I trust,
neither extraordinary nor disrespectful.   They attack nobody
and menace nobody.   And yet, sir, the gentleman's optics
have discovered, even in the mere expression of this
sentiment, what he calls the very spirit of the Missouri
question!   He represents me as making an onset on the whole
South, and manifesting a spirit which would interfere with
and disturb their domestic condition!   Sir, this injustice
no otherwise surprises me than as it is committed here, and
committed without the slightest pretence of ground for
it. . . .
     When the present Constitution was submitted for the
ratification of the people, there were those who imagined
that the powers of the government which it proposed to
establish, might, perhaps, in some possible mode, be exerted
in measures tending to the abolition of slavery.   This
suggestion would, of course, attract much attention in the
Southern conventions.   In that of Virginia, Governor
Randolph said: "I hope there is none here, who,
considering the subject in the calm light of philosophy,
will make an objection dishonorable to Virginia--that at the
moment they are securing the rights of their citizens, an
objection is started that there is a spark of hope that
those unfortunate men now held in bondage, may, by the
operation of the general government, be made free."
     At the very first Congress, petitions on the subject
were presented, if I mistake not, from different States.
The Pennsylvania society for promoting the abolition of
slavery took the lead, and laid before Congress a memorial,
praying Congress to promote the abolition by such powers as
it possessed.   This memorial was referred, in the House of
Representatives, to a select committee, consisting of Mr.
Foster of New Hapmshire, Mr. Gerry of Massachusetts, Mr.
Huntington of Connecticut, Mr. Lawrence of New York, Mr.
Sinnickson of New Jersey, Mr. Hartley of Pennsylvania, and
Mr. Parker of Virginia--all of them, sir, as you will
observe, Northern men, but the last.   This committee made a
report, which was committed to a committee of the whole
House, and there considered and discussed on several days;

and being amended, although without material alteration, it was made to express three distinct propositions, on the subject of slavery and the slave trade. First, in the words of the Constitution, that Congress could not, prior to the year 1808, prohibit the migration or importation of such persons as any of the States then existing should think proper to admit. Second, that Congress had authority to restrain the citizens of the United States from carrying on the African slave trade, for the purpose of supplying foreign countries. On this proposition, our early laws against those who engage in that traffic are founded. The third proposition, and that which bears on the present question was expressed in the following terms:

"<u>Resolved</u>, That Congress have no authority to interfere in the emancipation of slaves, or in the treatment of them in any of the States; it remaining with the several States alone to provide rules and regulations therein, which humanity and true policy may require."

This resolution received the sanction of the House of Representatives so early as March, 1790. And now, sir, the honorable member will allow me to remind him that not only were the select committee who reported the resolution, with a single exception, all Northern men, but also that of the members then composing the House of Representatives, a large majority, I believe nearly two-thirds, were Northern men also.

The House agreed to insert these resolutions in its journal; and from that day to this, it has never been maintained or contended that Congress had any authority to regulate or interfere with the condition of slaves in the several States. No Northern gentleman, to my knowledge, has moved any such question in either House of Congress.

The fears of the South, whatever fears they might have entertained, were allayed and quieted by this early decision; and so remained, till they were excited afresh, without cause, but for collateral and indirect purposes. When it became necessary, or was thought so, by some political persons, to find an unvarying ground for the exclusion of Northern men from confidence and from the lead in the affairs of the Republic, then, and not till then, the cry was raised, and the feeling industriously excited, that the influence of Northern men in the public councils would endanger the relation of master and slave. For myself, I claim no other merit than that this gross and enormous injustice toward the whole North has not wrought upon me to change my opinions or my political conduct. I hope I am above violating my principles, even under the smart of injury and false imputations. Unjust suspicions and undeserved reproach, whatever pain I may experience from them, will not induce me, I trust, nevertheless, to overstep the limits of constitutional duty, or to encroach on the rights of others. The domestic slavery of the South I leave where I find it--in the hands of their own governments. It is their affair, not mine. . . . But I am resolved not to submit in silence to accusations, either against myself, individually, or against the North, wholly unfounded and unjust; accusations which impute to us a disposition to evade the constitutional compact, and to extend the power of the government over the internal laws and domestic condition

of the States. All such accusations, wherever and whenever
made, all insinuations of the existence of any such
purposes, I know and feel to be groundless and injurious.
And we must confide in Southern gentlemen themselves; we
must trust to those whose integrity of heart and magnanimity
of feeling will lead them to a desire to maintain and
disseminate truth, and who possess the means of its
diffusion with the Southern public; we must leave it to them
to disabuse that public of its prejudices. But, in the
meantime, for my own part, I shall continue to act justly,
whether those toward whom justice is exercised receive it
with candor. . . .
    But as to the Hartford Convention, sir, allow me to say
that the proceedings of that body seem now to be less read
and studied in New England than further south. . . .
    Having dwelt long on this convention, and other
occurrences of that day, in the hope, probably (which will
not be gratified), that I should leave the course of this
debate to follow him, at length, in those excursions, the
honorable member returned and attempted another object. He
referred to a speech of mine in the other House, the same
which I had occasion to allude to myself the other day, and
has quoted a passage or two from it with a bold, though
uneasy and laboring air of confidence, as if he had detected
in me an inconsistency. Judging from the gentleman's
manner, a stranger to the course of the debate, and to the
point in discussion, would have imagined from so triumphant
a tone that the honorable member was about to overwhlem me
with a manifest contradiction. Any one who heard him, and
who had not heard what I had, in fact, previously said, must
have thought me routed and discomfited, as the gentleman had
promised. Sir, a breath blows all this triumph away. There
is not the slightest difference in the sentiments of my
remarks on the two occasions. What I said here on Wednesday
is in exact accordance with the opinion expressed by me in
the other House in 1825. Though the gentleman had the
metaphysics of Hudibras, though he were able
    "To sever and divide
    A hair 'twixt north and northwest side,"
he could not insert his metaphysical scissors between the
fair reading of my remarks in 1825, and what I said here
last week. There is not only no contradiction, no
difference, but, in truth, too exact a similarity, both in
thought and language, to be entirely in just taste. I had
myself quoted the same speech, had recurred to it, and spoke
with it open before me, and much of what I said was little
more than a repetition from it. In order to make finishing
work with this alleged contradiction, permit me to recur to
the origin of this debate and review its course. . . .
    We approach, at length, sir, to a more important part
of the honorable gentleman's observations. Since it does
not accord with my views of justice and policy to give away
the public lands altogether, as mere matter of gratuity, I
am asked by the honorable gentleman on what ground it is
that I consent to vote them away in particular instances?
How, he inquires, do I reconcile with these professed
sentiments my support of measures appropriating portions of
the lands to particular roads, particular canals, particular

rivers, and particular institutions of education in the
West? This leads, sir, to the real and wide difference, in
political opinion, between the honorable gentleman and
myself.   On my part, I look upon all these objects as
connected with the common good, fairly embraced in its
object and its terms; he, on the contrary, deems them all,
if good at all, only local good.   This is our difference.
The interrogatory which he proceeded to put, at once
explains this difference. "What interest," asks he, "has
South Carolina in a canal in Ohio?" Sir, this very question
is full of significance. It develops the gentleman's whole
political system; and its answer expounds mine. Here we
differ.   I look upon a road over the Allegheny, a canal
round the falls of the Ohio, or a canal or railway from the
Atlantic to the Western waters, as being an object large and
extensive enough to be fairly said to be for the common
benefit.   The gentleman thinks otherwise, and this is the
key to opine his construction of the powers of the
government. He may well ask: What interest has South
Carolina in a canal in Ohio? On his system, it is true, she
has no interest.   On that system, Ohio and Carolina are
different governments and different countries: connected
here, it is true, by some slight and ill-defined bond of
union, but, in all main respects, separate and diverse.   On
that system, Carolina has no more interest in a canal in
Ohio than in Mexico. The gentleman, therefore, only follows
out his own principles; he does no more than arrive at the
natural conclusions of his own doctrines; he only announces
the true results of that creed, which he has adopted
himself, and would persuade others to adopt, when he thus
declares that South Carolina has no interest in a public
work in Ohio. Sir, we narrow-minded people of New England
do not reason thus.   Our notion of things is entirely
different. We look upon the States, not as separated, but
as united.   We love to dwell on that union, and on the
mutual happiness which it has so much promoted, and the
common renown which it has so greatly contributed to
acquire.   In our contemplation, Carolina and Ohio are parts
of the same country; States, united under the same general
government, having interests, common, associated,
intermingled.   In whatever is within the proper sphere of
the constitutional power of this government, we look upon
the States as one. We do not impose geographical limits to
our patriotic feeling or regard; we do not follow rivers and
mountains, and lines of latitude, to find boundaries beyond
which public improvements do not benefit us. We who come
here as agents and representatives of these narrow-minded
and selfish men of New England consider ourselves as bound
to regard, with an equal eye, the good of the whole, in
whatever is within our power of legislation. Sir, if a
railroad or canal, beginning in south Carolina and ending in
South Carolina, appeared to me to be of natural importance
and national magnitude, believing, as I do, that the power
of government extends to the encouragement of works of that
description, if I were to stand up here, and ask: What
interest has Massachusetts in a railroad in South Carolina?
I should not be willing to face my constituents. These same
narrow-minded men would tell me that they had sent me to act
for the whole country, and that one who possessed too little

comprehension, either of intellect or feeling; one who was not large enough, both in mind and in heart, to embrace the whole, was not fit to be entrusted with the interest of any part.   Sir, I do not desire to enlarge the powers of the government, by unjustifiable construction; nor to exercise any not within a fair interpretation.   But when it is believed that a power does exist, then it is, in my judgment, to be exercised for the general benefit of the whole.   So far as respects the exercise of such a power, the States are one.   It was the very object of the Constitution to create unity of interests to the extent of the powers of the general government.   In war and peace we are one; in commerce, one, because the authority of the general government reaches to war and peace, and to the regulation of commerce.   I have never seen any more difficulty in erecting lighthouses on the lakes than on the ocean; in improving the harbors of inland seas than if they were within the ebb and flow of the tide; or of removing obstructions in the vast streams of the West more than in any work to faciliate commerce on the Atlantic coast.   If there be any power for one, there is power also for the other; and they are all and equally for the common good of the country. . . .

These, sir, are the grounds succinctly stated on which my votes for grants of lands for particular objects rest; while I maintain, at the same time, that it is all a common fund for the common benefit.   And reasons like these, I presume, have influenced the votes of other gentlemen from New England!   Those who have a different view of the powers of the government, of course, come to different conclusions on these as on other questions.   I observed, when speaking on this subject before, that, if we looked to any measure, whether for a road, a canal, or anything else, intended for the improvement of the West, it would be found that, if the New England ayes were struck out of the lists of votes, the Southern noes would always have rejected the measure.   The truth of this has not been denied and cannot be denied.   In stating this, I thought it just to ascribe it to the constitutional scruples of the South rather than to any other less favorable or less charitable cause. . . .

In 1820 (observe, Mr. President, in 1820), the people of the West besought Congress for a reduction in the price of lands.   In favor of that reduction, New England, with a delegation of forty members in the other House, gave thirty-three votes, and one only against it.   The four Southern States, with fifty members, gave thirty-two votes for it and seven against it.   Again, in 1821 (observe again, sir, the time), the law passed for the relief of the purchasers of the public lands.   This was a measure of vital importance to the West, and more especially to the Southwest.   It authorized the relinquishment of contracts for lands, which had been entered into at high prices, and a reduction in other cases of not less than thirty-seven and one-half per cent on the purchase money.   Many millions of dollars--six or seven, I believe, at least, probably much more--were relinquished by this law.   On this bill, New England, with her forty members, gave more affirmative votes than the four Southern States, with their fifty-two or three

members.
The tariff, which South Carolina had an efficient hand in establishing, in 1816, and this asserted power of internal improvement, advanced by her in the same year, and, as we have seen, approved and sanctioned by her Representatives in 1824, these two measures are the great grounds on which she is now thought to be justified in breaking up the Union, if she sees fit to break it up!

I may now safely say, I think, that we have had the authority of leading and distinguished gentlemen from South Carolina, in support of the doctrine of internal improvement. I repeat that, up to 1824, I for one followed South Carolina; but, when that star, in its ascension, veered off, in an unexpected direction, I relied on its light no longer.

Here the Vice-President, Mr. Calhoun, said: "Does the chair understand the gentleman from Massachusetts to say that the person now occupying the chair of the Senate has changed his opinions on the subject of internal improvements?"

From nothing ever said to me, sir, have I had reason to know of any change in the opinions of the person filling the chair of the Senate. If such change has taken place, I regret it. I speak generally of the State of South Carolina. Individuals, we know there are, who hold opinions favorable to the power. An application for its exercise, in behalf of a public work in South Carolina itself, is now pending, I believe, in the House, presented by members from that State. . . .

The bill of 1827, limited, as I have said, to the single object in which the tariff of 1824 had manifestly failed in its effect, passed the House of Represenatives, but was lost here. We had then the Act of 1828. I need not recur to the history of a measure so recent. Its enemies spiced it with whatsoever they thought would render it distasteful; its friends took it, drugged as it was. Vast amounts of property, many millions, had been invested in manufactures, under the inducements of the Act of 1824. Events called loudly, as I thought, for further regulation, to secure the degree of protection intended by that act. I was disposed to vote for such regulation, and desired nothing more; but certainly was not to be bantered out of my purpose by a threatened augmentation of duty on molasses, put into the bill for the avowed purpose of making it obnoxious. The vote may have been right or wrong, wise or unwise; but it is little less than absurd to allege against it an inconsistency with opposition to the former law. . . .

The gentleman, sir, has spoken at large of former parties, now no longer in being, by their received appellations, and has undertaken to instruct us, not only in the knowledge of their principles, but of their respective pedigrees also. He has ascended to the origin and run out their genealogies. With most exemplary modesty he speaks of the party to which he professes to have belonged himself, as the true pure, the only honest, patriotic party, derived by regular descent from father to son from the time of the virtuous Romans! Spreading before us the family tree of political parties, he takes especial care to show himself snugly perched on a poplar bough! He is wakeful to the

expediency of adopting such rules of descent as shall bring
him in, in exclusion of others, as an heir to the
inheritance of all public virtue and all true political
principle. His party and his opinions are sure to be
orthodox; heterodoxy is confined to his opponents. He
spoke, sir, of the Federalists, and I thought I saw some
eyes begin to open and stare a little when he ventured on
that ground. I expected he would draw his sketches rather
lightly when he looked on the circle around him, and
especially if he should cast his thoughts to the high places
out of the Senate. Nevertheless, he went back to Rome, ad
annum urbe condita, and found the fathers of the Federalsits
in the primeval aristocrats of that renowned empire! He
traced the flow of Federal blood down through successive
ages and centuries till he brought it into the veins of the
American Tories (of whom, by the way, there were twenty in
the Carolinas for one in Massachusetts). From the Tories he
followed it to the Federalists; and as the Federal party was
broken up, and there was no possiblity of transmitting it
further on this side the Atlantic, he seems to have
discovered that it has gone off, collaterally, thought
against all the canons of descent, into the Ultras of
France, and finally become extinguished, like exploded gas,
among the adherents of Don Miguel! This, sir, is an
abstract of the gentleman's history of Federalism. I am not
about to controvert it. It is not at present worth the
pains of refutation; because, sir, if at this day any one
feels the sin of Federalism lying heavily on his conscience,
he can easily procure remission. He may even obtain an
indulgence, if he be desirous of repeating the same
transgression. It is an affair of no difficulty to get into
the same right line of patriotic descent. A man nowadays is
at liberty to choose his political parentage. He may elect
his own father. Federalist or not, he may, if he choose,
claim to belong to the favored stock, and his claim will be
allowed. He may carry back his pretensions just as far as
the honorable gentleman himself; nay, he may make himself
out the honorable gentleman's cousin, and prove
satisfactorily that he is descended from the same political
great-grandfather. All this is allowable. We all know a
process, sir, by which the whole Essex Junto could, in one
hour, be all washed white from their ancient Federalism, and
come out, every one of them, an original Democrat, dyed in
the wool! Some of them have actually undergone the
operation, and they say it is quite easy. The only
inconvenience it occasions, as they tell us, is a slight
tendency of the blood to the face, a soft suffusion, which,
however, is very transient, since nothing is said by those
whom they join calculated to deepen the red on the cheek,
but a prudent silence observed in regard to all the past.
Indeed, sir, some smiles of approbation have been bestowed,
and some crumbs of comfort have fallen not a thousand miles
from the door of the Hartford Convention itself. And if the
author of the Ordinance of 1787 possessed the other
requisite qualifications, there is no knowing,
notwithstanding his Federalism, to what heights of favor he
might not yet attain. . . .
    Sir, let me recur to pleasing recollections--let me

indulge in refreshing remembrances of the past--let me remind you that in early times no States cherished greater harmony, both of principle and feeling, than Massachusetts and South Carolina. Would to God that harmony might again return! Shoulder to shoulder they went through the Revolution--hand in hand they stood round the administration of Washington and felt his own great arm lean on them for support. Unkind feeling, if it exist, alienation and distrust, are the growth, unnatural to such soils, of false principles since sown. They are weeds, the seeds of which that same great arm never scattered.

Mr. President, I shall enter on no encomium upon Massachusetts--she needs none. There she is--behold her, and judge for yourselves. There is her history; the world knows it by heart. The past, at least, is secure. There is Boston, and Concord, and Lexington, and Bunker Hill--and there they will remain forever. The bones of her sons, falling in the great struggle for independence, now lie mingled with the soil of every State, from New England to Georgia; and there they will lie forever. And, sir, where American liberty raised its first voice; and where its youth was nurtured and sustained, there it still lives, in the strength of its manhood and full of its original spirit. If discord and disunion shall wound it--if party strife and blind ambition shall hawk at and tear it--if folly and madness--if uneasiness, under salutary and necessary restraint shall succeed to separate it from that union by which alone its existence is made sure, it will stand, in the end, by the side of that cradle in which its infancy was rocked; it will stretch forth its arm with whatever of vigor it may still retain, over the friends who gather round it; and it will fall at last, if fall it must, amid the proudest monuments of its own glory, and on the very spot of its origin.

There yet remains to be performed, Mr. President, by far the most grave and important duty, which I feel to be devolved on me by this occasion. It is to state and to defend what I conceive to be the true principles of the Constitution under which we are here assembled. . . .

I understand the honorable gentleman from South Carolina to maintain that it is a right of the State Legislatures to interfere, whenever, in their judgment, this government transcends its constitutional limits, and to arrest the operation of its laws.

I understand him to maintain this right; as a right existing under the Constitution, not as a right to overthrow it on the ground of extreme necessity, such as would justify violent revolution.

I understand him to maintain an authority, on the part of the States, thus to interfere, for the purpose of correcting the exercise of power by the general government, of checking it and of compelling it to conform to their opinion of the extent of its powers.

I understand him to maintain that the ultimate power of judging of the constitutional extent of its own authority is not lodged exclusively in the general government or any branch of it; but that, on the contrary, the States may lawfully decide for themselves, and each State for itself, whether in a given case the act of the general government transcends its power.

I understand him to insist that if the exigency of the case, in the opinion of any State government, requires it, such State government may, by its own sovereign authority, annul an act of the general government which it deems plainly and palpably unconstitutional.

This is the sum of what I understand from him to be the South Carolina doctrine, and the doctrine which he maintains. I propose to consider it and compare it with the Constitution. . . .

[Mr. Hayne here rose. He did not contend, he said, for the mere right of revolution, but for the right of constitutional resistance. What he maintained was that, in case of a plain, palpable violation of the Constitution by the general government, a State may interpose, and that this interposition is constitutional.]

So, sir, I understood the gentleman, and am happy to find that I did not misunderstand him. What he contends for is that it is constitutional to interrupt the administration of the Constitution itself in the hands of those who are chosen and sworn to administer it, by the direct interference in form of law of the States in virtue of their sovereign capacity. The inherent right in the people to reform their government I do not deny; and they have another right, and that is to resist unconstitutional laws without overturning the government. It is no doctrine of mine that unconstitutional laws bind the people. The great question is: Whose prerogative is it to decide on the constitutionality or unconstitutionality of the laws?. . . . I say the right of a State to annul a law of Congress cannot be maintained but on the ground of the inalienable right of man to resist oppression; that is to say, upon the ground of revolution. I admit that there is an ultimate violent remedy above the Constitution and in defiance of the Constitution, which may be resorted to when a revolution is justified. But I do not admit that under the Constitution, and in conformity with it, there is any mode in which a State government, as a member of the Union, can interfere and stop the progress of the general government, by force of her own laws, under any circumstances whatever.

This leads us to inquire into the origin of this government and the source of its power. Whose agent is it? Is it the creature of the State Legislatures, or the creature of the people? If the government of the United States be the agent of the State governments, then they may control it, provided they can agree in the manner of controlling it; if it be the agent of the people, then the people alone can control it, restrain it, modify, or reform it. It is observable enough that the doctrine for which the honorable gentleman contends leads him to the necessity of maintaining, not only that this general government is the creature of the States, but that it is the creature of each of the States severally; so that each may assert the power for itself of determining whether it acts within the limits of its authority. It is the servant of four and twenty masters, of different wills and different purposes, and yet bound to obey all. This absurdity (for it seems no less) arises from a misconception as to the origin of this government and its true character. It is, sir, the people's Constitution, the people's government; made for the people, made by the people, and answerable to the people. The people of the United States have declared that this Constitution shall be the supreme law. We must either admit the proposition, or dispute their authority. The States are, unquestionably, sovereign, so far as their sovereignty is not affected by this supreme law. But the State Legislatures, as political bodies, however sovereign, are yet not sovereign over the people. So far as the people have given power to the general government, so far the grant is unquestionably good, and the government holds of the people, and not of the State governments. We are all agents of the same supreme power, the people. The general government and the State governments derive their authority from the same source. Neither can, in relation to the other, be called primary, though one is definite and restricted and the other general and residuary. The national government possesses those powers which it can be shown the people have conferred on it, and no more. All the rest belong to the State governments or to the people themselves. So far as the people have restrained State sovereignty, by the expression of their will, in the Constitution of the United States, so far, it must be admitted, State sovereignty is effectually controlled. I do not contend that it is, or ought to be, controlled further. The sentiment to which I have referred propounds that State sovereignty is only to be controlled by its own "feeling of justice"; that is to say, it is not to be controlled at all; for one who is to follow his own feelings is under no legal control. Now, however men may think this ought to be, the fact is that the people of the United States have chosen to impose control on State sovereignties. There are those, doubtless, who wish they had been left without restraint; but the Constitution has ordered the matter differently. To make war, for instance, is an exercise of sovereignty; but the Constitution declares that no State shall make war. To coin money is another exercise of sovereign power; but no State is at liberty to coin money. Again, the Constitution says that no sovereign State shall be so sovereign as to make a treaty. These prohibitions, it must be confessed, are a control on the State sovereignty of South Carolina, as well as of the other States, which does not arise "from her own feelings of honorable justice." Such an opinion, therefore, is in defiance of the plainest provisions of the Constitution. . . .

I must now beg to ask, sir, whence is this supposed right of the States derived?--where do they find the power to interfere with the laws of the Union? Sir, the opinion which the honorable gentleman maintains is a notion, founded in a total misapprehension, in my judgment, of the origin of this government and of the foundation on which it stands. I hold it to be a popular government erected by the people; those who administer it, responsible to the people; and itself capable of being amended and modified, just as the people may choose it should be. It is as popular, just as truly emanating from the people, as the State governments. It is created for one purpose; the State governments for another. It has its own powers; they have theirs. There is

no more authority with them to arrest the operation of a law
of Congress than with Congress to arrest the operation of
their laws. We are here to administer a Constitution
emanating immediately from the people, and trusted by them
to our administration. It is not the creature of the State
governments. It is of no moment to the argument, that
certain acts of the State Legislatures are necessary to fill
our seats in this body. That is not one of their original
State powers, a part of the sovereignty of the State. It is
a duty which the people, by the Constitution itself, have
imposed on the State Legislatures, and which they might have
left to be performed elsewhere, if they had seen fit. So
they have left the choice of President with electors; but
all this does not affect the proposition, that this whole
government, President, Senate and House of Representatives,
is a popular government. It leaves it still all its popular
character. The governor of a State (in some of the States)
is chosen, not directly by the people, but by those who are
chosen by the people, for the purpose of performing, among
other duties, that of electing a governor. Is the
government of the State, on that account, not a popular
government? This government, sir, is the independent
offspring of the popular will. It is not the creature of
State Legislatures; nay, more, if the whole truth must be
told, the people brought it into existence, established it,
and have hitherto supported it, for the very purpose among
others, of imposing certain salutary restraints on State
sovereignties. The States cannot now make war; they cannot
contract alliances; they cannot make, each for itself,
separate regulations of commerce; they cannot lay imposts;
they cannot coin money. If this Constitution, sir, be the
creature of State Legislatures, it must be admitted that it
has obtained a strange control over the volitions of its
creators.
    The people, then sir, erected this government. They
gave it a Constitution, and in that Constitution they have
enumerated the powers which they bestow on it. They have
made it a limited government. They have defined its
authority. They have restrained it to the exercise of such
powers as are granted; and all others, they declare, are
reserved to the States or the people. But, sir, they have
not stopped here. If they had, they would have accomplished
but half their work. No definition can be so clear as to
avoid possibiity of doubt; no limitation so precise as to
exclude all uncertainty. Who, then, shall construe this
grant of the people? Who shall interpret their will, where
it may be supposed they have left it doubtful? With whom do
they repose this ultimate right of deciding on the powers of
the government? Sir, they have settled all this in the
fullest manner. They have left it with the government
itself, in its appropriate branches. Sir, the very chief
end, the main design, for which the whole Constitution was
framed and adopted, was to establish a government that
should not be obliged to act through State agency, or depend
on State opinion and State discretion. The people had had
quite enough of that kind of government under the
Confederacy. Under that system the legal action--the
application of law to individuals--belonged exclusively to

the States.   Congress could only recommend--their acts were
not of binding force till the States had adopted and
sanctioned them.   Are we in that condition still?   Are we
yet at the mercy of State discretion and State construction?
Sir, if we are, then vain will be our attempt to maintain
the Constitution under which we sit.

     But, sir, the people have wisely provided, in the
Constitution itself, a proper suitable mode and tribunal for
settling questions of constitutional law.   There are, in the
Constitution, grants of powers to Congress, and restrictions
on these powers.   There are also prohibitions on the States.
Some authority must therefore necessarily exist, having the
ultimate jurisdiction to fix and ascertain the
interpretation of these grants, restrictions, and
prohibitions.   The Constitution has itself pointed out,
ordained, and established that authority.   How has it
accomplished this great and essential end?   By declaring,
sir, that "the Constitution and the laws of the United
States, made in pursuance thereof, shall be the supreme law
of the land, anything in the Constitution or laws of any
State to the contrary notwithstanding."

     This, sir, was the first great step.   By this the
supremacy of the Constitution and laws of the United States
is declared.   The people so will it.   No State law is to be
valid, which comes in conflict with the Constitution, or any
law of the United States passed in pursuance of it.   But who
shall decide this question of interference?   To whom lies
the last appeal?   This, sir, the Constitution itself decides
also by declaring "that the judicial power shall extend to
all cases arising under the Constitution and laws of the
United States."   These two provisions, sir, cover the whole
ground.   They are, in truth, the keystone of the arch.   With
these it is a Constitution; without them it is a
Confederacy. . . .

     They would inquire whether it was not somewhat
dangerous to resist a law of the United States.   What would
be the nature of their offence, they would wish to learn, if
they by military force and array resisted the execution in
Carolina of a law of the United States, and it should turn
out, after all, that the law was constitutional?   He would
answer, of course, treason.   No lawyer could give any other
reason.   John Fries, he would tell them, had learned that
some years ago.   How, then, they would ask, do you propose
to defend us?   We are not afraid of bullets, but treason has
a way of taking people off that we do not much relish.   How
do you propose to defend us?   "Look at my floating banner,"
he would reply; "see there the nullifying law!"   Is it your
opinion, gallant commander, they would then say, that if we
should be indicted for treason, that same floating banner of
yours would make a good plea in bar?   "South Carolina is a
sovereign state," he would reply.   That is true--but would
the judge admit our plea?   "These tariff laws," he would
repeat, "are unconstitutional, palpably, deliberately,
dangerously."   That all may be so; but if the tribunal
should not happen to be of that opinion, shall we swing for
it?   We are ready to die for our country, but it is rather
an awkward business, this dying without touching the ground!
After all, that is a sort of hemp tax worse than any part of
the tariff. . . .

If anything be found in the national Constitution, either by original provision, or subsequent interpretation, which ought not to be in it, the people know how to get rid of it. If any construction be established, unacceptable to them, so as to become, practically, a part of the Constitution, they will amend it, at their own sovereign pleasure; but while the people choose to maintain it, as it is; while they are satisfied with it, and refuse to change it, who has given, or who can give, to the State Legislatures a right to alter it, either by interference, construction, or otherwise? Gentlemen do not seem to recollect that the people have any power to do anything for themselves; they imagine there is no safety for them any longer than they are under the close guardianship of the State Legislatures. Sir, the people have not trusted their safety, in regard to the general Constitution, to these hands. They have required other security, and taken other bonds. They have chosen to trust themselves, first, to the plain words of the instrument, and to such construction as the government itself, in doubtful cases, should put on its own powers, under their oaths of office, and subject to their responsibility to them; just as the people of a State trust their own State governments with a similar power. Secondly, they have reposed their trust in the efficacy of frequent elections, and in their own power to remove their own servants and agents, whenever they see cause. Thirdly, they have reposed trust in the judicial power, which, in order that it might be trustworthy, they have made as respectable, as disinterested, and as independent as was practicable. Fourthly, they have seen fit to rely, in case of necessity, or high expediency, on their known and admitted power, to alter or amend the Constitution, peaceably and quietly, whenever experience shall point out defects or imperfections. And, finally, the people of the United States have, at no time, in no way, directly or indirectly, authorized any State Legislature to construe or interpret their high instrument of government; much less to interfere, by their own power, to arrest its course and operation.

If, sir, the people, in these respects, had done otherwise than they have done, their Constitution could neither have been preserved, nor would it have been worth preserving. And, if its plain provisions shall now be disregarded, and these new doctrines interpolated in it, it will become as feeble and helpless a being as its enemies, whether early or more recent, could possibly desire. It will exist in every State, but as a poor dependent on State permission. It must borrow leave to be and it will be no longer than State pleasure or State discretion sees fit to grant the indulgence and to prolong its poor existence.

But, sir, although there are fears, there are hopes also. The people have preserved this, their own chosen Constitution, for forty years and have seen their happiness, prosperity and renown grow with its growth, and strengthen with its strength. They are now, generally, strongly attached to it. Overthrown by direct assault, it cannot be; evaded, undermined, nullified, it will not be, if we, and those who shall succeed us here, as agents and representatives of the people, shall conscientiously and vigilantly discharge the two great branches of our public trust--faithfully to preserve and wisely to administer it.

Mr. President, I have thus stated the reasons of my dissent to the doctrines which have been advanced and maintained. I am conscious of having detained you and the Senate much too long. I was drawn into the debate with no previous deliberation such as is suited to the discussion of so grave and important a subject. But it is a subject of which my heart is full, and I have not been willing to suppress the utterance of its spontaneous sentiments. I cannot, even now, persuade myself to relinquish it without expressing once more, my deep conviction, that since it respects nothing less than the Union of the States, it is of most vital and essential importance to the public happiness. I profess, sir, in my career, hitherto, to have kept steadily in view the prosperity and honor of the whole country, and the preservation of our Federal Union. It is to that Union we owe our safety at home and our consideration and dignity abroad. It is to that Union that we are chiefly indebted for whatever makes us most proud of our country. That Union we reached only by the discipline of our virtues in the severe school of adversity. It had its origin in the necessities of disordered finance, prostrate commerce and ruined credit. Under its benign influence, these great interests immediately awoke as from the dead and sprang forth with newness of life. Every year of its duration has teemed with fresh proofs of its utility and its blessings; and, although our territory has stretched out wider and wider, and our population spread further and further, they have not outrun its protection or its benefits. It has been to us all a copious fountain of national, social and personal happiness. I have not allowed myself, sir, to look beyond the Union to see what might lie hidden in the dark recess behind. I have not coolly weighed the chances of preserving liberty when the bonds that unite us together shall be broken asunder. I have not accustomed myself to hang over the precipice of disunion to see whether, with my short sight, I can fathom the depth of the abyss below; nor could I regard him as a safe counsellor in the affairs of this government, whose thoughts should be mainly bent on considering not how the Union should be best preserved, but how tolerable might be the condition of the people when it shall be broken up and destroyed. While the Union lasts we have high, exciting, gratifying prospects spread out before us, for us and our children. Beyond that I seek not to penetrate the veil. God grant that in my day, at least, that curtain may not rise. God grant that, on my vision, never may be opened what lies behind. Whey my eyes shall be turned to behold, for the last time, the sun in heaven, may I not see him shining on the broken and dishonored fragments of a once glorious Union; on States dissevered, discordant, belligerent; on a land rent with civil feuds, or drenched, it may be, in fraternal blood! Let their last feeble and lingering glance rather behold the gorgeous ensign of the Republic, now known and honored throughout the earth, still full high advanced, its arms and trophies streaming in their original lustre, not a stripe erased or polluted, nor a single star obscured, bearing for

its motto no such miserable interrogatory as, "What is all
this worth?" nor those other words of delusion and folly,
"Liberty first and union afterward"; but everywhere, spread
all over in characters of living light, blazing on all its
ample folds, as they float over the sea and over the land,
and in every wind under the whole heavens, that other
sentiment, dear to every true American heart--Liberty and
Union, now and forever, one and inseparable!

The Seventh of March Address (1850)

I wish to speak today, not as a Massachusetts man, nor as a Northern man, but as an American and a member of the Senate of the United States. It is fortunate that there is a Senate of the United States; a body not yet moved from its propriety, nor lost to a just sense of its own dignity and its own high responsibilities, and a body to which the country looks, with confidence, for wise, moderate, patriotic, and healing counsels.

It is not to be denied that we live in the midst of strong agitations and are surrounded by very considerable dangers to our institutions and government. The imprisoned winds are let loose. The East, the North, and the stormy South combine to throw the whole sea into commotion, to toss its billows to the skies, and disclose its profoundest depths. I do not affect to regard myself, Mr. President, as holding, or fit to hold, the helm in this combat with the political elements; but I have a duty to perform, and I mean to perform it with fidelity, not without a sense of existing dangers, but not without hope. I have a part to act, not for my own security or safety, for I am looking out for no fragment upon which to float away from the wreck, if wreck there must be, but for the good of the whole and the preservation of all; and there is that which will keep me to my duty during this struggle, whether the sun and the stars shall appear for many days. I speak today for the preservation of the Union. "Hear me for my cause." I speak today out of a solicitous and anxious heart, for the restoration to the country of that quiet and that harmony which makes the blessings of this Union so rich and so dear to us all. These are the topics that I propose to myself to discuss; these are the motives, and the sole motives, that influence me in the wish to communicate my opinions to the Senate and the country; and if I can do anything, however little, for the promotion of these ends, I shall have accomplished all that I expect.

We all know, sir, that slavery has existed in the world from time immemorial. There was slavery in the earliest periods of history among the Oriental nations. There was slavery among the Jews; the theocratic government of that people issued no injunction against it. There was slavery among the Greeks. At the introduction of Christianity, the

Roman world was full of slaves, and I suppose there is to be found no injunction against that relation between man and man in the teachings of the Gospel of Jesus Christ or of any of His Apostles.

Now, sir, upon the general nature and influence of slavery there exists a wide difference of opinion between the Northern portion of this country and the Southern. It is said, on the one side, that, although not the subject of any injunction or direct prohibition in the New Testament, slavery is a wrong; that it is founded merely in the right of the strongest; and that it is an oppression, like unjust wars, like all those conflicts by which a powerful nation subjects a weaker to its will; and that, in its nature, whatever may be said of it in the modifications which have taken place, it is not according to the meek spirit of the Gospel. It is not "kindly affectioned"; it does not "seek another's, and not its own"; it does not "let the oppressed go free." These are sentiments that are cherished, and of late with greatly augmented force, among the people of the Northern states. They have taken hold of the religious sentiment of that part of the country, as they have, more or less, taken hold of the religious feelings of a considerable portion of mankind. The South, upon the other side, having been accustomed to this relation between the two races all their lives; from their birth, having been taught, in general, to treat the subjects of this bondage with care and kindness, and I believe, in general, feeling great kindness for them, have not taken the view of the subject which I have mentioned. There are thousands of religious men, with consciences as tender as any of their brethren at the North, who do not see the unlawfulness of slavery; and there are more thousands, perhaps, that, whatsoever they may think of it in its origin, and as a matter depending upon natural rights, yet take things as they are, and, finding slavery to be an established relation of the society in which they live, can see no way in which, let their opinions on the abstract question be what they may, it is in the power of this generation to relieve themselves from this relation. And candor obliges me to say that I believe they are just as conscientious, many of them, and the religious people, all of them, as they are at the North who hold different opinions.

There are men who, with clear perceptions, as they think, of their own duty, do not see how too eager a pursuit of one duty may involve them in the violation of others, or how too warm an embracement of one truth may lead to a disregard of other truths just as important. As I heard it stated strongly, not many days ago, these persons are disposed to mount upon some particular duty, as upon a war horse, and to drive furiously on and upon and over all other duties that may stand in the way. There are men who, in reference to disputes of that sort, are of opinion that human duties may be ascertained with the exactness of mathematics. They deal with morals as with mathematics, and they think what is right may be distinguished from what is wrong with the precision of an algebraic equation. They have, therefore, none too much charity toward others who differ from them. They are apt, too, to think that nothing is good but what is perfect, and that there are no

compromises or modifications to be made in consideration of
difference of opinion or in deference to other men's
judgment. If their perspicacious vision enables them to
detect a spot on the face of the sun, they think that a good
reason why the sun should be struck down from heaven. They
prefer the chance of running into utter darkness to living
in heavenly light, if that heavenly light be not absolutely
without any imperfection. . . .
     But we must view things as they are. Slavery does
exist in the United States. It did exist in the states
before the adoption of this Constitution, and at that time.
Let us, therefore, consider for a moment what was the state
of sentiment, North and South, in regard to slavery--in
regard to slavery at the time this Constitution was adopted.
A remarkable change has taken place since; but what did the
wise and great men of all parts of the country think of
slavery then? In what estimation did they hold it at the
time when this Constitution was adopted? It will be found,
sir, if we will carry ourselves by historical research back
to that day, and ascertain men's opinions by authentic
records still existing among us, that there was not
diversity of opinion between the North and the South upon
the subject of slavery. It will be found that both parts of
the country held it equally an evil, a moral and political
evil. It will not be found that, either at the North or at
the South, there was much, though there was some, invective
against slavery as inhuman and cruel. The great ground of
objection to it was political; that it weakened the social
fabric; that, taking the place of free labor, society became
less strong and labor less productive; and therefore we find
from all the eminent men of the time the clearest expression
of their opinion that slavery is an evil. They ascribed its
existence here, not without truth, and not without some
acerbity of temper and force of language, to the injurious
policy of the mother country, who, to favor the navigator,
had entailed these evils upon the colonies. . . . You
observe, sir, that the term slave or slavery is not used in
the Constitution. The Constitution does not require that
"fugitive slaves" shall be delivered up. It requires that
persons held to service in one state, and escaping into
another, shall be delivered up. Mr. Madison opposed the
introduction of the term slave or slavery into the
Constitution; for he said that he did not wish to see it
recognized by the Constitution of the United States of that
there could be property in men. . . .
     Here we may pause. There was, if not an entire
unanimity, a general concurrence of sentiment running
through the whole community, and especially entertained by
the eminent men of all parts of the country. But soon a
change began, at the North and the South, and a difference
of opinion showed itself; the North growing much more warm
and strong against slavery, and the South growing much more
warm and strong in its support. Sir, there is no generation
of mankind whose opinions are not subject to be influenced
by what appear to them to be their present emergent and
exigent interests. I impute to the South no particularly
selfish view in the change which has come over her. I
impute to her certainly no dishonest view. All that has

happened has been natural. It has followed those causes
which always influence the human mind and operate upon it.
What, then, have been the causes which have created so new a
feeling in favor of slavery in the south, which have changed
the whole nomenclature of the south on that subject, so
that, from being thought and described in the terms I have
mentioned and will not repeat, it has now become an
institution, a cherished institution, in that quarter; no
evil, no scourge, but a great religious, social, and moral
blessing as I think I have heard it latterly spoken of?   I
suppose this, sir, is owing to the rapid growth and sudden
extension of the cotton plantations of the south. So far as
any motive consistent with honor, justice, and general
judgment could act, it was the cotton interest that gave a
new desire to promote slavery, to spread it, and use its
labor. . . .
     Now, as to California and New Mexico, I hold slavery to
be excluded from these territories by a law even superior to
that which admits and sanctions it in Texas, I mean the law
of nature, of physical geography, the law of the formation
of the earth. That law settles forever, with a strength
beyond all terms of human enactment, that slavery cannot
exist in California or New Mexico. . . .
     Sir, wherever there is a substantive good to be done,
wherever there is a foot of land to be prevented from
becoming slave territory, I am ready to assert the principle
of the exclusion of slavery. I am pledged to it from the
year 1837; I have been pledged to it again and again; and I
will perform these pledges; but I will not do a thing
unnecessarily that wounds the feelings of others or that
does discredit to my own understanding.
     Mr. President, in the excited times in which we live,
there is found to exist a state of crimination and
recrimination between the North and South. There are lists
of grievances produced by each; and those grievances, real
or supposed, alienate the minds of one portion of the
country from the other, exasperate the feelings, and subdue
the sense of fraternal affection, patriotic love, and mutual
regard. I shall bestow a little attention, sir, upon these
various grievances existing on the one side and on the
other. I begin with the complaints of the South. I will
not answer, further than I have, the general statements of
the honorable Senator from South Carolina [Calhoun], that
the North has prospered at the expense of the South in
consequence of the manner of administering this government,
in the collection of its revenues, and so forth. These are
disputed topics, and I have no inclination to enter into
them. But I will allude to other complaints of the South,
and especially to one which has, in my opinion, just
foundation; and that is, that there has been found at the
North, among individuals and among legislators, a
disinclination to perform fully their constitutional duties
in regard to the return of persons bound to service who have
escaped into the free states. In that respect, the South,
in my judgment, is right, and the North is wrong. Every
member of every Northern legislature is bound by oath, like
every other officer in the country, to support the
Constitution of the United States; and the article of the
Constitution which says to these states that they shall

deliver up fugitives from service is as binding in honor and conscience as any other article. . . .

Complaint has been made against certain resolutions that emanate from legislatures at the North, and are sent here to us, not only on the subject of slavery in this District, but sometimes recommending congress to consider the means of abolishing slavery in the states. . . .

Then, sir, there are the abolition societies of which I am unwilling to speak, but in regard to which I have very clear notions and opinions. I do not think them useful. I think their operations for the last twenty years have produced nothing good or valuable. At the same time, I believe thousands of their members to be honest and good men, perfectly well-meaning men. They have excited feelings; they think they must do something for the cause of liberty; and, in their sphere of action, they do not see what else they can do than to contribute to an abolition press, or an abolition society, or to pay an abolition lecturer. I do not mean to impute gross motives even to the leaders of these societies, but I am not blind to the consequences of their proceedings. I cannot but see what mischief their interference with the South has produced. And is it not plain to every man? Let any gentleman who entertains doubts on this point recur to the debates in the Virginia House of Delegates in 1832, and he will see with what freedom a proposition made by Mr. Jefferson Randolph, for the gradual abolition of slavery, was discussed in that body. Everyone spoke of slavery as he thought; very ignominious and disparaging names and epithets were applied to it. The debates in the House of Delegates on that occasion, I believe, were published. They were read by every colored man who could read, and to those who could not read those debates were read by others. At that time Virginia was not unwilling or afraid to discuss this question, and to let that part of her population know as much of the discussion as they could learn. That was in 1832. As has been said by the honorable member from South Carolina, these abolition societies commenced their course of action in 1835. It is said, I do not know how true it may be, that they sent incendiary publications into the slave states; at any rate, they attempted to arouse, and did arouse, a very strong feeling; in other words, they created great agitation in the North against Southern slavery. Well, what was the result? The bonds of the slaves were bound more firmly than before, their rivets were more strongly fastened. Public opinion, which in Virginia had begun to be exhibited against slavery, and was opening out for the discussion of the question, drew back and shut itself up in its castle. I wish to know whether anybody in Virginia can now talk openly, as Mr. Randolph, Governor McDowell, and others talked in 1832, and sent their remarks to the press? We all know the fact, and we all know the cause; and everything that these agitating people have done has been, not to enlarge, but to restrain, not to set free, but to bind faster, the slave population of the South.

There are also complaints of the North against the South. I need not go over them particularly. The first and gravest is that the North adopted the Constitution, recognizing the existence of slavery in the states, and recognizing the right, to a certain extent, of the representation of slaves in Congress, under a state of sentiment and expectation which does not now exist; and that by events, by circumstances, by the eagerness of the South to acquire territory and extend her slave population, the North finds itself, in regard to the relative influence of the South and the North, of the free states and the slave states, where it never did expect to find itself when they agreed to the compact of the Constitution. They complain, therefore, that, instead of slavery being regarded as an evil, as it was then, an evil which all hoped would be extinguished gradually, it is now regarded by the South as an institution to be cherished, and preserved, and extended; an institution which the south has already extended to the utmost of her power by the acquisition of new territory.

Well, then, passing from that, everybody in the North reads; and everybody reads whatsoever the newspapers contain; and the newspapers . . . are careful to spread about among the people every reproachful sentiment uttered by any Southern man bearing at all against the North; everything that is calculated to exasperate and to alienate; and there are many such things, as everybody will admit, from the South, or from portions of it, which are disseminated among the reading people; and they do exasperate, and alienate, and produce a most mischievous effect upon the public mind at the North. . . .

There is a more tangible and irritating cause of grievance at the North. Free blacks are constantly employed in the vessels of the North, generally as cooks or stewards. When the vessel arrives at a Southern port, these free colored men are taken on shore, by the police or municipal authority, imprisoned, and kept in prison till the vessel is again ready to sail. This is not only irritating, but exceedingly unjustifiable and oppressive. Mr. [Samuel] Hoar's mission, some time ago, to South Carolina was a well-intended effort to remove this cause of complaint. The North thinks such imprisonments illegal and unconstitutional; and as the cases occur constantly and frequently they regard it as a grievance.

Now, sir, so far as any of these grievances have their foundation in matters of law, they can be redressed, and ought to be redressed; and so far as they have their foundation in matters of opinion, in sentiment, in mutual crimination and recrimination, all that we can do is to endeavor to allay the agitation, and cultivate a better feeling and more fraternal sentiments between the South and the North.

Mr. President, I should much prefer to have heard from every member on this floor declarations of opinion that this Union could never be dissolved than the declaration of opinion by anybody that, in any case, under the pressure of any circumstances, such a dissolution was possible. I hear with distress and anguish the word "secession," especially when it falls from the lips of those who are patriotic, and known to the country, and known all over the world for their political services. Secession! Peaceable secession! Sir, your eyes and mine are never destined to see that miracle. The dismemberment of this great country without convulsion!

The breaking up of the fountains of the great deep without ruffling the surface! Who is so foolish--I beg everybody's pardon--as to expect to see any such thing? Sir, he who sees these states, now revolving in harmony around a common center, and expects to see them quit their places and fly off without convulsion, may look the next hour to see the heavenly bodies rush from their spheres, and jostle against each other in the realms of space, without causing the wreck of the universe. There can be no such thing as a peaceable secession. Peaceable secession is an utter impossibility. Is the great Constitution under which we live, covering this whole country, is it to be thawed and melted away by secession, as the snows on the mountain melt under the influence of a vernal sun, disappear almost unobserved, and run off? No, sir! No, sir! I will not state what might produce the disruption of the Union; but, sir, I see as plainly as I can see the sun in heaven what that disruption itself must produce; I see that it must produce war. . . .

And, now, Mr. President, instead of speaking of the possibility or utility of secession, instead of dwelling in those caverns of darkness, instead of groping with those ideas so full of all that is horrid and horrible, let us come out into the light of the day; let us enjoy the fresh air of Liberty and Union; let us cherish those hopes which belong to us; let us devote ourselves to those great objects that are fit for our consideration and our action; let us raise our conceptions to the magnitude and the importance of the duties that devolve upon us; let our comprehension be as broad as the country for which we act, our aspirations as high as its certain destiny; let us not be pygmies in a case that calls for men. Never did there devolve on any generation of men higher trusts than now devolve upon us, for the preservation of this Constitution and the harmony and peace of all who are destined to live under it. Let us make our generation one of the strongest and brightest links in that golden chain which is destined, I fondly believe, to grapple the people of all the states to this Constitution for ages to come. We have a great, popular, constitutional government, guarded by law and by judicature, and defended by the affections of the whole people. No monarchical throne presses these states together, no iron chain of military power encircles them; they live and stand under a government popular in its form, representative in its character, founded upon principles of equality, and so constructed, we hope, as to last forever. In all its history it has been beneficent; it has trodden down no man's liberty; it has crushed no state. Its daily respiration is liberty and patriotism; its yet youthful veins are full of enterprise, courage, and honorable love of glory and renown. Large before, the country has now, by recent events, become vastly larger. This Republic now extends, with a vast breadth, across the whole continent. The two great seas of the world wash the one and the other shore. We realize, on a mighty scale, the beautiful description of the ornamental border of the buckler of Achilles:

"Now, the broad shield complete, the artist crowned
With his last hand, and poured the ocean round;

In living silver seemed the waves to roll,
And beat the buckler's verge, and bound the whole."

Chronology of
Major Speeches

Fourth of July Address, Hanover, New Hampshire, July 4, 1800.

Fourth of July Address to the Washington Benevolent Society, Portsmouth, New Hampshire, July 4, 1812.

First Settlement of New England, Plymouth, Massachusetts, December 22, 1820.

The Revolution in Greece, House of Representatives, Washington, D.C., January 19, 1824.

The Tariff, House of Representatives, Washington, D.C., April 1-2, 1824.

First Bunker Hill Address, Charlestown, Massachusetts, June 17, 1825.

Eulogy to Adams and Jefferson, Boston, Massachusetts, August 2, 1826.

The Second Reply to Hayne, Senate, Washington, D.C., January, 26-27, 1830.

The Knapp-White Murder Case, Salem, Massachusetts, August 6, 1830.

The Character of Washington, Washington, D.C., February 22, 1832.

The Presidential Veto of the United States Bank Bill, Senater, Washington, D.C., July 11, 1832.

Debate on the Force Bill, Senate, Washington, D.C., February 16, 1833.

A Redeemable Paper Currency, Senate, Washington, D.C., February 22, 1834.

The Appointing and Removal Power, Senate, Washington, D.C., February 16, 1835.

On the Loss of the Fortification Bill, Senate, Washington, D.C., January 14, 1836.

Reception at Madison, Madison, Indiana, June 1, 1837.

Slavery in the District of Columbia, Senate, Washington, D.C., January 10, 1838.

Reply to Calhoun, Senate, Washington, D.C., March 22, 1838.

Address to the Whig Young Men's Convention, Washington, D.C., May 9, 1840.

A Uniform System of Bankruptcy, Senate, Washington, D.C., May 18, 1840.

Address in Saratoga, Saratoga, New York, August 24, 1840.

The Completion of the Bunker Hill Monument, Charlestown, Massachusetts, June 17, 1843.

Objects of the Mexican War, Senate, Washington, D.C., March 2, 1848.

The Exclusion of Slavery from the Territories, Senate, Washington, D.C., August 12, 1848.

The Seventh of March Address, Senate Chamber, Washington, D.C., March 7, 1850.

The Seventeenth of July Address, Senate, Washington, D.C., July 17, 1850.

Addition to the Capitol, Washington, D.C., July 4, 1851.

Bibliographic Essay

This bibliography is divided into five sections for the reader's convenience. The first discusses various locations where the papers of Webster can be found. The second section discusses the question of authentication of texts. The third section examines biographies of Webster with an emphasis on their usefulness to this study and other rhetorical studies. The fourth section comments on the most important rhetorical studies done on Webster's rhetoric. The final section comments on general sources of use to this study and to other studies of American public address in the first half of the nineteenth century. My object is to provide the reader with a guide to the available literature on Webster and to evaluate that literature in terms of its usefulness to further critical analysis.

I. RESEARCH COLLECTIONS AND COLLECTED PAPERS

The almost 2,000 documents that make up the papers of Daniel Webster written prior to 1820 are located in the Baker Library at Dartmouth College. This collection includes a draft of Webster's argument for the Dartmouth College Case. Reference libraries often make these papers available on microfilm. The 41-reel microfilm edition was published in 1971. The most relevant reels for rhetorical scholars are numbers 30 through 37, the Congressional documents. Selected libraries usually have the documents under these listings:

Guide and Index to the Microfilm: Microfilm Edition of the Papers of Daniel Webster, ed. Charles M. Wiltse. Ann Arbor, Michigan, 1971.

The Papers of Daniel Webster, ed. Charles M. Wiltse and others, are being issued in fourteen volumes. Of most interest to rhetorical scholars are two volumes entitled The Papers of Daniel Webster: Speeches and Formal Writings, in two volumes, edited by Charles M. Wiltse and Alan R. Berolzheimer. Hanover: University Press of New England, 1987. Charles M. Wiltse has a distinguished career as an editor and compiler of historic papers. Though his work on Jefferson and Calhoun is thorough, he will be remember more for the stupendous job he has done on the Webster papers.

In 1974, housed in Baker Library at Dartmouth, he began to
compile The Papers of Daniel Webster.   The microfilm
edition, broken into four sections, is now complete.
"Guides" to the microfilm editions have been put together
and Wiltse has moved to the task of publishing useful
volumes in print from the materials he has gathered.   The
two volumes reviewed here are result of this fourteen volume
project.   They constitute what will be released in print of
the speeches and formal writings of Daniel Webster.   The
first volume runs from Webster's first entry into politics
in 1800 to the tariff battles of 1833.   The second volumes
covers discourse up to his death in 1852.

The work done on the speeches is meticulous.
Newspaper, pamphlet, and shorthand versions of the text were
compared on a word by word basis.   Footnotes dot the text
explaining which paragraph or word or section was in which
version of which speech.   Other footnotes explain arcane
references and historically relevant facts.   In fact, the
Reply to Hayne is printed twice, the only speech that is,
because the differences between the delivered version, as
best it can be reconstituted, and the published version are
deemed so important by Wiltse.   Each speech is preceded by a
few paragraphs which attempt to establish a historical
setting for the speech and a paragraph which traces its
"publication history."   The publication history will prove
very useful to rhetorical scholars because it explains
which text was used in the volume and why.   It cites
variant texts from the one used.

At the end of each volume is a "Calendar" of speeches
and formal writings and an index.   The "Calendar" includes
the date and location of each speech or writing that is not
included in the volume, along with the most authoritative
source in which to find it.   The "Calendar" informs the
reader by a simple comparison with the table of contents of
which speeches are not included in the volume while at the
same time providing a chronology of Webster's rhetorical
career.   Rhetorical scholars will be disappointed to learn
that the only forensic speech included is from the Knapp-
White murder case.   The others are relegated to volume three
of the Legal Papers in this same project though their dates
and location are given in the "Calendar" in these volumes.

Other biases further reduced the number of speeches
included in these volumes.   For example, the editors claim
that they include only one speech on the tariff because
Webster's speeches on the subject after 1824 are "little
more than special pleading for special interests."   The fact
of the matter is that several speeches are included which do
address the tariff, notably the Reply to Hayne.   Neither
Bunker Hill Address is included because the editors prefer
the Eulogy to Adams and Jefferson, and yet they have room
for both speeches delivered during the 1850 Compromise
debates.   Webster's Plymouth Oration with its incredibly
powerful attack on slavery is left out, but such minor
speeches as the one on the Cumberland Road Bill are
included.   While the first volume claims to begin in 1800,
it only does so in the "Calendar."   The first speech printed
in the Rockingham Memorial of 1812.   In fact, there seems to
be a general prejudice against epideictic speeches since the
Character of Washington is also excluded, but many

deliberative speeches of lesser consequence are included.

Another 2,500 items can be found at the New Hampshire Historical Society in Concord. Much of this correspondence is between family members and is often highly personal in nature. Of most importance to rhetorical scholars are his outlines for the reply to Hayne (January, 1830) and for the Seventh of March Address of 1850.

Webster's papers have also been collected at the Massachusetts Historical Society in Boston where they are often found in other collections. The National Archives in Washington, D.C., holds many papers generated by Webster's political career. Of more use is the collection of approximately 3,000 papers at the Library of Congress, including the Congressional Globe and The Register of Debates in Congress, the latter edited by Gales and Seaton.

Also available at the Library of Congress are microfilms of various newspapers cited in this study. These are helpful in assessing the milieu of a speech and the reaction to it. Furthermore, since newspapers were highly partisan, one can deduce the reactions of party leaders to speeches by reading the reviews printed in the papers. The Boston Atlas, New York Tribune, and New York Evening Post were papers that leaned toward the Democratic party. The New York Herald was a Whig paper favorable to merchant and industrial interests. The Albany Argos generally favored the American plan but supported Free Soil platforms and Martin Van Buren. The Vicksburg Weekly Whig often praised Webster's efforts at compromise as did the New Orleans Picayune, the Daily Advertiser, the National Intelligencer, the Charleston Mercury, Boston Courier, the Quawka Spectator, the Washington Union, and the Philadelphia Evening Bulletin.

II. AUTHENTIC TEXTS

Many distinguished scholars have written about the life of Webster. Some scholars have undertaken the examination of single speeches or rhetorical situations. But none have executed a complete rhetorical biography. This study attempts to fill that void. The second part of this volume contains six of the most prominent speeches Webster delivered, two each from the forensic, ceremonial, and deliberative categories. In the early nineteenth century, it was not uncommon for speeches to take three or four hours to deliver. For that reason, I have edited five of the speeches and printed in full only "The First Bunker Hill Address," also known as "Laying the Cornerstone of the Bunker Hill Monument." In editing, I have tried to preserve a sense of style, the entire narrative, and all arguments. Diversions, repetitions, and otherwise superfluous passages have been cut.

One difficulty with building a collection of speeches is determining the authenticity of the text. Most of the speeches included here come from the National Edition of The Writings and Speeches of Daniel Webster published in New York in 1903 in eighteen volumes. That edition was carefully prepared by James W. McIntyre, who in attempting to provide the most accurate texts, relied on earlier collections, such as the one put together by Charles Haddock, a professor of Rhetoric at Dartmouth and a nephew of Webster's. Unfortunately, most of Webster's major speeches were edited by him after they were delivered and before they were published. Thus, they are not entirely representative of what he actually said on the floor of the Senate, on a patriotic holiday, or before a jury. However, eye witnesses and newspaper accounts indicate that the extant texts are very close to Webster's actual speeches. His memory was phenomenal; his brain, which was weighed and measured after his death, was found to be much larger than most. He was able to speak from notes and soon after reproduce the entire speech. Where direct transcriptions occurred, as in the Dartmouth College case, it is clear that Webster was faithful to the original remarks and they do not differ markedly in published form. The same conclusion is reached by examining newspaper accounts, or by drawing the text from The Register of Debates, the National Intelligencer, or the Congressional Globe. Where Webster was unable or unwilling to reconstruct a speech, there were usually reporters or congressional recorders on hand. For example, the debate with Hayne printed in this book is drawn from The Register of Debates in Congress (vol. VI, part I, Washington, 1830) which was printed from on-the-spot transcriptions. This 30,000-word version is more accurate than the final published and edited version, which was polished by Webster. The Seventh of March, 1850 Compromise Address is drawn from the Congressional Globe (March 7, 1850, Appendix I, pp. 476-84) because Webster provided it to the Globe three days after he delivered it and edited it from the version printed the day after the speech in the National Intelligencer. The changes he made are minor and indicate that he was concerned with accuracy, not audience. The pamphlet version of the speech that Webster circulated in the North was changed in at least two ways. First, Webster removed a remark that infuriated Abolitionists; in it, he claimed that Abolitionists had enough money to buy every slave in Maryland his or her freedom. Second, he added a passage chiding the South for removing "free colored sea men" from commercial vessels. Therefore, wherever possible, the most immediate and accurate version of the speech as delivered is included herein.

Other sources for speeches by Webster include the following:

Works of Daniel Webster (Boston: Little, Brown and Company, 1877) is the seventeenth edition of a series that began in 1830 when Webster had another twenty-two years to live. The collection was first called Speeches and Forensic Arguments and edited by Webster's nephew, Professor Haddock. It was revised in 1835, 1843 and finally in 1851. This last authorized version was edited by Edward Everett, Webster's prote'ge' and the man who spoke before Lincoln at Gettysburg. We can assume that Everett knew Webster's style well and had an astute appreciation of speech making.

Ives, S. B., and W. Ives, The Knapp-White Trial (Salem, 1830). This volume contains the first trial in Salem and was re-edited in Boston in 1830 to include the second trial and Webster's summation to the jury.

Great Speeches of Daniel Webster (Boston: Little, Brown, and Co., 1879) was an attempt by editors at the publishing company to create a popular book of Webster's most famous orations. Unfortunately, in almost every case, it contains the most polished version of the text and therefore, not always the one actually uttered.

Oliver, Robert T., and Eugene White, Selected Speeches from American History (Boston: Allyn and Bacon, 1966). This carefully constructed volume contains only one speech by Webster. It is one of the few available and authenticated versions of Webster's "Reception at Madison Address."

Baird, A. Craig, American Public Addresses, 1740-1952 (New York: McGraw-Hill, 1956). This anthology contains three of Webster's speeches, all of which are drawn from the Writings and Speeches of Daniel Webster. They include the Knapp-White Murder Case, the Reply to Hayne, and the Seventh of March Address. Each is heavily edited to fit into the volume.

III. SELECTED BIOGRAPHIES

Knapp, Samuel, Life of Daniel Webster (1831). Knapp published the first book-length biography of Webster soon after the Webster-Hayne debate. Knapp was a graduate of Dartmouth and an ardent admirer of Webster. By the time of Webster's death, six books on his speaking or speeches had been published. None were distinguished, some were printed only for the royalties they would bring, and almost all of them were flattering of Webster to a fault.

More useful to scholars have been the books published since Webster's death. Here is a list of the most prominent:

Webster, Fletcher, Private Correspondence of Daniel Webster (Boston, 1857) 2 vols. Fletcher Webster, Webster's last living child, published the correspondence in honor of his father. (Fletcher was killed while leading a company in the Civil War.) The book is a treasure trove of information about Webster. Most important for public address are the things Webster said about rhetoric. Volume 1 contains Webster's "Autobiography," and there on pages 9 through 11 is Webster's heartfelt description of his earliest speaking, including his stage fright and failure, over which he "wept bitter tears of mortification." Later on page 465, Webster spoke about the importance of empathy, "[M]ake me think as he thinks, and feel as he feels." In volume 2, on page 16 he shared the tricks of the trade with his son, calling one "honest quackery." The Private Correspondence is essential reading for anyone seeking to understand Webster's early training, his assessment of other speakers, and his rhetorical roots. Webster's writings in these two volumes also indicates a healthy interest in the criticism of public address. He wanted to know what made it work; in no case was he satisfied with mystical explanations. The correspondence reveals what his speeches confirm: that Webster was a very practical and pragmatic man.

Lanman, Charles, The Private Life of Daniel Webster (New York, 1852). This book is typical of a spate of volumes published upon Webster's death. It attempts to get at the personal life of Webster, speculating on such subjects as his love for children and his religious conviction. It is probably no more accurate than Parson Weems writing on George Washington.

Smucker, Samuel M., The Life, Speeches, and Memorials of Daniel Webster (Philadelphia: Duane Rulison, 1861). Smucker's tribute to Webster was biased but faithful. It contains Webster's best speeches but is limited in two ways. First, the speeches included have been edited and are drawn from reprinted versions somewhat removed from the actual speaking event. Second, Smucker's admiration for Webster prevents him from writing objectively about the great leader. Smucker was interested in oratory and has a healthy respect for the art form.

Curtis, George T., Life of Daniel Webster (New York: Appleton, 1872) 2 vols. The "T." in Curtis' name stands for Ticknor. He was a direct descendent of George Ticknor and Edward Curtis, the close friends and travelling companions of Webster. Grace Webster and Anna Ticknor were also close, though Grace was the wallflower compared to Anna's role as outgoing hostess. This two-volume work is both a biography and a collection of Webster's letters. Since the biography is authorized and uses the letters for support, direct claims have an air of credibility about them. For example, in volume 1 on page 90, Curtis claims that Webster emulated Jeremiah Mason's plain, direct style and supports his claim with a citation from one of Webster's missives.

Harvey, Peter, Reminiscences and Anecdotes of Daniel Webster (Boston, limited edition, 1877, published posthumously by Little, Brown and Company in 1921). Harvey was a close friend of Webster's. Webster often confided in Harvey, wrote intimate letters to him, and considered him one of the most broad-minded and unselfish men in America. If one is looking for evidence of Webster's anguish during the 1850 Compromise debates, it can be found in Harvey's collection. If one seeks Webster's view of English speakers, it can be found in Harvey's book. Perhaps no collection other than Fletcher Webster's gives the reader a more personal look at Daniel Webster than does Harvey's.

Lodge, Henry Cabot, Daniel Webster (Boston: Houghton Mifflin, 1884, reprinted in New York by Chelsea House in 1980 with an introduction by Charles M. Wiltse). Lodge fancied himself as a historian, but in fact was much better as a senator who used historical data to buttress his arguments. Using local sources and being biased against slavery and the South, Lodge wrote an unflattering and often inaccurate biography that condemns Webster for being a political compromiser. The book was published as volume 21 in the American Statesmen Series commissioned by Houghton Mifflin Publishers. Given Lodge's enormous influence in Massachusetts and on its educational institutions, it should come as no surprise that his version of Webster's life prevailed for generations in New England's popular culture.

Van Tyne, Claude H., The Letters of Daniel Webster (New York, 1902). Less complete than other collections, this one represents a selected view of Webster's interests. It is inferior to Fletcher Webster's two-volume set and to Curtis's work, but it does include several passages that

reveal Webster's views on education.   For example, Webster
believed in a solid philosophical foundation before one
started writing material to be published or speaking in
public, was fond of public education and thought lawyers
should be well versed in Greek, Latin, and French along with
their native English.   Tyne focuses more than others on
Webster's penchant for clear, clean, parsimonious style.
His book may be the best in terms of representing Webster's
notion that style should serve function and ostentation
should be avoided.   Tyne fails to point out, however, that
Webster often violated his own stylistic principles.

   Fuess, Claude M., _Daniel Webster_ (Boston: Little,
Brown, and Co., 1930).   This study is carefully done and
perhaps the first with enough distance from Webster to be
called objective and genuinely reliable with regard to
interpretations of events.   The manuscript was republished
by Da Capo Press of New York in 1968 as two volumes with
illustrations and a bibliography.   Fuess provides a
detailed political analysis along with an excellent picture
of the culture of the time.   He carefully establishes
speaking situations and events leading up to major
addresses.   No scholar writing on Webster can afford to
ignore this work.

   Brown, Norman D., _Daniel Webster and the Politics of
Availability_ (Athens: University of Georgia Press, 1969).
This work concentrates on the tensions within political
parties from 1815 to the time of Webster's death in 1852.
It gives readers an excellent look at the death of the
Federalist party and the impact that had on Webster.   It
also examines the rise of the Whig party and the role
Webster played in constructing the Whig platform.   The
book's emphasis on presidential politics renders a clear
picture of the battle for power fought between the
principals of the time, particularly John Quincy Adams,
Andrew Jackson, Henry Clay, William Seward, Zachary Taylor,
John C. Calhoun, Lewis Cass, James Polk, Martin Van Buren,
and of course, Webster.   No source does a better job of
reviewing what actually occurred at the national party
conventions during Webster's lifetime, a lifetime in which
he often sought but never obtained the Whig nomination.

   Current, Richard N., _Daniel Webster and the Rise of
National Conservatism_ (Boston: Little, Brown, and Co.,
1955).   This book is commended for two reasons: it is the
first careful historical study of Webster in the modern era
and it provides a better understanding of Webster's notion
of national conservatism than any other work.   This latter
point is important because Webster's development of
national conservatism in the court system and the Congress
was his greatest legacy.   Through it, he helped Marshall
establish the authority of the Supreme Court, limit the
power of the states, and strengthen the sanctity of private
contracts.   National conservatism also complemented Clay's
American System, which gave the Whigs a platform with a
truly universal appeal.

   Baxter, Maurice G., _Daniel Webster and the Supreme
Court_ (Amherst: University of Massachusetts Press, 1966).
This study authoritatively examines Webster's career before
the bar.   Its strengths include a clear explication of the

law and the context of each case. It is Baxter who confirms
that the Supreme "Court borrowed heavily from Webster's
briefs." He gives us the important counts of cases won and
lost, and the number of times Webster appeared with various
other lawyers. Baxter, however, is no rhetorician. While
he understands the power of an argument, he evidences little
feel for style in language and the full gamut of persuasive
tools.

    Lewis, Walker, Speak for Yourself, Daniel: A Life of
Webster in His Own Words (Boston: Houghton Mifflin, 1969).
Like a modern version of Smucker, this book attempts to
popularize Webster by using his own words drawn for the most
part from his speeches and correspondence.

    Bartlett, Irving H., Daniel Webster (New York: W. W.
Norton, 1978). Between the Current and Peterson volumes,
the most credible is Bartlett's. While he admits to not
fully developing Webster's legal career, he does provide the
most comprehensive personal examination of any historian to
date. To read Bartlett is to get to know Webster. Passages
such as this one illustrate the point: "Whenever he thought
about his father he became a little boy again." Bartlett
also stresses the important role rhetoric plays in American
history. For example, the second reply to Hayne is treated
on pages 116-21 and then referred to often in other relevant
parts of the book. Like Peterson, Bartlett is not a
rhetorical critic, but he does understand the paradox of
Daniel Webster and the importance of language to his genius.
For example, Bartlett writes, "The fact that Webster was
read so much more widely than any other public man of his
time, that he was looked upon as a literary giant as well as
a great lawyer, orator, and statesman contributed heavily to
his enormous visibility before the American public." This
passage reveals Bartlett's appreciation of the role of the
orator in American society; that appreciation is evident
throughout his study.

    Dalzell, Robert F., Daniel Webster and the Trial of
American Nationalism: 1843-1852 (Boston: Houghton Mifflin,
1973). Dalzell's book is a political history that traces
emerging issues from the war with Mexico through the death
of Webster. It is a careful book which provides an
excellent background to the speeches of Webster from the
time he became Secretary of State in the Harrison-Tyler
administration to his death in 1852.

    Nathans, Sydney, Daniel Webster and Jacksonian
Democracy (Baltimore: Johns Hopkins University Press,
1973). Nathans is concerned with interaction between
Webster and his arch enemies in the new, that is to say,
Jacksonian Democratic party. Webster fought with them over
the tariff, the bank, internal improvements, and western
land development. In the background, Clay, more often in
support than opposition, and Calhoun, more often in
opposition than support, play supporting roles. While other
books do a better job of describing Webster's philosophical
foundation and political platform, few do a better job than
this one of describing the Jacksonian platform and why it
was at odds with Webster's.

    Peterson, Merrill D., The Great Triumvirate: Webster,
Clay, and Calhoun (New York: Oxford University Press,
1987). Peterson's long and distinguished career as a

history professor at the University of Virginia and writer
on American history culminates in this 573-page work on the
"great triumvirate." Peterson, who had concentrated his
work on the Founders, particularly Jefferson, here turns his
attention to the second generation of American leaders.
Among its other virtues, this work brings together all the
previous work that has been done on the three legislative
leaders and enlightens those moments where their paths
cross. Many of those occasions include debates in the House
of Representatives and in the United States Senate.   For
example, Peterson spends ten pages on the famous
Webster-Hayne debates, Calhoun's involvement, and the
issues surrounding them.   He mentions the first
confrontation between Clay and Webster in the House.   But
Peterson's view is the view of a historian, not the view of
a rhetorical scholar.   He relies on secondary sources and
eye witness accounts to assess the merits of speeches rather
than analyzing the audience and the rhetorical opportunities
available.   While he often recites the main lines of
argument presented in a speech, he does not often examine
organization, style, delivery or other means of persuasion.
Such an examination, of course, is not his charge and would
greatly expand his undertaking.   He does provide for the
rhetorical scholar a solid portrait of the times, the events
and the major characters.   This information is useful in
constructing the milieu of a given speech and assessing the
role the speech played in American history.   Those who wish
to study the life and oratory of Webster will be
particularly interested in what Peterson has to say about
literary influences on Webster (pp. 29, 32, 35, 37, 400),
Webster's training for law practice (pp. 31-34, 97-98), his
performance before the Supreme Court (pp. 98-104, 250-51,
396-97), his oratorical prowess (pp. 105-12, 175, 181,
295-96, 400-402, 462-64), and his campaigning in the
election of 1840 (pp. 293-96). Peterson's material is well
documented and his notes lead the reader to source material
that is useful in rhetorical analysis.   His references to
Webster's writings, letters, and speeches are clear and easy
to find among the documents cited above.   But the reader
would be wise to keep in mind that Peterson's goal is to
examine the golden age of republican democracy in America
which spans the years from the war of 1812 to the Compromise
of 1850.   That this period of time also happens to be the
golden age of American oratory is coincidental to Peterson
and a minor focus, though he does acknowledge his three
protagonists gained their fame through their rhetorical
abilities.   One does not find in Peterson's notes any
references to works by rhetorical scholars.

IV.   SELECTED CRITICAL STUDIES

     Foster, Herbert D., "Webster's Seventh of March Speech
and the Secession Movement, 1850," American Historical
Review, 27 (1922), 245-70.   Foster's study was an early
attempt to bring the tools of historicism to an event that
had been treated either mythically or with prejudice by
Henry Cabot Lodge and other biographers of Webster.

Foster's discussion of the legislative debate is useful for the facts it provides about the sequence of events. It also attempts to correlate those events with occurrences outside the Congress that helps one to evaluate the effectiveness of Webster. For example, Foster points out that Webster's rhetoric cooled talk of secession. To support this point, he examines the rise and fall of the clamor for secession in the South and measures that against the timing and distribution of Webster's speeches. Foster was also the first to prove that Webster's reputation in the North was much less damaged than Lodge and others claimed. But Foster either ignored or did not have access to some of the newspapers of the period and therefore, does not provide a detailed look at the audience. That confines his rhetorical judgments considerably. Foster, who had a love for Dartmouth, also wrote "Webster and Choate in College," Dartmouth Alumni Magazine, (April-May, 1927) in which he described the courses and textbooks Webster was exposed to in college.

Arntson, Paul, and Craig R. Smith, "The Seventh of March Address: A Mediating Influence," Southern Speech Communication Journal, 40 (1975), 288-301. Professor Arntson and I completed this article in order to correct two standard interpretations of Webster's speech in the 1850 Compromise debates. The first interpretation, propagated by John F. Kennedy in Profiles in Courage, is that Webster was heroic to take a stand that saved the Union despite the fact that he would be vilified in Massachusetts and the North. Kennedy's error was to assume that Abolitionists were in the majority and that they were the only opinion leaders in the North in general and in Massachusetts in particular. The second interpretation, put forward by Henry Cabot Lodge in 1884, historian and senator from Massachusetts, is that Webster's contemporary critics were correct and that the speech was corrupt and rightly condemned. Lodge relies on the same sources as Kennedy to reach his conclusion but instead of portraying Webster as a courageous hero, he paints him as a pandering politician who had lost sight of his moral compass. Our examination of political voting and newspapers of the time indicates that Abolitionists were in the minority and that Webster consolidated pro-Union and conservative sentiment in the North with his first major speech in the 1850 Compromise debates. We argue that Webster was heroic in the sense that he need not have entered the battle, nor violated instructions from his state legislature. Instead, at Clay's behest, Webster supported the Compromise and achieved a remarkable amount of consensus among northerners who were in the majority but much less vocal than the Abolitionists. We also make clear that the Free Soil movement was divided between those who sought to exclude slavery from the territories and those who sought to abolish it altogether. The former had a conservative interest in expanding into the West and farming the land. Webster appealed to this group with his support of Union and the American System and by warning them that a failure to achieve compromise would result in an end to their dreams. The latter branch of the Free Soil group was in the minority and Webster sought in his rhetoric to isolate them from the mainstream of northern thinking.

Howell, Wilbur S., and Hoyt H. Hudson, "Daniel Webster," in A History and Criticism of American Public Address, eds. Norbert Brigance and Marie Hochmuth (New York: Russell and Russell, 1960), vol. 2, pp. 665-733. This essay provides a catalogue of Webster's best rhetorical moments. It is a straight forward assessment of Webster as public speaker. Like the present study, it divides Webster's rhetoric into the traditional genre of Aristotelian criticism. However, unlike the present study, it does not examine the interstices between the genre and therefore, is unable to account fully for Webster's effectiveness. With the exception of speech texts, the authors rely heavily on secondary sources. For that reason, their assessment of Webster's milieu is flawed and judgments about his speeches often lack credibility. The criticism they attempt is normative and prescriptive; it assumes that rhetorical standards can be established and used independent of audience analysis, particularly when it comes to style. While such criticism is possible of literature, it is not valid in rhetorical studies because the standards of assessment for the most part must be deduced from an analysis of the audience. However, the authors do spend some time discussing the changes Webster made in various drafts of his speeches and do a credible job of describing how Webster constructed certain speeches.

Black, John W., "Webster's Peroration in the Dartmouth College Case," Quarterly Journal of Speech, 23 (1937), 636-42. This essay concentrates on style, organization, ethos, pathos, and logos. Black's detailed understanding of language--he eventually moved his academic focus to linguistics--allows him to unpack the connotations of style prevalent in Webster's speech. Black then explains how this stylistic supremacy worked to reinforce the emotional tone of the speech and to enhance the credibility of Webster. Black also examines the lines of argument in the speech and why they are so important in persuading various courts to Webster's point of view.

Mills, Glen E., "Daniel Webster's Principles of Rhetoric," Speech Monographs, 9 (1942), 124-40. Mills's essay was drawn from the dissertation he completed at the University of Michigan in 1941. It differs from a standard rhetorical biography by attempting to deduce a set of rhetorical principles from the corpus of Webster's works. The strongest part of the essay is the opening section on "His Training." Relying on Fletcher Webster's compilation of Webster's Private Correspondence (see above), Mills reveals that Webster's immersion in the classics was deep and included such rhetorical works as Cicero's de Oratore and Lord Kames's Elements of Criticism. Mills reconstructs, in brief, Webster's course of study at Exeter Academy and at Dartmouth with an emphasis on what kinds of speaking assignments were made. Mills concludes the section by stating, "[T]he principal factors which produced his guiding principles were his knowledge of rhetoric, the development of his judgment, and his ability to profit from criticism and observation." Mills then proceeds to deduce the various principles upon which Webster relied. The description suffers in two ways: first, Mills places the principles into standard Aristotelian categories; second, he selects the principles from Webster's speeches without a careful examination of the audience for the speeches. The first problem causes Mills to overlook such strategies as the use of progressive and fugal form in Webster's most important speeches. The latter problem causes Mills to ignore the subtlety and flexibility of Webster's method. Nonetheless, the catalogue of principles is a useful one and reveals how complex Webster's understanding of rhetorical theory was. It includes Webster's view of the audience, the message, and the speaker. In short, it answers the question, did Webster know what he was doing when he did it. Also of interest is the advice that Webster gave to speakers in his letters. For example, though Webster was the master of style, Mills found evidence in Webster's papers that the orator thought it less important than other principles of rhetoric. Whether Webster was being disingenuous or indicating that style simply came naturally to him, Mills does not conjecture.

Bradley, H. A., and James A. Winans, Daniel Webster and the Salem Murder Trial (Columbia: University of Missouri Press, 1956). This study of the Knapp-White murder case is detailed and comprehensive. The authors possess a detailed understanding of rhetoric, particularly its use in judicial narratives. They provide an excellent depiction of the crime, its impact upon the town of Salem, and all of the events that lead up to the famous set of trials. They also perform a splendid analysis of Webster's speech in terms of its logic, its emotion, its style, and its impact on the jury. The present study attempts to advance this analysis by focusing on Webster's use of repetition and fugal form. However, such additional strategies should be understood as second to the main thrust of Webster's summations: to paint a believable picture of the events surrounding the murder. Bradley and Winans superbly explicate Webster's narrative abilities in this case.

Eisenstadt, A. A., "Daniel Webster and the Seventh of March," Southern Speech Journal, 20 (1954), 136-47. This article represents the traditional view of Webster's speech. The author argues that Webster gave a stylistically sound address which offended northern sensibilities.

V.   GENERAL SOURCES

Hamilton, Holman, Prologue to Conflict: The Crisis and Compromise of 1850 (New York: W. W. Norton, 1964). For analysis of Webster's immediate audience in the 1850 Compromise debates, no source is better than this one. Hamilton's dissection of the membership of the House and Senate is exhaustive and invaluable. His understanding of the issues and how each member of Congress viewed them is also very impressive and tremendously useful to the rhetorical critic. For example, Hamilton explains why it took the House sixty-three ballots to organize for the session in which the compromise debates took place. He divides Whigs and Democrats between northern and southern, slave and free, and pro-western versus anti-expansion. He also explains the fault lines that divided the Free Soil party and how they grew out of the divisions in the American Anti-Slavery Society.

Craven, Avery, The Coming of the Civil War (Chicago: University of Chicago Press, 1963). Craven carefully traces the roots of the conflict of 1861-65. In the course of his study, he provides useful information for the time period from 1833 to 1852.

John, Allen, and Dumas Malone, eds., Dictionary of American Biography (New York: Charles Scribner's Sons, 1960). This useful reference volume is helpful in determining the character of the persons who engaged Webster in debate and heard him speak before the Supreme Court. The eleven volumes contain extensive biographies of important Americans written by experts in history, law, political science, and the social sciences. For the purposes of this study, the biographies of important lawyers such as Choate and Gore and of Supreme Court justices such as Marshall, Taney, Story, and Washington were used to supplement other means of audience analysis. The biographies detail the background of each justice in terms of where they were raised and how they were selected for the bench. The biographies also reveal the justices' voting patterns and leanings on constitutional questions.

Chase, Harold, Samuel Krislov, Keith O. Boyum, and Jerry N. Clark, comp., Biographical Dictionary of the Federal Judiciary (Detroit: Gale Research, 1976). This volume focuses on prominent jurists, particularly Supreme Court justices. It provides a careful analysis of their careers that is useful in reconstructing the audience Webster faced when he argued before the Supreme Court. Such reconstruction includes attitudes on constitutional issues, party affiliation, voting records, and biographies.

Myert, Gustavus, The History of the Supreme Court of the United States (New York: Bert Franklin, 1968). This is a reprint of the 1912 edition, which concentrated solely on the Supreme Court. It examines major decisions and all of the justices of the Supreme Court in some detail up to the Warren court.

Swisher, Carl B., ed., The History of the Supreme Court of the United States (New York: Macmillan Publishing, 1974) 11 vols. Like the aforementioned sources in this section, this eleven volume set is invaluable in reconstructing Webster's forensic world. It provides extremely useful case histories and biographical information on Supreme Court justices.

Aristotle, Rhetoric, trans. W. Rhys Roberts (New York: Random House, 1954). While the Lane Cooper version is easier to understand, this version is more accurate and that becomes crucial when applying Aristotle's principles to American public address. This work is seminal to all rhetorical studies and easily the most useful book ever written on the subject. Aristotle avoided the dogmatism of Plato and the overly formalistic prescriptions of the Romans by basing his system in the audience. Aristotle's method of deriving a rhetorical theory was ingeniously simple. He watched effective orators and then watched their audiences. By closely examining the interaction between the two he generated a set of questions useful in almost any

rhetorical setting. It is for those questions that
Aristotle is to be valued; his answers, while on the mark
for Athens, do not always work in America. On the other
hand, some of his judgments are uncanny in their aptness for
our time. The book is a complete catalogue of rhetorical
strategies ranging from how to appear credible before an
audience to developing a fitting style for a given occasion.
     Oliver, Robert T., History of Public Speaking in
America (Boston: Allyn and Bacon, 1965). Oliver helped to
put the field of American public address on the map with
this ambitious undertaking. While his analysis of Clay,
Calhoun, and Webster relies heavily on secondary sources,
Oliver's own criticism is fresh and informative. In the
short essays, Oliver examines the major positions orators
took on the issues, lists their major speeches, and writes
about how each thought of the art of public speaking. His
assessment of Webster's Seventh of March Address is
problematic because it does not credit Webster with forming
a consensus of opinion among a majority of northerners.
     Lynd, Staughton, Class Conflict, Slavery, and the
United States Constitution (New York: Bobbs-Merrill, 1967).
In ten well written and informative essays, Lynd describes
the social milieu which surrounded the major issues during
the founding of the nation. This study is particularly
useful to understanding the emergence of the slavery issue
during Webster's career. It also examines the important
philosophical questions that undergirded the writing of the
Constitution. That information is important to the proper
understanding of Webster's court cases and his career as a
speaker in Congress.
     Current, Richard N., T. Harry Williams, and Frank
Freidel, American History: A Survey (New York: Alfred A.
Knopf, 1963). Anyone who analyzes American public address
needs a solid reference history of the United States. I
have found none better than this book for analysis of the
period leading up to the Civil War. These facts also led to
my preference for this text over others: Current has written
a serious and useful book on Webster (see above); Williams
in all of his works has a wonderful understanding of and
respect for rhetorical analysis; and Freidel has long been
known for his brilliant work at Harvard. The book is filled
with useful charts, maps, appendices, and a detailed index.
It also contains a copy of the Constitution and the
Declaration of Independence. In its thousand pages, the
authors provide not only political and military histories,
they analyze the society and its culture. The latter is
particularly important to understanding the American
audience that Webster faced when he gave ceremonial speeches
or distributed his speeches as pamphlets.

Index

About the Author

CRAIG R. SMITH received his B.A. degree from the University of California in 1966 with honors, his M.A. from the City University of New York in 1967, and his Ph.D. from Pennsylvania State University in 1969. Smith has taught rhetorical theory and criticism, argumentation, and American public address at San Diego State University, the University of Virginia, and the University of Alabama in Birmingham, where he also served as Communication Arts Division Chair. Currently, Smith is professor of speech communication at California State University, Long Beach, and serves as president of the Freedom of Expression Foundation, a non-profit organization dedicated to publishing research on the impact of twentieth-century technology on First Amendment rights. His publications include numerous articles on Daniel Webster's speaking and a book on the 1850 Compromise.